THE ANCIENT ORIENT

The Ancient Orient

An Introduction to the Study
of the Ancient Near East

Wolfram von Soden

Translated by
Donald G. Schley

WILLIAM B. EERDMANS PUBLISHING COMPANY
GRAND RAPIDS, MICHIGAN

Gracewing.

Library of Congress Cataloging-in-Publication Data

Soden, Wolfram von, 1908-
[Einführung in die Altorientalistik. English]
The ancient Orient: an introduction to the study of the ancient Near East /
Wolfram von Soden; translated by Donald G. Schley.
p.   cm.
Includes bibliographical references and index.
ISBN 0-8028-0142-0 (pbk.)
1. Middle East — Civilization — To 622. I. Title.
DS57.S5813 1993
939′.4 — dc20   93-36268
CIP

Gracewing ISBN 0 85244 252 1

Contents

Contents

Translator's Preface

Ever since Prof. Dr. Rykle Borger suggested in 1989 that I carry out this translation, I have looked forward to the day when this text would be available in English. I had two main purposes in mind: first, I wanted a concise, yet comprehensive text for use in my classes in ancient Western history, and second, I wanted one which could also serve as a background text on the ancient Near East, to be used in conjunction with classes in biblical studies. Wolfram von Soden's text is excellently suited to both purposes. With regard to ancient Western civilization, von Soden takes the kind of broad, yet intensively textually based approach that could only be expected from the author of the *AHw* (*Akkadisches Handwörterbuch*) and the master of the field of Assyriology. As an historian, he makes serious contributions to the hitherto neglected areas of economic history (especially chs. VII-IX, which cover agriculture, artisanry, and trade) and ancient Mesopotamian science (ch. XI). These topics are treated in connection with other topics as well, such as religion (ch. XII) and literature (ch. XIII). The book succeeds in tying these several themes together across many chapters by means of the copious in-text references (which the author originally made in terms of page references, but which I have altered to references to chapter and section [e.g., VII.2b] to facilitate the speed of editing and publication). As a basic history text, the work is notable for its breadth of cultural history, in which von Soden also treats the history of language (ch. III) and the history of writing (ch. IV). At the same time, von Soden gives a first-rate treatment of Mesopotamian religion from the standpoint of the history of religions, even pointing up the specific connections between early religion, magic, and medical practice. The chapter on science (ch. XI) is one of the most outstanding features of the work as a history of civilization. Here, von Soden is at pains to indicate both the origins of Mesopotamian science in the Sumerian concept of order, expressed in terms of the voluminous lists, and its development down to the time of the Greeks, when Thales of Miletus became the first to predict a total solar eclipse using the Babylonian records of solar observations (XI.9). Von Soden includes in this treatment a critical analysis of the strengths and weaknesses of ancient Mesopotamian science and mathematics, and his suggestions for their eclipse by the classical Greeks. His presentation of the multilingual lists of grammatical expressions and vocabulary terms is the first time, to my knowledge, that the beginnings of the discipline of philology in ancient Mesopotamia have been made available in a general work. Of special note throughout is von Soden's own profound interest in intellectual history in all its aspects, and what he calls "humanity in its wholeness," that is, how the study of the ancient Orient informs our understanding of humankind and the great issues of human existence. The entire work is structured as an extended inquiry into the ancient world, and areas where evidence is lacking, or where further investigation is required, are painstakingly noted. Above all, the book is a model of good historical thinking and analysis, which one will want one's students to emulate (and which is so straightforward as to allow this).

For all of these reasons, von Soden's treatment represents the first comprehensive, interdisciplinary presentation of ancient Near Eastern civilization in a form that is at once expressly related to Western history, intensive in its portrayal of Near Eastern civilization itself, and novelle in its interest in heretofore neglected aspects of that civilization (e.g., science, economics, intellectual history, et al.).

The text can also serve the more particular use of providing a background work in ancient Near Eastern civilization for students of the Bible. There are several reasons, in fact, for preferring such a general work which does not seek to give a specific treatment of Israelite history. To begin, the history and religion of Israel are, necessarily, subsets of the study of the ancient Orient. Thus, if a student wishes to understand the history, culture, and religion of Israel, he or she must first know something of the historical context of Israel, which is to say, of the ancient Orient. While von Soden alludes to this fact in his first chapter, he also recognizes (as one who has written extensively in Old Testament) that the study of Israel and its religion has long since existed as a separate discipline of its own. Thus, ancient Israel must remain a separate, though related, field to which only occasional reference is made.

Still, for the practiced student of the Bible, this presentation of ancient Mesopotamian civilization is extremely illuminating for Israelite life and institutions. For example, the treatment of the state and society and the limitations of the power of the monarchy, even under the patriarchal absolutism of a Hammurabi, effectively dispel the modern Western prejudice that the ancient Mesopotamian potentates held a view similar to the seventeenth- and eighteenth-century European belief in the divine right of kings. Von Soden also notes that political usurpers of the royal throne, beginning with Sargon of Akkad, generally justified their actions by appeal to divine election or favor. Here, one must only think of David of Judah or Jehu of Israel.

The role of the king in psalmody is highlighted in the chapter on literature, raising again the question of the historicity of the biblical tradition of David's authorship of some of the psalms. It is of note here that the largest single category of ancient Mesopotamian psalms comprises, as in the Hebrew Bible, the psalms of individual lament, and outstanding examples of royal laments are attested as well. Wisdom is also treated and is one of the areas in which the author sees actual dependence of Israelite literature on its Mesopotamian antecedents. Interestingly enough, direct connections between the Babylonian account of Creation are downplayed, if not denied outright.

So also can von Soden's treatment of women be as easily applied to Israel: marriage by simple purchase was overturned at the latest in the third millennium. Thus, women were not chattel property by any means, and contempt for one's mother was no less a sin than contempt for one's father. Here, again, the work avoids the modern Western prejudice that all previous societies were absolutely paternalistic (on the Roman model of the father's right of imperium over members of his household). Still, women did hold what can only be called a second-class status, although one which was in many ways strictly protected (though childless wives were at a particular disadvantage in divorce). Conversely, the Middle Assyrian Laws, which granted the husband the right to mutilate his wife's face for certain offenses (even to twisting off her ears!), represent a particular setback for women, though nothing of the sort is to be found elsewhere, either in Babylonia or Israel. The exclusion of women from judgeships may have its one possible exception in the biblical figure of Deborah. There will be some debate about this, since for the Deuteronomistic historian all deliverers are also judges. Nonetheless, the depiction of the Israelites coming to Deborah in judgment is unique in the entire book of Judges and may not, therefore, be the result of deuteronomistic redaction.

In the areas of law and religion, the student will be interested to note that the concept of law as a divine command emerged for the first time in Hammurabi's Babylon, and along with this, the idea of universal sin. At such points, one sees that Israel's relationship to ancient Mesopotamian civilization ran to the deepest levels. At the same time, as von Soden is careful to point out in his final summation, one should be careful not to attribute all such correspondences to direct dependence of Israel on Babylon, as pan-Babylonians such as Hugo Winckler had done. Rather, von Soden seems to reach back to the long-ignored concept of an *Ur-Semitic* religion, and argues that common elements of this religion emerged in different places (e.g., Amorite Babylon and Israel) and then independently developed further. Direct dependence probably does exist, however, in the myth of the Flood, in which the accounts of the sending out of the birds are so similar in the Babylonian and Hebrew versions.

The chapter on building, art, and music (ch. XIV), as well as other aspects, recalls much of the incidental background to 1-2 Kings. Thus, the mention of the occasional dedication of horses to the temples in the chapter on agriculture (ch. VII) recalls the horses dedicated to the sun, at the entrance to the temple in Jerusalem (2 Kings 23:11). The Syrian art of ivory-carving had its late representatives in Megiddo and Samaria, and the importance of mixed-form creatures in ancient Oriental iconography and the intricate wood panels, decorated with carved reliefs, which are described in connection with other ancient temples were also characteristic of Solomon's. The importance of music in general is noted, and there is a brief, though intensive treatment of instruments and the possibilities regarding systems of notation. A brief reference to the important role of music in the Jerusalem cult does, as the author notes, still leave essential questions unanswered.

Although one of von Soden's purposes was to limit direct references to Israel, I have taken the liberty of making mostly parenthetical notations in the text to aid the student of the Bible. These are, for the most part, brief and unobtrusive, and more would have been possible. I thought this necessary because most students reading this book will not bring with them the extensive knowledge of biblical literature and history which will allow them to make maximum use of its strengths. This fact has to do with unfortunate cultural, political, and educational trends in this country over the last four decades, and should not be laid at the door of the students themselves. Moreover, knowledge of the ancient world among students is almost nonexistent. To the extent that many students will have a sense of, or an interest in, the ancient world, however, this will most often be through the Bible. I hope, therefore, by the interjection of these notations, to draw out some of the connections between Israel and the ancient Orient in such a way as to excite the interest of the students in both Israel and the civilization of the ancient Near East.

Finally, I would like to thank the many people who have helped me in this project: Prof. Robert Sackett, my colleague at UCCS with whom I have discussed many translational difficulties, and Prof. John H. Hayes of Emory University, who read the final draft and updated many of the bibliographical references. I am also grateful to Professor von Soden for reading the final draft and updating the notes, which are a key element in the work. Above all, I am indebted to my teacher, Prof. Dr. Rykle Borger of the Seminar for Cuneiform Studies in Göttingen, who first suggested this project to me, and for the support given me by him and Dr. Wolfgang Schramm in my own introduction to the ancient Orient so long ago in Göttingen. This translation is dedicated to them.

The University of Colorado,   DONALD G. SCHLEY
Colorado Springs
November, 1992

Foreword

At last, after long years of delay, I can present my introduction to the ancient Orient. Understandably, there are many things that cannot be treated here, but I am nevertheless satisfied with this short presentation. I have thus mentioned, in chapters I and XV, some essential perspectives by which I have allowed myself to be guided in selecting material. I found it particularly important to show what the study of the ancient Orient has already accomplished for these select themes in a little over a century, and how much still remains to be done. I would be pleased if one or another of these stimuli would be taken up by younger scholars for further investigation. It was particularly distressing that the limited scope of the undertaking permitted neither extensive illustration nor excerpts of translation to illustrate the texts. Therefore, the notes, which of course enumerate only a very small portion of the most important academic works, make special reference to works translated in recent decades. Regrettably, I had to forego completely a chapter on the history of the discipline. The notation of names, dates, and some particular accomplishments alone would have brought little reward without placing them in the context of the history of the discipline, a task impossible to accomplish in a few sentences. From those scholars already at work at the turn of the century, to whom we are indebted even today, I would like to name as representative here only Heinrich Zimmern (1862-1931), the founder of the discipline of the history of ancient Near Eastern religions; Bruno Meissner (1868-1947), the author of the first great portrait of Babylonian-Assyrian culture; and François Thureau-Dangin (1872-1944), the master of many fields of philology.

I have maintained the standardized spellings of ancient names without employing special signs for transliteration. Thus I write Gilgamesh and not Gilgameš. Words from the ancient languages are otherwise transliterated in terms of their original spellings.

Abbreviations

1. General

Akk.   Akkadian
Arab.   Arabic
Aram.   Aramaic
Ass.   Assyrian
Bab.   Babylonian
Gk.   Greek
Heb.   Hebrew
Hitt.   Hittite
Lat.   Latin
Sum.   Sumerian

2. Periodicals and Serials

AfO   *Archiv für Orientforschung* (Graz)
AHw   Wolfram von Soden, *Akkadisches Handwörterbuch*, I-III (Wiesbaden, 1958-1981)
ANET   *Ancient Near Eastern Texts*, ed. J. B. Pritchard, 3rd ed. (Princeton, 1969)
AnOr   Analecta orientalia (Rome)
AOAT   Alter Orient und Altes Testament (Neukirchen-Vluyn)

CAD	*The Assyrian Dictionary of the Oriental Institute of the University of Chicago* (Chicago, 1956–)
HKL	*Handbuch für Keilschriftliteratur,* ed. R. Borger, vols. I-III (Berlin, 1967-1975)
JCS	*Journal of Cuneiform Studies* (New Haven, Cambridge, Mass.)
JNES	*Journal of Near Eastern Studies* (Chicago)
MDOG	*Mitteilungen der Deutschen Orient-Gesellschaft* (Berlin)
MSL	Materials for the Sumerian Lexicon (Rome)
Or	*Orientalia,* New Series (Rome)
OrAnt	*Oriens antiquus* (Rome)
RA	*Revue d'assyriologie et d'archéologie orientale* (Paris)
RLA	*Reallexikon der Assyriologie,* ed. E. Ebeling-B. Meissner (Berlin, 1932–)
RSO	*Rivista degli studi orientali* (Rome)
UF	*Ugarit-Forschungen* (Neukirchen-Vluyn)
WZKM	*Wiener Zeitschrift für die Kunde des Morgenlandes* (Vienna)
ZA	*Zeitschrift für Assyriologie* (Berlin)

Other periodicals are cited in nonabbreviated form. In connection with dates, the designation B.C. is normally omitted.

CHAPTER I

The Term "Ancient Orient" and Its Demarcation

Orient is not a term of physical geography, as is also true of the designation Near East, which comprises the same region. Therefore, Orient has no clear geographical demarcation. In our linguistic usage, the Orient comprises the Near East with Egypt and Iran (in contrast to the typical American usage, which identifies the "Orient" with East Asia). In the north the Black Sea, the Caucasus, and the Caspian Sea form reasonably clear natural boundaries, as does the Indian Ocean in the southeast. The boundaries of the Orient were never constant in relation to adjacent cultures in the Mediterranean region, in northeast Africa, in eastern Iran, or later, the Occident, Central Asia, and India. While Islam was the definitive power of the Orient in the Middle Ages, extending far beyond the actual confines of the Orient, there was no comparably dominant power in the pre-Hellenistic ancient Orient, primarily because the differences between the cultures of this region were too great, despite important commonalities, and the boundaries too unstable. Egypt, plainly cut off to the east by the Red Sea and the Sinai desert, created hieroglyphics as a writing system used only there, and in many respects had a development all its own. It has therefore become customary to reckon Egypt to the ancient Orient only in the wider sense of the word, and to apply this term in normal usage only to ancient Western Asia, without western Asia Minor but with western Iran.

A special position within the discipline assumes the people of Israel being the bearer of the oldest religion of revelation. The biblical scholarship of Christians and Jews has occupied itself for centuries with the

1

Cuneiform tablet (about 600) containing a map of the world showing the surrounding oceans (ring) and designating Babylon as the Center. *(Trustees of the British Museum)*

Israelites, and for them the ancient Orient is the environment of the Bible. Thus many orientalists, especially in the early years of our discipline, were by no accident theologians. Because of the present significance of its religion, Israel remains a central theme of biblical scholarship. For this reason, Israel does not constitute one of the main areas of ancient Oriental studies, and only occasional references to Israel must suffice here.

The study of the ancient Orient has grown out of Assyriology, as it is often called today — that is, out of the study of ancient Mesopotamia, where about five thousand years ago humanity's oldest system of writing, the later cuneiform, came into existence. Babylonia and Assyria stand at the center of this discipline with their high, widely radiating culture. Yet they cannot be considered in complete isolation from the other cultures of ancient Western Asia, which we call the cuneiform cultures because of the predominant form of writing which for so long was exclusively used there. Since these cultures present us with their own manifold problems, according to the respective state of the development of their languages and literatures, no scholar can deal with all of these simultaneously in a thorough fashion, and such a brief Introduction as this can do them even less justice. Therefore, this volume is relieved of its burden with regard to these cultures by several other texts which are devoted specifically to them. Accordingly, the ancient Hittites of Asia Minor, who spoke predominantly Indo-European languages, should receive their own separate treatment. A few small textbook volumes deal with further topics from the ancient Orient.[1] Besides Babylon, Assyria, and Mesopotamia, then, one must here incorporate early northern Syria and, in further sections, Elam in the southeast and pre-Armenian Urartu in the north.

Phoenician alphabetic writing, which could be used by more than the members of an intensively schooled scribal caste, appeared in Syria-Palestine around 1200. In somewhat altered form this writing was taken over early on by the ancient South Arabians, who, so far as we know, had until that time been without writing. Yemen, the center of ancient South Arabian culture, was far removed from Babylon as well as from

---

1. Among these are G. Wilhelm, *Grundzüge der Geschichte und Kultur der Hurriter* (Darmstadt, 1982); and H. J. Nissen, *The Early History of the Ancient Near East 9000-2000 B.C.* (Chicago, 1988). Cf. further A. Moortgat, *Einführung in die Vorderasiatische Archäologie* (Darmstadt, 1971).

Syria and Egypt. For this reason the influence of these much older cultures did not have as much effect there, and a culture which was in many respects independent took shape — a culture which deserves its own separate treatment. Still, South Arabia can receive occasional mention here. Syria, conversely, remained a part of the ancient Western Asian cultural circle even after the acquisition of alphabetic writing; accordingly, it cannot be completely overlooked. Particular presentations will be dedicated to the culture of Ugarit and the history of the Phoenicians, who, with their colonization of wide reaches of the Mediterranean region, grew beyond the confines of the ancient Orient.

It is not the task of an Introduction into so wide a field to compile as many facts, individual observations, and discoveries as possible, as in the case of a compendium. Rather, one must proceed from the recognition that a single individual can no longer survey the profusion of written sources, artistic compositions, and archaeological monuments. The mass of these materials increasingly forces one to specialize, and thereby gives rise to the danger that the view of the whole of the ancient Orient will be lost. The first priority must therefore be to indicate what is common to the successive historical periods, cultures, and regions, and at the same time to present the often essential differences, which are frequently neglected. All of this can, of course, be carried out only by means of select examples. These should make it clear that essential knowledge frequently remains inaccessible even to the meticulous specialist, not least of all in his or her own field of specialization, if there is too narrow a concentration on certain periods or areas. Thus we must reckon with the particular situation of our discipline at the present.

Because of the close ties of Assyriology to biblical studies, historical and religio-historical questions long stood in the foreground of research. The discovery of the stela containing the Code of Hammurabi and of thousands of legal documents at an early stage, however, drew the attention of legal historians to the ancient Orient. The myriads of economic documents, on the other hand, were studied with far less intensity, although that changed about forty years ago when the investigation of the material basis of life came strongly to the fore. Even the significance which the nature of the land had for humanity received increased consideration. These developments led to important new areas of knowledge and opened the way for many lines of inquiry which scarcely would have been considered earlier. The socio-historical investigations which subsequently received priority often forced the study of the problems of intellectual history too far into the background; for a time these were even dismissed as less relevant than the problems of social and economic history. Over and against these issues, it seems to me essential, even in the ancient Orient, to inquire into humanity in its wholeness. This means, for example, that we must take the phenomenon of Babylonian science rather seriously. Such an approach leads to shifts in emphasis, in contrast to many other presentations of the last decade. Textual evidence and phenomena which are often insufficiently appreciated must be emphasized more heavily here. Some essential aspects of ancient Oriental art must also be drawn into the discussion. The progressive separation of the development of historical-philological study from that of the study of artistic monuments in Near Eastern studies has had unfortunate consequences.[2]

2. The only comprehensive work on Mesopotamia with numerous samples of texts is still B. Meissner, *Babylonien und Assyrien,* 2 vols. (Heidelberg, 1920-1925). The great work, *L'Alba della civiltà* (Turin, 1976), ed. S. Moscati *et al.;* vol. 1: *La società;* 2: *L'economia;* 3: *Il pensiero,* is treated in *Altvorderasien und Ägypten.* See further, among others, H. Schmökel, H. Otten, V. Maag, and T. Beran, *Kulturgeschichte des Alten Orients: Mesopotamien, Hethiterreich, Syrien-Palästina, Urartu* (Stuttgart, 1961); A. L. Oppenheim, *Ancient Mesopotamia: Portrait of a Dead Civilization,* 2nd ed. (Chicago, 1977). H. W. F. Saggs is responsible for several major comprehensive works in English: *The Greatness That Was Babylon,* 2nd ed. (New York, 1991); *The Might That Was Assyria,* 2nd ed. (New York, 1991); *Civilization before Greece and Rome,* and one in German, *Mesopotamien: Assyrer, Babylonier, Sumerer* (Zürich, 1966); also see below, ch. III, n. 19, and ch. V, n. 1.

CHAPTER II

The Scene

W estern Asia was the scene of the ancient Oriental cultures. It comprises the southwestern part of the mighty landmass of Asia and contains regions of quite diverse character and unequal possibilities for cultivation. The Euphrates and Tigris, the only two great rivers of the region, flow from where they emerge from the mountainous land of eastern Anatolia, along with their lesser tributaries, through the predominantly hilly area of northern Mesopotamia, and then through the almost completely level floodplain of southern Iraq. Since the transition to civilization succeeded here some five thousand years ago, and similarly in the Nile Valley and the plain of the Indus, the opinion was long accepted that even in still earlier times the great river plains had offered the circumstances most conducive to the development of agrarian cultures. We know today that this is not correct. In fact, the floodplains, even in Iraq, were for a long time largely uninhabitable. This was because people could neither tame the floodwaters and put them to use nor make adequate preparations for the dry season. Some lesser plains bordering the high mountain ranges offered far more congenial conditions, and for this reason these were settled much earlier than the river valleys. From these small settlements on the edge of the mountains people first descended gradually into the plains, in order to make them habitable.[1]

1. Significant works on geography for ancient Western Asia include: E. Wirth, *Agrargeographie des Irak* (Hamburg, 1962); *Syrien: Eine geographische Landeskunde* (Darmstadt, 1971); W.-D. Hütteroth, *Türkei* (Darmstadt, 1982); E. Ehlers, *Iran: Grundzüge einer geographischen Landeskunde* (Darmstadt, 1980).

Foundations of the Hanging Gardens of Babylon. Nebuchadnezzar II (605-562) designed this system of terraces supported by arches to remind his bride Amytis of her mountainous homeland, Media. *(Jack Finegan)*

High mountains, along with the intercalated steppes and the great deserts of Arabia and Iran, occupy extensive areas of Western Asia. Moreover, diverse sub-alpine mountain zones are found primarily in the west, often with attractive conditions for settlement. The high, jagged mountain ranges, with occasional volcanoes and few passes, reach heights of over 5000 m. in eastern Anatolia and Iran as well as in the Caucasus. The mountains range to more than 3000 m. in Yemen and Oman, as they frequently do in Asia Minor and in some places in Syria. The vast desert steppe in the Arabian interior offered scant possibilities for settlement down to modern times. In the area of the mountains bordering the western part of the peninsula, the natural preconditions for continuous occupation were found in various locations, just as they were in the eastern districts, which were not too far removed from the coast. If our understanding is correct, Yemen became the most significant cultural region of Arabia at an early date. Little is known of copper-rich Oman in ancient times.

In Iran and Asia Minor, high regions with fair possibilities for trade were generally interspersed with smaller valley regions cut off from one another by high mountain chains. These, in turn, could be controlled from the center only with difficulty. Some of these valleys were partially filled by great inland seas. Salt seas with no outlet were the very deep Lake Van and the shallow Urmia. Lake Sevan (or Gökcha) had an outlet to the north.

Although seas form the greater part of the boundaries of Western Asia, these seas had only limited significance for the adjacent lands. Sources are lacking for possible trade on the Caspian Sea, and the Black Sea was not widely navigated until the time of the Greeks. The situation of the Mediterranean and Aegean Seas was completely different, since the jagged shore of western Asia Minor was open along its entire length. There were, however, no great harbors on the southern coast of Asia Minor, and this was especially true of the Syrian coast. Still, the Syrian coast was of some limited importance for the interior lands beyond the range of the coastal mountains. As with the Persian Gulf and the Red Sea, the shores of the Indian Ocean are extremely hot in the summer. For this reason they are suitable for permanent settlements only in certain places. In spite of this, seaborne commerce around the Arabian peninsula and extending as far as the Indus Valley must have played a considerable role early on.

While the topography of the vast regions of Western Asia has only been altered in individual places in the last six thousand years, there were certainly changes in the climate and the water level in the rivers and seas even before the encroachment of humankind in recent times. The study of these changes by geographers and climatologists is today only in its inception, but it must be appropriately considered by orientalists, who can themselves contribute to resolving some of the problems. It has long been known that in the Mesopotamian plain the Tigris and Euphrates, as with many rivers which do not flow constantly through desert and steppe, often altered their courses, and that through alluvial deposits the Persian Gulf was forced back considerably. This latter process was admittedly viewed incorrectly as being steady and continual, since no exact observations of the rivers and the Gulf were available. As elsewhere, the tides had a strong effect in the vicinity of the river mouth. Together with the rivers, they alternately influenced the salt table and, consequently, grain production in the areas subject to flooding. While this is not the place to present these complicated

8

processes in detail, it must be pointed out that they did occasionally influence political configurations.

The most important causative factor for changes in the rivers of Iraq and elsewhere was, and is, the climate. The new science of paleoclimatology, in conjunction with paleobotany and other sciences, has focused on study of the climate in the distant past.[2] If, at the end of the last Ice Age, the sea level lay approximately 110 m. below the present level because the ice had taken a great deal of the water out of circulation, the rivers, insofar as they had not previously trickled away, must have sought their way to the sea through deep canyons. About sixteen thousand years ago the slowly rising sea began to fill the Persian Gulf once again. Around 4000 especially heavy rainfall and the melting ice resulted in the water in the sea being temporarily higher than it is today. At that time, large parts of the desert became passable steppe, and steppe became arable land. This, in turn, made possible folk migrations, which will be mentioned later. Agriculture was possible on the basis of rainfall at that time in vast expanses of Western Asia, which later reverted to steppe and became dependent on irrigation. After about 3000 a very long, progressive drying-out phase set in. During this period, the possibilities for rain-based agriculture gradually decreased, until they almost disappeared in Babylonia. Today the southern boundary for rain-based agriculture, which demands a minimum rainfall of 250-350 mm. per annum, runs through northern Mesopotamia. In ancient times it may from time to time have lain to the north or south. As far as I know, exact studies of this problem are lacking. Nor is it known in detail whether rain-based agriculture was possible in Asia Minor and Iran everywhere and at all times outside the deserts and salt steppes.

An exact study of the indications of rain in the ancient texts can still yield important results for agriculture in regions without a great network of canals. The fact that the Akkadian word for sandstorm, *ašamšutu,* is not frequently attested, as compared with present climatic conditions, indicates that west of the lower Euphrates desert and desert steppe had not penetrated nearly as far as in modern times, prior to the

2. Using the results of measurements that the German research vessel *Meteor* obtained, W. Nützel and others presented important studies of the rise of the water level in the Persian Gulf at the end of the last Ice Age and on drainage and salination in southern Iraq in *MDOG,* 107, 109, 111, 113 (1975-1981). See also Nützel, "Kann die Naturwissenschaft der mesopotamischen Archäologie neue Impulse geben?" *ZA* 66 (1976): 120ff.

installation of the great irrigation projects of the last decades. Even here, however, the fragmentary literary tradition offers only indeterminate, preliminary generalizations.[3]

We can give only provisional and minimal answers to the questions regarding forestation. It is highly probable that the mountain ranges of Asia Minor and Iran, as well as Syria, were predominantly forested in the corresponding altitudes, although deforestation by humans aiming to acquire space for settlement and cultivation took place very early. Cuneiform texts report great, partially impenetrable forests in the mountain ranges bordering the plains. Despite the massive deforestation carried out by Near Eastern monarchs in search of good building timber, Syria and southern Asia Minor contained great cedar and cypress forests as late as the middle of the first millennium B.C. To what extent the mountains surrounding Arabia were forested in ancient times still requires investigation. Unequivocal testimony about larger forests in the plains and hill country does not exist, as far as I can tell. The words for forest frequently encountered in the texts no doubt designate for the most part only larger groves and woods, perhaps in the vicinity of rivers. With the method of pollen analysis, which formerly was largely neglected in excavations, one will henceforth be able to obtain clear results at many sites. There was scarcely any reforestation, aside from the creation of smaller woods or parks.

The centers of settlement within a region, which were not always at the same place in different periods, pose not only an historical but also a geographical problem. Why were some cities and thickly populated districts, following natural catastrophes or those caused by humans, rather quickly rebuilt while others were completely abandoned, in some cases until today? The shift in water resources, occasionally through human agency, was certainly a frequent reason for the erection of new settlements on other sites. Modern aerial photography allows one to recognize ancient riverbeds better than was previously possible. If regular watering was absent in a district which had been abandoned on account of a water shortage, salination of the soil was generally unavoidable. Such a development made a new beginning difficult. This is still the case today, and under earlier circumstances it would have

3. A recently developed plan to use the written sources to research climatic changes following the last Ice Age also offers hope for important results for ancient Western Asia.

been impossible. In researching these causes, natural science and archaeology must again work closely together. This kind of investigation is still in its infancy despite much survey work, in part because no agreement yet exists on the appropriate methods. The study of ancient economic documents yields very important information on many places. Such documents are available for some periods and cities in great quantity, but in other cases they are completely lacking for long periods of time.

In the mountains, other reasons could lead to the displacement of centers of settlement, such as landslides or the exhaustion of rich deposits of natural resources. Enemies occasionally not only destroyed settlements, but also rendered the arable land useless by sowing salt in it. The ceremonial cursing of all those who would begin rebuilding such a place was as a rule effective for only a short time, as, for example, with Hattusas around 1800 (cf. also Jericho's destruction by the Israelites and the Roman destruction of Carthage). Still, the power of foreign gods in whose names such cursing was carried out was not fundamentally doubted.

The significance of the natural resources which could be exploited using the methods then available, and for those regions with little possibility for cultivation and animal husbandry, can be mentioned only briefly here, since they will be treated later. Vast stretches of Western Asia, above all those outside the mountainous regions, were poor in natural resources, and therefore lacked economic autonomy. For these, trading over wide areas was a necessity of life.

CHAPTER III

Peoples and Cultures
in the Ancient Orient

The excavations of the last 140 years, and the simultaneous intensive plundering of ancient sites, have made known to us a superabundance of cultural remains from ancient Near Eastern peoples that can no longer be surveyed by any single person; a great deal more lies unpublished in museums. Yet this massive amount of material is distributed very unevenly over both the region and the historical periods. Even in Babylonia and Assyria there are epochs for which we know very little. For the remaining regions the gaps in our knowledge are larger still. By sheer coincidence, we are dependent in many areas upon sometimes very extensive, sometimes lesser, or sometimes nonexistent finds. Consequently, a presentation of the history and cultures which has been weighed from all perspectives and which in every case draws out that which is essential is, and will long remain, impossible. Both points of emphasis and gaps in the treatment will always be determined in part by the respective availability or lack of material. We will do well if we always remain aware of this fact.

A very brief delineation of the historical periods is necessary, since this overview focuses primarily on those time frames which we call "historical," insofar as the term "history" can be used here. Events of considerable historical ramifications have taken place all over the earth for many millennia. These events only first become "historical" in the complete sense of the word, however, when they are recorded, as a rule, through writing or, less often, in pictures, whether this occurred immediately after the events took place or whether they were recorded later on the basis of oral tradition, by historically aware peoples (e.g., the

Assyrian soldiers lead away captive peoples, with women seated in an ox-drawn cart. Alabaster relief from Ashurbanipal's palace at Nineveh (668-633). *(Louvre)*

patriarchal traditions of Israel). That which was never recorded, and which has fallen into oblivion, remains an "historical" event only in a limited sense. Thus we term "prehistoric" those epochs in which nothing had yet been written down, without thereby assuming that events of great significance had not yet taken place. The historical era began in this sense first in Babylonia and Egypt, with the earliest meager attestation around 3000; such history did not begin in northern Syria and parts of Mesopotamia and Elam until after 2500; elsewhere it began still more recently, in many places not until 1000 or later.

For a long time scholars have sought to deduce especially important developments, for example, folk migrations, from cultural changes which can be read in archaeological remains, particularly in the ceramic materials. Thus, archaeological evidence has long been interpreted in a strongly historical fashion. Yet there can be frequent and substantial changes in the ceramic style, even if no other people has come onto the scene. In other cases, very important events, such as the invasion of Asia Minor by the people later known as the Hittites, cannot be read at all in the contemporary archaeological finds. Conclusions based on ceramic evidence and miniature sculpture can be drawn only in rare cases, and then only with great care. To these rare cases I would reckon the transition from the painted Samarra pottery to the Tell Halaf pottery in Mesopotamia and Assyria in the fifth millennium. In this case, the differences in theme and means of depiction are so great that the assumption of a change in style alone is insufficient to explain the data. One must therefore postulate two cultures of very different types.[1]

The study of language and comparative linguistics offers better possibilities for drawing conclusions about migrations in prehistoric times. New languages are never established anywhere without the immigration of new ethnic groups. One can determine the influences of other languages on the basis of vocabulary and certain grammatical phenomena. Earlier languages in a country often continue to affect more recent languages there as a substratum, even when the older languages are no longer spoken. New ruling classes, conversely, influence the languages of the subjugated, often as a superstratum (see below, pp. 16, 19-20, 21-22). In early times, however, the effects of substratum as well as superstratum languages are only partially recognizable.

If we want to designate the populations attested in the sources appropriately, we will have considerable difficulty with a terminology that allows for too little differentiation. For lack of a better term, we speak of "peoples" when the large living-communities of the same language and culture so designated would be better characterized by a neutral term with less content. A term such as "ethnic group" may fit better, but today this is used primarily in connection with the designation of minority groups in opposition to a people identified with a state. In connection with the political entities of the ancient Orient, we will scarcely have to deal with "tribes." Similarly, the modern term "nation" is not at all applicable to antiquity. In the linguistic usage of the ancient Orient itself, only Israel developed an unequivocal term for itself as a people, and subsequently confirmed this self-identification through its history. People everywhere else were characterized only according to their origin in a particular land or according to their membership in a social group, insofar as one does not speak merely of "humankind."

1. On the Samarra and Tell Halaf ware, cf. A. Parrot, *Sumer* (Munich, 1960), 44ff., with illustrations.

1. The Ancient Oriental Cultures before 3000: The Sumerians

Settlements in the mountainous regions of ancient Western Asia were primarily, though not continuously, occupied as early as the Paleolithic Age. The beginning of rain-based agriculture at suitable sites around 6000 first created the necessary preconditions for permanent settlements in the pre-ceramic Neolithic Age, as these are also found toward the end of the sixth millennium in Mesopotamia. After about 5000 arose the rich, colored ceramic cultures of the Chalcolithic Age. Little by little, these developed without interruption into the high Mesopotamian cultures on hand when writing was invented. The manifold accomplishments of these earlier cultures cannot be presented in detail here.[2] Still, they presuppose the formation of a society based on a division of labor which freed large groups of the population — such as artisans, merchants, and cultic and administrative personnel — from the production of food, as well as on an advanced technology for the production of clay vessels using the potter's wheel, metallurgy, and the mass production of heavily used objects. Many new possibilities were opened for the timeless concern with artistic forms.

Skilled crafts, sculpture, and the remains of cultic installations testify to differentiated religious conceptions (see below, XIV.1, 2). Nevertheless, we can scarcely infer anything historically, even of a provisional nature, from the extremely rich archaeological finds of the fifth and fourth millennia. The possibilities of reaching some conclusions on the basis of later textual witnesses are very meager as well.

We can say with great certainty that prior to the last centuries of the fourth millennium, during the Chalcolithic Age, neither Semitic-speaking groups nor Sumerians belonged to the presumably light-skinned inhabitants of Western Asia. Ancient geographic names, as well as pre-Sumerian loanwords and other occasional phenomena of the linguistic substratum in Sumerian and Akkadian, permit some conclusions concerning their languages. As yet there have been no individual investigations of these problems. For example, place names with -a/ill-, as in the Babylonian *Kazallu* and *Babillu* (later in Akkadian interpreted as *Bāb-ili*, "the gate of God"), *Urbillu/Arbela* in Assyria, and

2. On this point, compare H. J. Nissen, *The Early History of the Ancient Near East*; and A. Moortgat, *Die Entstehung der sumerischen Hochkultur* (Leipzig, 1945).

Hapalla in Asia Minor, are dispersed over wide areas. Names with *a/i/ utt-*, which later appear mostly in nasal forms, have their center in Asia Minor and extend as far as Greece. I mention here from Mesopotamia and Syria only *Kaḫat*, *Elu/aḫu/at*, and *Ugarit*, from Asia Minor *Burušḫattum/Burušḫanta*, *Šinaḫuttum*, and *Lalanta*, as well as *Olynth* and *Corinth* in Macedonia and Greece. Finally, in an extensive area stretching from Asia Minor over Syria and on to Egypt, the substratum language does not generally differentiate between *l* and *r*, above all at the beginnings of words. It is still much too early for an historical interpretation of these and other linguistic phenomena which can be observed over broad sections of Western Asia; but this will be an important task for future scholarship.

The characteristic parts of the nominal vocabulary of a language spoken in the fourth millennium in Babylon can be derived from other sources besides geographic names. According to Benno Landsberger's procedure, this language should be designated "proto-Euphratic." From this language (among others), Sumerian borrowed professional designations such as *nangar* ("carpenter"), *ašgab* ("leather worker"), and *sanga* ("priest"); these show us how far the division of labor in Babylonia had progressed by that time. It appears that dialects of another language were spoken in Assyria and in the western Zagros. These can be called "proto-Tigridic" or, even though the more ambiguous designation makes it less suitable, "Subaraic."[3] The variations in the languages correspond to considerable differences in the simultaneous and apparently equally developed cultures in the south and north: the Uruk culture and the Tepe Gawra culture.[4]

According to the learned tradition in Babylonia, terrible and catastrophic floods took place in the fourth millennium, where they fell upon a very ancient urban culture in the land. These floods provided the occasion for the formation of the myth of the Flood. The extremely high ages attributed to the "kings before the Flood" should not mislead us into discarding this whole tradition as a product of fantasy (see below, V.3).

The designation Sumerians is derived from the Babylonian name

3. The basis for the term Subaraic is the Akkadian term *Šubartum*, later *Subartu*, which originally designated Assyria but later referred to a much larger region. Subaraic was earlier called Hurrian; today, however, it is a collective term for languages unknown to us in the Zagros region, primarily at the dawn of history.

4. Cf. Nissen, 71ff.

for southern Babylonia — Sumer; the actual Sumerian name for the land was Kengi(r), "civilized land." Today it is generally recognized that the Sumerians were not the oldest inhabitants of the land, and there have been different opinions as to their origin. Since the discovery of the Indus civilization about seventy years ago, however, it has been almost universally accepted that the Sumerians immigrated from the east. This immigration could have succeeded entirely by land if the Sumerians immigrated from somewhere in northern India, because in the fourth millennium the barrier to great folk migrations, the eastern Iranian deserts of Lut and Kavir, were passable and even partially inhabitable — at least periodically — as a result of the much more moist climate (see above, ch. II). Migratory movements through the southern Iranian coastal region, which was in all probability extremely hot even at that time, were just as improbable as the long sea route through the Persian Gulf. Whether migrations across eastern Arabia should be considered, following the crossing of the Gulf of Oman, may perhaps be shown for the first time by the excavations recently begun in Oman. It has already been established that trade relations existed between the region of the Indus and Babylonia at an early date, with intermediate stations on the islands of Bahrain and Failaka. What led to the westward migration of the Sumerian groups, whose language may have been related to the Dravidian languages of India, will probably never be understood. Likewise the age of migration in the last quarter of the fourth millennium will hardly be more precisely understood. It appears that the Sumerians settled southern Babylonia densely enough to enable them to establish their language only as far north as Nippur. Further north there would have been trade centers and perhaps some cultic centers as well. The Sumerian language still presents us with manifold problems.[5]

5. The agglutinative (i.e., not changing the root words) Sumerian is reckoned among the ergative languages, which are characterized by a passive conception of verbs. For some time, these verb forms have been under renewed discussion from many angles, especially the difficulty of analyzing them on account of their long chains of prefixes. On the structure of the language, cf. W. H. P. Römer, *Einführung in die Sumerologie*, 2nd ed. (Nimwegen, 1982), 27ff., and the literary overview on pp. 17ff.; cf. also M.-L. Thomsen, *The Sumerian Language: An Introduction to Its History and Grammatical Structure*, 2nd ed. (Copenhagen, 1987). A lexicon which takes into account the many individual studies and glossaries is needed; some larger projects are in preparation: cf. Å. Sjöberg, *The Sumerian Dictionary*, 2 [B] (Philadelphia, 1984); 1a [J] (1993).

2. The Semites in Western Asia

a. Northeast and North Semites

Under the designation "Semites" we group together those peoples who speak Semitic languages. It was long accepted that the original homeland of the Semites lay in Arabia, since Arabia had been the point of departure for Semitic migrations from a very early period. Against this assumption stands the primary fact that Arabia, which in large part is extremely arid, makes a poor cradle for emergent peoples. But more important than this is the fact that the Semitic languages are inflected languages — that is, they alter the roots of their words. The Semitic languages share this property with only the Hamitic languages of Africa and the Indo-Germanic or Indo-European languages of Europe and Asia. This fact compels us to assume that these three language families developed in neighboring regions, since the emergence of the inflected language-type must be regarded as a one-time development in the history of languages.[6] Since the Semites and Hamites may have emerged from northwest Africa, one should also seek the earliest speakers of inflected languages in the area of northwest Africa and western Europe. About nine to twelve thousand years ago, the Hamito-Semitic peoples, who are much more strongly differentiated from Indo-European peoples than they are among themselves, must have become autonomous and gradually developed an identity separate from the Indo-Europeans. Because written sources are entirely lacking, almost nothing is known of the early forms of the Hamitic languages, which differ a good deal from each other. The Hamites must have occupied wide stretches of North Africa very early on, and long remained there, in large part untouched by further contact with the high civilizations of the Mediterranean region.

Of the Semites, the ancestors of the later Berbers remained in North Africa, and thus in contact with Northwest Hamites. Other groups migrated away to the east. The conditions for the later crossing of desert regions were particularly favorable as a result of the unusually moist climate after the middle of the fifth millennium (see above, ch. II). Large groups settled in Egypt, and in the ancient Egyptian language both Semitic and Hamitic elements can be ascertained. Other Semitic

6. All other languages are agglutinative (see above, n. 5).

groups had reached Western Asia by the fourth millennium. Parts of these may have made their way across Lower Egypt and the Sinai peninsula, while others may have traveled by way of Nubia or southern Egypt and the Red Sea until they reached western Arabia. All further clues to a more precise account are at present lacking. Until recently, early Semitic language inscriptions from the middle of the third millennium were known only from Babylonia. Then, in 1975 a comprehensive archive of clay tablets was uncovered at Tell Mardikh, the site of ancient Ebla, about 60 km. southwest of Aleppo. To our surprise, this discovery showed that as early as 2400 there had been a North Syrian kingdom, whose inhabitants had in large part spoken and written a Semitic language. This tremendous find brought new knowledge, but at the same time it presented us with a multiplicity of new problems.[7]

Previously it was held without question that Akkadian, designated as "Northeast Semitic," represented the most ancient Semitic cultural language, along with the Semitic components of ancient Egyptian. Now we have reason to assume that the first Semites came to Mesopotamia and northern Babylonia not much later than the arrival of the Sumerians in the south, that is, toward the end of the fourth millennium. In the Jemdet Nasr period (named after a site excavated near Kish), which follows immediately upon the period of the invention of writing, there may have been states ruled by Semites and perhaps even an occasional Semitic empire. Very old Semitic loanwords in Sumerian make such an assumption attractive. According to the reigning consensus, the Canaanites were the next wave of Semites; their presence in Western Asia can be demonstrated from about 2000 on (see below, section 2b). I had already concluded on the basis of many hundreds of Semitic names in early antiquity, which are neither Akkadian nor Canaanite, that one must reckon with a further group of Semites. As a designation for these I suggested first of all "Old Amorites," but later substituted the neutral expression "North Semites."[8] Now we have learned from the archives at Ebla that the predominant rulers in North Syria in the middle of the third millennium were North Semites and not, as had first been sup-

7. G. Pettinato, *The Archives of Ebla: An Empire Inscribed in Clay* (Garden City, N.Y., 1981); and P. Matthiae, *Ebla: An Empire Rediscovered* (Garden City, 1981), report on the initial works. Numerous texts with word lists or indices have already been published; a grammar and lexicon are yet to come.

8. Cf. preliminarily, W. von Soden, "Das Nordsemitische in Babylonien und Syrien," *La Lingua di Ebla* (Naples, 1981), 355ff.; further studies are in process.

posed, Canaanites or Northeast Semites with a "West Akkadian" language (for the relationship of Eblaite to the later Ugaritic, see below, section 2b). We must now assume, moreover, that North Semites had settled in northern Syria much earlier, since the strong influence of a non-Semitic substratum can be recognized in Eblaite. That leads to a further question, namely, whether the North Semites really immigrated into Syria-Mesopotamia after the Northeast Semites, or whether this actually occurred before the arrival of the Northeast Semites. If the latter is true, the earliest Semites in Babylonia must have been North Semites, although we know nothing for certain about their language. They would then have been subjugated by the Northeast Semites about five hundred years later. The effects of a linguistic substratum (e.g., on the pronunciation of specifically Semitic sounds such as the laryngeals) can be observed in early ancient Akkadian down to the time of the Dynasty of Akkad about 2300, though much less frequently than in Eblaite. This fact could speak for a much earlier arrival of Semitic-speaking peoples in Mesopotamia than had heretofore been supposed. We can only pose the question of the time of the arrival of Northeast and North Semitic peoples in Syria and Mesopotamia provisionally, since research on Eblaite is only in its inception and early ancient Akkadian is insufficiently known. Without new discoveries in northern Babylonia from the middle of the third millennium, we will hardly acquire more clarity. Akkadian itself developed in Babylonia and Assyria in many variant ways.[9]

b. The Northwest Semites: Canaanites and Aramaeans

While we provisionally understand the earliest Semites as historical only as they settled in cities, the picture for the later groups of Semites is much more variegated, and thus more realistic. Shortly before 2000 pressure for migration began to build in the area of western Arabia and southern Palestine. Wars and, in areas of declining fertility, the pressure of overpopulation may have been the cause for this. The main destina-

9. For the grammar, cf. W. von Soden, *Grundriss der akkadischen Grammatik,* 2nd ed. with additions. AnOr 33 (1969). The recent dictionaries include *The Assyrian Dictionary of the Oriental Institute of the University of Chicago,* ed. A. L. Oppenheim and E. Reiner (Chicago, 1956–); and W. von Soden, *Akkadisches Handwörterbuch,* 3 vols. (Wiesbaden, 1958-1981).

tions of these migrations had for some time been Syria and Mesopotamia. Many tribal groups long remained nomadic shepherds, while
others engaged in the cultivation of grain as seminomads or trans-
humants. Still others managed to gain a foothold in the cities, often
even seizing the political leadership there. The Northwest Semitic and
Old Canaanite dialects which they spoke never became written languages, as far as we know, although many Canaanite words are found
in the Babylonian texts, primarily those from early second millennium
Mari on the middle Euphrates. On the evidence of their Canaanite
names, many Old Canaanites came to Babylonia as mercenary soldiers
and workers at the time of the Third Dynasty of Ur, soon after 2000.
There they were called "Amurru" (= west)-people; accordingly, many
today refer to them as Amorites.[10] In Babylonia, too, many Amurru-
people rose through military command to positions as rulers of cities,
and even kings of larger areas. Since new waves of Canaanites continued
to come to Babylonia over many decades, the mass of Amurru-people
remained a dependent population, often of low status.

After the middle of the second millennium the Old Canaanites no
longer appear as a separate population group in Babylonia and Mesopotamia. Rather, they were in constant conflict with arriving Hurrian
groups as they increasingly prevailed in Syria-Palestine, probably
strengthened by clans of people speaking the same language entering
the land from the southwest. The Canaanites established their domi-
nance primarily in the coastal cities south of Latakia. We designate them
Phoenicians in imitation of the Greeks, and their language we call
Phoenician. Scarcely anything is known of the population strata in Syria
at that time. In any case, there were considerable differences between
the coastal cities and the interior. Clans of seminomads in the region
of the arable steppe and nomads in the desert steppes to the east certainly caused turmoil in many places.

Near Latakia, the port city of Ugarit held a peculiar position, with
its dependent lands in the interior. Here Ugaritic was written and spoken
alongside Akkadian and, less frequently, Hurrian. Ugaritic was originally
a North Semitic language (see above, section 2a), but it was later influ-

---

10. The Amorites in this sense are not identical with the Amorites often named
in the Old Testament. The term Amurru or the designation Old Canaanites (earlier the
less appropriate term East Canaanites) is therefore to be preferred. On this topic cf.
G. Buccellati, *The Amorites of the Ur III Period* (Naples, 1966).

enced by a Canaanite superstratum as well, without becoming, as many think, a Canaanite language.[11] After the destruction of Ugarit around 1200, Ugaritic quickly fell out of use.

The people of Israel spoke a Canaanite language, Hebrew, and their tribes may be reckoned predominantly to the Canaanites. The highly complex relations in Palestine after 1400 cannot be treated here.

The colonizing efforts of the Phoenicians, who had become sea-farers, finally led many of them out of the ancient Orient completely and into the wide realm of the Mediterranean Sea and beyond. The official language in most of these colonies, which later achieved auton-omy, was Punic. This was originally a Phoenician dialect and is known to us primarily from North Africa. Whether Semites comprised an essential element in the population in Crete during the Minoan Age, as many propose, is highly questionable.[12]

After 1300, the Assyrians encountered new nomadic Semitic groups in Mesopotamia who were soon building fortified settlements. The Assyrians called these *Aḫlamu* — "new troops" — and later *Aramu* — "Aramaeans."[13] They were successfully kept out of Babylonia and Assyria until ca. 1050. Nevertheless, because they continually increased in number despite devastating wars, at least partially through further reinforcements from the region of Arabia, they gradually occupied the plains and the smaller cities in Babylonia after 1000 and established themselves sporadically in Assyria. After 900 the Aramaeans formed an increasingly greater portion of the population of Mesopotamia, above all through the great deportations. The first Aramaean states in Syria came into existence perhaps already before 1000, but we know hardly anything of them. The state of Damascus was particularly powerful. In northern Syria the Aramaeans steadily infiltrated the remaining states of the Hittite Empire and finally occupied them entirely.

We know almost nothing about the languages of the Arameans

11. Cf. C. H. Gordon, *Ugaritic Textbook*. AnOr 38 (1965), with grammar and glossary; no lexicon is yet available.

12. Cf. J. Friedrich–W. Röllig, *Phönizisch-punische Grammatik*. AnOr 46 (1970); S. Segert, *A Grammar of Phoenician and Punic* (Munich, 1976); see below, n. 14; for Crete, Babylonian *Kaptaru*, Hebrew *Kaphtor*, cf. M. Weippert–V. Herrmann, "Kreta," *RLA* VI (1981): 225ff.

13. The origin of the word *Aramu* is unknown. Old Aramaic is first attested around 900; on this and the Imperial Aramaic of the Persian Empire, cf. S. Segert, *Altaramäische Grammatik mit Bibliographie, Chrestomathie und Glossar* (Leipzig, 1975).

before about 900, since only a few names are known to us. Inscriptions in the Phoenician alphabetic writing first appear in small quantities after 850. The names and foreign words of Aramaic origin in Assyrian and Babylonian texts come from previously little-used supplementary sources. Through the Neo-Assyrian Empire, and still more through the succeeding Chaldean and Achaemenaean Empires, ancient Aramaic became a kind of *lingua franca* throughout Western Asia. Under the Achaemenaeans and afterward, Aramaic became the administrative and literary language in the western part of the empire; this we call "Imperial Aramaic."[14] The literary languages of the Jews, Christians, and Mandaeans later evolved from Imperial Aramaic, but the study of these no longer belongs to the discipline of ancient Oriental studies. One cannot speak of an Aramaean people during any period.

After around 1100, Aramaic tribes became the first camel Bedouin in Western Asia. Whether they or the Arabs further to the south first domesticated the dromedary, so that the ass and onager could be relieved as beasts of burden over wide reaches of desert, is still unknown.[15] In connection with the earliest Aramaeans in the second millennium and their relation to the Canaanites, there are still controversial questions. Some are of the opinion that there are signs of "Proto-Aramaeans" already early in the second millennium, for example, in the Old Babylonian letters from Mari. From this it is further concluded that the Israelite tribes were partially Aramaeans. Nor do all recognize a separate family of Aramaic languages within Northwest Semitic. Space does not permit discussion of the arguments brought to bear on this debate.[16]

c. South Arabians and North Arabians

Among the Semitic groups who did not migrate to the north, a separate Semitic language type developed which is called Southwest Semitic. The

14. The Imperial Aramaic of the Old Testament is called Biblical Aramaic. See above, n. 13, and C.-F. Jean–J. Hoftijzer, *Dictionnaire des Inscriptions sémitiques de l'Ouest* (Leiden, 1960), for Phoenician-Punic and early Aramaic.

15. Cf. W. Heimpel, "Kamel," *RLA* V (1980): 330ff. (see below, VII.2b, and p. 93, n. 13).

16. On the same subject, cf. S. Moscati, A. Spitaler, E. Ullendorff, W. von Soden, *An Introduction to the Comparative Grammar of the Semitic Languages* (Wiesbaden, 1964), 7ff. and 171ff. (bibliography).

most ancient representative of this language type is Old South Arabian with its main dialects, Sabaean, Minaean, Qatabanic, and Hadramautic, which we know from thousands of stone and metal inscriptions from the period between 1000 B.C. and A.D. 600, though almost nothing is known of earlier periods. The South Arabians inhabited the southwest part of Arabia with the partially fertile mountains of Yemen in the center. Related groups settled across the Red Sea in Nubia and became the ancestors of the later Ethiopians.[17] As a result of the great distances and the great deserts which separated them from the other cultural centers of the ancient Orient, the South Arabians had little contact with the rest of Western Asia, apart from trade and individual military engagements. Sabaean is therefore a separate subdiscipline of ancient Oriental studies, to which only a separate treatment can do justice.

The West and North Arabians of central Arabia enter the light of history soon after the South Arabians. Their language is the most important representative of Late Semitic and is called North Arabian. The Assyrians knew them from 853 on as warlike Bedouin with whom they repeatedly had to fight in Syria and, later, Babylonia. West Arabian oasis-cities such as Tema are occasionally mentioned after about 750, and for a short time around 550 these became a part of the Chaldean Empire as far as Yatrib (today Medina). The cuneiform texts hand down a few Arabic names and words, but inscriptional witnesses for Arabic are first known from a much later time. The Arabs did not attain substantial significance for the ancient Orient even in its late period.

3. Hurrians and Urartians

The Hurrians, who came out of northwest Iran and encompassed wide stretches of Western Asia with their migrations, consequently became one of the most important factors in the history of the second millennium. Their language is attested in different dialects and is a so-called ergative language. It is still only partially understandable, partly because of many variables in the cuneiform writing. The available sources

17. Despite a plethora of individual studies, there is still no comprehensive presentation of the history and culture of the South Arabians in antiquity. When Semites first reached Nubia and, further to the south, Ethiopia has still not been clarified; cf. the preliminary treatment of C. Conti Rossini, *Storia d'Ethiopia*, I (Bergamo, 1928). Perhaps there were various waves of immigrants.

throw only spotlights on the history of the Hurrians. Little is known of their first thrusts to the west toward the end of the third millennium. From the middle of the second millennium until about 1200, only Babylonia was never subjugated to rule by Hurrian groups. Hurrians simultaneously played a considerable role in the history of the Hittite Empire, and they were the strongest population group in the Mittanian kingdom. For their language, history, culture, and religion, I refer the reader to G. Wilhelm, *Grundzüge der Geschichte und Kultur der Hurriter* (see ch. I, n. 1). However, since the history and culture of Assyria and Syria were both strongly determined by the Hurrians, they must be treated briefly.

Armenia was probably one of the main regions of Hurrian settlement as early as the second millennium. Still, we learn nothing of the emergence of a greater state there until after 900, when the kingdom of Urartu came into existence. It had its center on Lake Van and in the eighth century its political influence occasionally stretched far beyond its own borders, even as far as Syria. In the ensuing struggles with the Assyrians this kingdom was severely weakened, until the Scythians conquered it after 600. The cultural attainment of the Urartians (whom the Greeks called Alarodians) is significant in many areas, including metallurgy. The Urartian language is a form of later Hurrian and is attested predominantly in royal inscriptions; it has not been sufficiently studied.[18]

4. Peoples and Cultures in Western Iran

a. Elamites, Gutians, and Kassites

In southern Iran, especially in the province of Khuzistan, lay the homeland of the Elamites, who probably settled there in the fourth millennium. The Elamite language, which was recorded in a starkly altered form of the Sumerian writing very early in the third millennium, can be related to no other known language and is only partially under-

18. Brief grammars are offered by I. M. Diakonoff, *Hurrisch and Urartäisch* (Munich, 1971); and G. A. Melikišvili, *Die urartäische Sprache*, with an appendix by M. Salvini (Rome, 1971) and a glossary with words which can already be interpreted. The two works differ in many particulars.

standable in its earlier stages. Neo-Elamite was one of the administrative languages of the Achaemenaean Empire. Although Elamite culture was influenced by Babylonia in many respects, it displays its own thoroughly peculiar impress and certainly had a strong effect on neighboring regions, just as it did later on the Achaemenaean Empire. In the infrequent times of political unity, there were transient attempts at empire-building.[19] Elam must repeatedly be discussed in this work.

Outside of Elam there were, as far as we know, no literate cultures in western Iran prior to the first millennium. We can accordingly say little of the tribes and ethnic groups of this region, most of whose names, along with their certainly variable fates, are known from the cuneiform sources from Urartu to Elam. Nor do we know whom we have to thank for the so-called Luristan bronzes which were created there over many centuries. The Babylonians and Assyrians knew their mountain neighbors primarily as reckless warriors from their incursions into the plains, and in their counterstrikes they dealt with them with similar severity. Twice peoples from western Iran were able to establish themselves in Babylonia for a rather long time.

When the Empire of Akkad crumbled, the Gutians to the east and north of Babylonia were able to establish a realm, the extent of which we are unable to ascertain. In the Sumerian literature, the period of the Gutians is depicted as a time of terror. We know some names of Gutian princes, but otherwise we know almost nothing of the Gutian language. The Assyrians named the successors of the Gutians the Quti. Next to these, the texts mention the often wildly warlike Lullubeans, or the Lullubu.

The Kassites (in Greek, the Kossaeans), who began to infiltrate Babylon from west-central Iran during the time of the successors to Hammurabi of Babylon, had a much greater significance for Babylonia. They first established themselves after 1680 in a northern border region, where they founded a dynasty which first ruled northern Babylonia and later the entire land for 450 years. The changes they wrought will be treated later. The Hurrian presence set the boundary of Kassite expansion in the region of Kirkuk. Inscriptions in the Kassite language have

19. On the history, cf. W. Hinz, *Das Reich Elam* (Stuttgart, 1964); and the sections on Elam by Hinz and R. Labat in the *Cambridge Ancient History*, II/1 and 2 (1963/1964). For the grammar of Elamite, concerning which there is still much controversy, cf. E. Reiner, "The Elamite Language," *Handbuch der Orientalistik*, 1:2/2 (Leiden, 1969), 54-118. See W. Hinz and H. Koch, *Elamisches Wörterbuch*, 2 vols. (Berlin, 1987).

not been preserved: their kings used Babylonian or late Sumerian. From the names, small word lists, and foreign loanwords in Akkadian, a few hundred Kassite words can still be recovered and partially interpreted, and the structure of the language can be deduced.[20] The Kassites were gradually assimilated into Babylonian society, which owed to them important impulses in the area of art.

Some of the Kassites remained in Iran, where they are mentioned in Assyrian texts as late as the seventh century. From changes in place names in the region of Lake Urmia and to the southeast, one can infer many struggles between Kassite and Hurrian tribes. Assyrian texts often mention a kingdom of Mane that lay between Assyria, Urartu, and the Medes in the district of Lake Urmia between about 850 and 650.[21]

b. Indo-Aryans, Medes, Cimmerians, and Persians

Indo-Aryan groups first arrived in Mesopotamia from eastern Iran around 1500 and established there the dynasty of the Mitannian kingdom (see below, V.6). Indo-Iranian terminology was also used in the business of horse breeding among the Hittites. The significance of these Indo-Aryans has long been overestimated and even today cannot be appropriately described; we know their language only from names and a few foreign loanwords in the cuneiform languages.[22]

The Medes in northwest Iran and the Persians in western Iran are first mentioned around 840, far to the northwest of their later homelands, in the inscriptions of the Assyrian king Shalmaneser III. A Median kingdom organized as a confederacy, later having Ecbatana (modern Hamadan) as its capital, is attested in Assyrian sources and by Greek historians, though these are certainly only partially reliable; Median inscriptions have not yet been recovered. The Cimmerians (biblical Gomer) were another highly militant Iranian people, first mentioned in 714; they immediately set the ancient kingdoms in terror and came

20. Cf. K. Balkan, *Kassitenstudien I: Die Sprache der Kassiten* (New Haven, 1954); J. A. Brinkman, "Kassiten," *RLA* V (1980): 464ff.

21. A recent synopsis of the research is still needed.

22. On the interpretations, many of which remain controversial, cf. A. Kammenhuber, *Die Arier im Vorderen Orient* (Heidelberg, 1968); M. Mayrhofer, *Die Arier im Vorderen Orient — ein Mythos?* (Vienna, 1974).

to power at many key points in Media. Their influence was limited by the Scythians who followed them. These latter were an Indo-European people but they were not Iranians, and they achieved a far greater cultural significance than the Cimmerians. Aside from some incursions, the Scythians remained outside the ancient Orient. They were unable to save the Assyrians from the Medes and Cimmerians.

For a long time, the Persians were unable to make headway against Media in the north and Elam in the south. After Elam had succumbed to the Assyrians, Cyrus II (the Great, 559-529) was able to conquer the kingdom of the Medes, Lydia, and the Chaldean Empire and establish a world empire, all within eleven years. The Medo-Persian Empire, its religion, and its art, as well as northern and eastern Iran, must be the focus of another volume.

5. Asia Minor: Proto-Hattians, Luwians, and Hittites

Which peoples inhabited Asia Minor, a region of extremely ancient culture, before 2000 and which languages were spoken there are questions which even today are almost completely beyond our knowledge. The western part of Asia Minor was probably already oriented toward the Aegean at an early date, while central and eastern Anatolia belonged to the ancient Orient. The Hattians or Proto-Hattians settled in northern Anatolia. They had already been there a long time in 2000, and their agglutinative language is fairly well-known to us from the archives of the Hittite capital of Hattusas. Ethnic groups having a different language must have been settled to the south, if we have correctly interpreted their names and loanwords in Old Assyrian and Hittite. Soon after 2000, Indo-European peoples came to Anatolia from either the east or the west, and by 1800 or shortly thereafter had subjugated much of the land to themselves, without completely suppressing the earlier inhabitants. These newcomers were the Hittites, who called themselves Nesians; they came with their relatives the Luwians and Paleans. The Hittites borrowed cuneiform from Mesopotamia and later even created a new system of hieroglyphics for Luwian. These languages comprise a single family within Indo-European. The culture of the Hittites was dependent upon Babylonian culture in many respects, but in many areas it was also creatively independent. The Hurrians, too, gained great importance in Hittite culture. The Hittites later encroached upon Syria and founded states there which survived to an extent long after the destruction of the Hittite Empire around 1200.[23]

6. The Coalescence of Peoples

We have attempted in all brevity to introduce the peoples and ethnic groups or tribes who, according to what we know, achieved some significance for the ancient Orient. Along with these peoples there were several more, concerning whom our current sources reveal nothing, or so little that we cannot evaluate their accomplishments. For this reason I have omitted these, including the many small groups in the high, mountain valleys whose names are recorded, as well as the small peoples adjacent to Israel (since the history of Israel deals with them). To this latter group belong primarily the Ammonites, Moabites, and Edomites of the Transjordan, whose languages are closely related to Hebrew but are attested only in a very few texts (such as the Mesha Inscription). The Philistines occupied the southwestern coast of Palestine from around 1200 on, but their presumably Indo-European language is still unknown to us. They came into their new-found land through the great storm of Sea Peoples, who had such momentous consequence for the eastern Mediterranean world — even the Hittite Empire and Ugarit succumbed to them.[24]

If we now consider the development of the whole, we will notice — outside the typical zones of retreat in the high mountain valleys — the preeminent tendency of smaller groups to coalesce into larger ones, which to be sure were in no way always unitary in anthropological terms but did often share a common language. This development was demanded above all by certain large states: initially by the Hittite Empire and later, on a far greater scale, by the Neo-Assyrian Empire, which created dependent states comprising various (and sometimes numerous) peoples or used mass deportations and forced resettlements. Such policy established new small groups of deportees, but these were unable to maintain their language in a foreign environment for more than a few generations. Certainly only in exceptional cases (as with the

23. An introduction is under preparation by E. Neu; cf. also A. Goetze, *Kleinasien* (Munich, 1957).

24. On the Sea Peoples and the Philistines, cf. F. Schachermeyr, *Die Levante im Zeitalter der Wanderungen vom 13. bis zum 11. Jahrhundert v. Chr.* (Vienna, 1982).

Judeans) could they succeed in holding fast to their religion for long periods of time, although forced conversions were certainly the rare exception in the ancient Orient. Even in the naming of children, people gradually sought to conform to the majority, since minorities did not stringently maintain their ties to one another (as in the cases of the biblical figures of Mordecai and Esther).

Which language prevailed in one of the great states depended in no way upon the will of the rulers. The Assyrians were just as incapable as the ancient ruling classes of the Babylonian cities had been of preventing Aramaic from becoming the language of the common people over time, even in the core districts of the Assyrian homeland. Aramaic was certainly written far more than we can prove today, since papyrus and leather survive as writing materials only in rare cases, and wax never.

Besides the wars and deportations, numerous infiltration movements had the effect of assimilating smaller peoples into larger ones, so that these smaller peoples disappeared from history without any catastrophes taking place. Toward the end of the second millennium, the Hurrians in Mesopotamia and the Kassites in Babylonia met this fate. Since a high degree of freedom of movement existed in the great states, ancient differences increasingly vanished. In this process, the initially strong impulse to throw off the rule of the great states gradually lost its intensity. As a result, when the Neo-Assyrian Empire collapsed, most provinces went over to the new lords, the Babylonians and the Medes, without a struggle. The entire Chaldean Empire, after brief fighting primarily over the capital city of Babylon, fell peacefully to Cyrus, the Persian king. The same thing occurred two hundred years later when Alexander the Great conquered the Achaemenaean Empire. Petty states founded by ambitious officials only rarely held out for longer periods of time. In the end, the advantages of a unified world came to be considered even more important than their drawbacks.

CHAPTER IV

Writing and Systems of Writing

1. Sumerian Writing and Cuneiform

The invention of writing was one of the most consequential innovations in human history. Millennia had already passed in which quite different technologies had been developed. Then an expanding economy and the agglomeration of a large mass of people within a confined space in Western Asia created a situation which could no longer be managed merely by the spoken word and improvised notes recording quantities of animals and objects. We have learned only recently that the earliest writing had precursors. Clay counting stones had already been used throughout Southwest Asia and Egypt for many hundreds of years. These had symbols for animals and certain objects scratched into them and were placed in the appropriate number in a pouch or clay holder. The use of plates with numerical points or marks followed. After the middle of the fourth millennium, clay tablets with distinctly differentiated numerical marks were introduced, as well as individual numerical stones, and, later on, cylinder seals.[1] Nevertheless, these improvisations became less and less sufficient for the increasingly complex demands which were being made on the marking system. Thus around 3000, the Sumerians in Uruk came upon the idea of creating hundreds of some-

1. The pioneering treatment is by D. Schmandt-Besserat, *An Archaic Recording System and the Origin of Writing.* Syro-Mesopotamian Studies I/2 (Malibu, 1977); an essay which goes further is "From Tokens to Tablets: A Re-evaluation of the So-called 'Numerical Tablets,'" *Visible Language* 15 (1981): 321ff.

31

Predynastic Sumerian tablets, inscribed with linear characters immediately derived from pictographs (Jemdet Nasr, 3100). They contain accounts of fields, crops, and commodities. *(Trustees of the British Museum)*

what abbreviated pictograms and many signs for numbers and measures. These pictograms were pressed into clay tablets with a reed stylus, making possible records not only for immediate use but for archival purposes as well. A few signs for certain adjectives, verbs, and abstract terms soon followed this initial development. It is impossible to say whether the transition to a genuine system of writing, representing audible words by means of visible signs, came about swiftly or demanded a longer amount of time. In any case, desperate administrators at that time gave impetus to a new creation, the possibilities and consequences of which no one in contemporary Sumer could have foreseen.

The further development of writing can be sketched here only with a few brief strokes. The pictograms were increasingly simplified, and the forms of the signs generally became abstract and geometric. Curved lines, which could be written in clay only with difficulty, were replaced by straight ones. Above all, deeper impressions were produced at the beginning of the lines through the pressure of the stylus. These impressions became increasingly broader until the middle of the third millennium, when distinctive, wedge-shaped signs became characteristic, and cuneiform became a distinctive writing system that could even be used on metal and stone. The particular writing traditions in Babylonia, Assyria, Syria, Asia Minor, and so forth led to variant forms for most signs. At first, writing was from top to bottom, but after about 2400 it was from left to right, whereby the signs were turned 90 degrees.[2]

The signs for Sumerian words had already been used at a very early stage for other homonyms as well; thus, for example, *ti*, "arrow," was also used for *ti(l)*, "life." Later, most signs became simultaneously word and syllabic signs and, in rare cases, bi-syllabic signs. Signs existed for single sounds only in the cases of the vowels *a, e, i, u,* and perhaps *o.* Partially as a result of the coinciding of originally variant signs — their number was greatly reduced in the course of time to about six hundred — many signs had multiple word and phonetic values quite early on. Since a series of signs could also stand for a word (e.g., A.TU.GAB.LIŠ for *asal,* "Euphrates

---

2. The fundamental work on the earliest writing by A. Falkenstein, *Archäische Texte aus Uruk* (Berlin, 1936), has been somewhat superseded by many new discoveries; a new, comprehensive work on the genesis of the Sumerian script and its transformation into cuneiform is H. J. Nissen and M. W. Green, *Zeichenliste der archaischen Texte aus Uruk* (Berlin, 1987).

poplar"), some signs even took on multiple meanings. With the aid of graphic determinatives for materials such as wood or copper, places, rivers, classes of persons, deities, and other things, the scribes sought to reduce the ambiguity of the polyphony of signs to a bearable mass, but they achieved thereby only limited success. Aids to our own reading very often are provided by variations in the writing, as when one could write a syllable such as *tar* as *ta-ar*, and when two or more signs could be used for many syllables in certain periods or in specific groups of texts.

The idea that it was possible to capture a language by means of writing soon traveled along the trade routes to the west and east. The Egyptians learned from the new art and soon created their own writing system — Egyptian hieroglyphics — which indicated vowels only in rare instances. In the East, neighboring Elam was the first to adopt the new writing with some modifications. In later centuries, these modifications led to still more pronounced changes, down to the time of the neo-Elamite script of the Achaemenaean period. A native proto-Elamite script remained in use only a short period of time. The idea of writing then migrated further eastward to India, where sometime later the Indus script developed, and still further, to China.[3]

In Babylonia itself, the most important event in the history of cuneiform was the adoption of the Sumerian writing system by the Semitic Akkadians at a still unknown time in the third millennium. This process was completed over a long period of time. Indeed, the absence of any systematic means for solving the problems inherent in this adoption shows that the Akkadians adapted the Sumerian writing system to a language with a completely different structure. By applying all mono-syllabic Sumerian words as syllabic signs, and by including several further signs, the Akkadians were able to create a purely syllabic script. Over time, this script would have made possible unequivocal transcriptions, even of sounds foreign to the Sumerian, such as emphatic consonants and laryn-geals. Yet not only did the Akkadians retain the polyphony of the Sumerian system, and in certain respects expand it, they also made the writing system still more complicated by adopting many hundreds of Sumerian words, and occasionally even complete verbal forms, as Sumerograms. Moreover, the initial transcription of the consonant phonemes was at first

3. The Indus script, which is preserved preponderantly on seal inscriptions, has still not been deciphered. It is possible that an early Dravidic language was written in this script in the third millennium.

very poor: *d, t,* and *ṭ, g, k,* and *q, b* and *p, z, s,* and *ṣ,* were at first only rarely differentiated by specific syllabic signs, as for example, *ga, ka,* and *qa.* After 2000 this situation improved, first in Babylonia and later in Assyria; but even in later times the above-mentioned sounds were from time to time written with only a single sign (e.g., *az = as = aṣ*), which in many cases may indicate the loss of audible differences in pronunciation. At the beginnings of syllables, for instance, *za* and *ṣa, dur* and *ṭur, bal* and *pal* were never written with different signs. *Bu* and *pu, di* and *ṭi,* and so forth were represented by different signs only in specific regions (e.g., Assyria) and at particular times. The manner of writing in the so-called border districts of Babylonian culture, in which foreign-language substrata or superstrata — Hurrian, Canaanite, and so forth — were active, made the irregularities of the phonetic transcriptions much greater still. Nevertheless, fewer signs were in use throughout those districts, and the polyphony was reduced.[4]

Anyone who works with Akkadian cuneiform texts must be familiar not only with the frequently changing forms of the signs, but also with the quite dissimilar writing conventions which persisted throughout all the respective centuries between the different lands and districts, as well as between the manifold genres of literary works, and between documents and letters. In this regard, one can gather a great deal from the available sign lists, but in no way everything one needs to decipher the script.[5] The difficulty of interpreting cuneiform texts is frequently increased by all of these factors; this has led many scholars to specialize in very specific groups of texts.

From this it can be seen that cuneiform, despite its difficulty and the absence of any other form of writing besides Egyptian hieroglyphics, was used in many countries in Western Asia, far beyond the region in

4. Because of the great differences in writing styles, a particular writing guide must have been available in each of the border districts; some of these have already been found.

5. The heretofore comprehensive list of word signs, which certainly has been somewhat superseded, has been incorporated by A. Deimel into the *Sumerisches Lexikon,* I (3rd ed.)-III (Rome, 1928-1937). The term "lexicon" corresponds only in part to the content. Cf. also F. Ellermeier, *Sumerisches Glossar,* I/1, 1: *Sumerische Lautwerte,* in 2 vols. (Nörten-Hardenberg, 1979-1980; no further volumes appeared); R. Borger, *Assyrisch-babylonische Zeichenliste,* in collaboration with F. Ellermeier. AOAT 33 (1978); supplementary volume, AOAT 33a (1981); W. von Soden–W. Röllig, *Das Akkadische Syllabar,* 4th ed. (Rome, 1991).

which the Babylonian-Assyrian language was established. Only recently have we discovered that the earliest adoption of writing in the West was of cuneiform, in which the Eblaite language was written from about 2400 or even somewhat earlier (see above, III.2a). Eblaite texts typically feature several narrow columns side by side, usually with very short lines. Neither all the signs nor all the phonetic values of the Sumerian writing system were taken over into Eblaite, as far as can be ascertained to date; however, several new phonetic values were introduced, and some syllabic signs thus became even more ambiguous than in Babylonia. What we find unusual at Ebla is that in documents, apart from the names, particles, and some few words, people wrote almost exclusively in Sumerograms, even for the verbal forms. As a result, we still do not know many of the most widely used Eblaite words. The syllabic writings cannot reproduce all of the Semitic consonants which must be presupposed for Ebla.[6] Whether the Ebla script remained in use long after the destruction of the city by Naram-Sin of Akkad is unknown. Some properties of the cuneiform of northern Syria in the time of Hammurabi make it probable that a writing tradition had been nurtured in that region over a long period of time.

Cuneiform was also adopted for the writing of Hurrian as early as the third millennium. Even in the second millennium, the Hurrians wrote almost entirely in the syllabic script at Old Babylonian Mari, at Ugarit, Mesopotamia, and Hattusas; they primarily used the C-V (consonant-vowel) and V-C (vowel-consonant) phonetic values; C-V-C phonetic values (e.g., *sar*) are found much more rarely. The Hurrian orthography distinguished remarkably few consonants.[7]

According to our knowledge, Assyrian merchants brought cuneiform to Asia Minor about 1900. They wrote their Old Assyrian letters and documents in cuneiform, in a style which deviated considerably from the Old Babylonian. After about 1500 the writing customs in Assyria changed sharply.

When the Hittites, Luwians, and Paleans came to Asia Minor they were not writing their languages, so far as we know, nor did they even adopt the writing style of the Assyrian merchants. After about 1600,

---

6. Cf. M. Krebernik, "Zu Syllabar und Orthographie der lexikalischen Texte von Ebla," *ZA* 72 (1982): 178ff.; 73 (1983): 1ff.

7. Cf. E. A. Speiser, *Introduction to Hurrian.* Annual of the American Schools of Oriental Research 20 (1940-1941).

however, some royal inscriptions allow us to recognize the influence of the scribal school in Old Babylonian Mari. The typical Old, Middle, and Neo-Hittite writing style of the capital of Hattusas must have had still other models which we are yet unable to identify. The Hittites did not adopt all Babylonian signs, and they sharply reduced the polyphony. The writing nonetheless became more complicated in that they added Akkadograms to the Sumerograms already present in Hittite texts; in this process, complete parts of sentences were often written entirely in Akkadian, although the languages in fact differed somewhat in word order. In particular, the genitive-attribute came first in Hittite, but in Akkadian it followed the connecting word (cf. Hitt. *parnas ishās,* "house-holder," = Akk. *bēl bītim*). For many Hittite words (e.g., "woman" and "son") we have only Sumerograms and Akkadograms.

The other languages of the kingdom of Hatti (see above, III.5) were also written in cuneiform (see below for Luwian, written in pictograms). Proto-Hattian texts from the pre-Hittite era have not been found. After the destruction of Hattusas around 1200, cuneiform was no longer written in Asia Minor, as far as we know. It may been in the same period that cuneiform fell out of use in Syria-Palestine as well, until the Assyrians reintroduced it in some cities around 850, as the Babylonians did later.

Finally, in the ninth century the Urartians of Armenia adopted cuneiform for their language in a greatly simplified form. They wrote primarily in a syllabic script but also used Sumero- and Akkadograms. We do not know whether the Medes occasionally used cuneiform.

2. The Hittite Hieroglyphs (the Luwian Pictograms)

Although the Hittites and Luwians normally wrote in cuneiform, they developed a system of picture-writing after 1500 using pictograms which had long been in use. This is attested for a long time only on the seals of Hittite kings and on rock reliefs (e.g., Yazilikaya) and was inspired by, though not dependent upon, the similar writing systems in Egypt and Crete (Minoan A). A mixed system of word symbols and syllabic writing, which still has not been fully deciphered, is extant. The longer inscriptions, often with alternating right- and left-running lines, derive largely from the states which succeeded the Hittite Empire between approximately 1200 and 700 in eastern Anatolia (e.g., Malatya), Cilicia (e.g., Karatepe, with a parallel Phoenician inscription), and Syria (e.g., Carchemish, Hamath). In rare cases people wrote on lead tablets. After 850, the Aramaic which was increasingly being spoken in Syria also appeared in inscriptions. The language of the hieroglyphic inscriptions is a Luwian dialect.[8] Pictograms of another type were also found on vessels and other objects in Urartu (see above). Whether one can speak with certainty about a hieroglyphic writing system peculiar to Urartu, however, is still disputed because of the dearth of available evidence; that writing was done either from right to left, or from left to right.[9]

3. The Phoenician Alphabetic Script and Its Predecessors

a. Scripts of the Early Second Millennium in Syria-Palestine

Certainly the desire to write in their own language and, especially, to loose themselves from the complicated writing systems of cuneiform in the north and Egyptian hieroglyphics in the south emerged among the western Canaanites early in the second millennium. The oldest witnesses to this are some stone and bronze inscriptions from Byblos. Here we can identify 114 writing signs, a few of which were still pictograms, but most of which were syllabic signs. Although some are of the opinion that certain Canaanite words can be recognized in these inscriptions, a real decipherment will not be possible without further discoveries.[10]

Numerous lesser remains of early writing systems have been discovered at primitive mining sites in the Sinai peninsula and southern Palestine. However, attempts to decipher the Sinai inscriptions, which have long been known, have not progressed beyond conjecture.

---

8. A synopsis of the previous research and its many controversies is lacking for both this script and hieroglyphic Luwian.

9. There is as yet no compilation of the monumental inscriptions.

10. On this and the other writing systems described here, cf. J. Friedrich, *Geschichte der Schrift unter besonderer Berücksichtigung ihrer geistigen Entwicklung* (Heidelberg, 1966), with many examples of the writing; M. Dietrich and D. Loretz, *Die Keilalphabete: Die phönizisch-Kanaanäischen und altarabischen Alphabete in Ugarit* (Münster, 1988).

b. Phoenician and the Other Semitic Alphabets

After the idea of writing was conceived, probably in Sumerian Uruk (see above), the second great achievement in this field was the transition from ideograms and syllabic writing to the isolation of individual phonetic sounds in the form of alphabetic writing. For this, too, we must assume a monogenetic origin, since all later alphabets were either derived from the Phoenician or were created under the influence of its derivatives. Sadly, we still do not know where and when the oldest alphabet came into existence. The oldest Phoenician inscription of significance, found on the sarcophagus of Aḥiram of Byblos, is to be dated around 1000. Smaller inscriptions with a similar orthography may be some centuries older. The discovery of Ugaritic cuneiform proves that the Phoenician alphabetic script cannot have come into existence much later than 1500, since the scribes at Ugarit adopted the principle of alphabetic writing and took over the Phoenician alphabet with certain alterations; even in the forms of the signs Ugaritic depended heavily on the Phoenician alphabet. The ancient port city of Byblos (Gebal) could have been the place where alphabetic writing was invented.

It is certain, moreover, that the Phoenicians consciously drew upon the Egyptian hieratic script. Wolfgang Helck[11] has compiled a list of signs of the hieratic script after which the most ancient signs were modeled; some signs were adopted almost unchanged. Thus the Phoenicians were able to indicate their consonantal phonemes much more exactly than had been possible with cuneiform. Still, as in Egyptian, the Phoenicians initially had to leave undetermined almost all vowels and, later, all short vowels. It has frequently been argued that the letters were initially syllabic signs; so, for example, *m* had originally been a *ma*. Even should that proposal be correct, the fact remains that *m* and *m* + a vowel were written with the same letters. The writing is from right to left.

As early as 1000 alphabetic writing was adopted in South Arabia. There the forms of the signs became more starkly geometric, and writing was either from right to left or from left to right, often with a change of direction in each line (the so-called bustrophedon-style). For the ancient Semitic consonants, which were particularly well preserved in Old South Arabic, seven further signs were added to the twenty-two Phoenician letters. From South Arabia alphabetic writing further mi-

11. "Zur Herkunft der sog. 'phoenizischen' Schrift," *UF* 4 (1972): 41-45.

grated to India, where it was considerably transformed by the introduction of vowel signs. Much later it came to Ethiopia, where it was written from left to right, as in India.[12]

Alphabetic writing for Aramaic spread quickly after 1000 in Syria-Palestine and in Mesopotamia. After 900 the Aramaeans began to introduce letters for initial *aleph* and the half-vowels *w* and *y*, as well as *h* instead of *aleph*, as designations for the long vowels *a, i/e,* and *u/o.* Additional signs for short vowels were first introduced in different systems after 500. Nevertheless, (North) Arabic and the other languages employing the Arabic script (e.g., Neo-Persian, Osmanic-Turkish until the time of Ataturk) have been written right down to the present without vowel signs.

We do not know when Israel adopted the Phoenician script with its ancient alphabet, which is still in use today. It must be assumed, however, that this took place under David at the latest. Moab and other neighboring states may have followed quickly. The script migrated westward with the Phoenician-Punic language, but it was not until a thousand years later that the Arabic script was developed out of the script of the Nabateans of southern Palestine, who wrote Aramaic; this script then became a worldwide script.

Even more significant was the adoption of the alphabetic script by the Greeks, which took place around 800 at the latest. Since these people were accustomed to writing with vowels, they made vowel letters out of six consonant signs which they found to be unnecessary; to these were added four letters, among them the *omega*. The Phoenician-Hebraic alphabet was only slightly altered, and all European alphabets were subsequently derived from the Greek script.

4. Alphabetic Scripts in Cuneiform: Ugaritic and the Old Persian Script

While the Phoenician-Aramaic alphabetic script scarcely affected Babylonian-Assyrian cuneiform, even into the later stages of cuneiform's development, at very different times this script gave rise to two short-lived alphabetic cuneiform scripts, one in Syria, the other in Iran.

---

12. Cf. the table of comparative scripts in M. Höfner, *Altsüdarabische Grammatik* (Leipzig, 1943), 6-7.

In second millennium Ugarit, people wrote first Babylonian and later Assyrian in normal cuneiform as in other Syrian cities. However, for the Ugaritic language (see above, III.2b), a new cuneiform with thirty very simple signs — none with more than seven wedge-impressions — was invented, in all probability shortly after 1400. The forms of these signs were partly dependent upon Babylonian cuneiform and partly on the as yet little-known early stage of the Phoenician script, while both the writing system and the alphabet were borrowed from the latter. The alphabet known from Ugaritic alphabetic tablets contains twenty-seven consonantal signs, five more than the later Phoenician-Aramaic. Three more were added to these for writing foreign words and the Hurrian language (see above, III.3). Since these (especially Indo-European) words could not be written entirely without vowel signs, two more signs were added to the *aleph* sign, allowing one to write *a, i,* and *u* with or without the *aleph* before or after. This system was used to some extent for Ugaritic, too. Numerous clay tablets written in this script were recently found outside of Ugarit. After the destruction of Ugarit around 1200, the writing doubtless fell out of use.[13]

Much later, in the sixth century, a greatly simplified form of cuneiform was invented, in all probability commissioned by the Achaemenaean king Darius I for his Old Persian rock inscriptions. This script contained signs for *a, i,* and *u* and thirty-three signs for consonants with a following vowel — usually *a,* occasionally *u* and *i;* these could also be read as vowelless. To these signs were added word signs with variations for land, earth, king, God, and Ahuramazda. The script represented the language insufficiently and was, as far as we can see, used only on stone and metal inscriptions (and on weights and seals). It did not survive the demise of the Achaemenaean Empire. In Iran during the Parthian and Sassanian Empires, a further development of the Aramaic script was employed.[14]

13. Cf. C. H. Gordon, *Ugaritic Textbook.* AnOr 38 (1965): 11ff.

14. Cf. writing tablets and attempts at writing in J. Friedrich–W. Röllig, *Phönizisch-punische Grammatik.* AnOr 46 (1970): 272.

CHAPTER V

The History of Ancient Western Asia:
The Historical Sources

It is not the task of this book to provide an overview of the history of the ancient Orient covering nearly three thousand years, since that has already been undertaken in other volumes.[1] The purpose here is only to characterize very briefly the main epochs in order to sketch out the historical framework for the following chapters. Moreover, it is necessary to identify the limits of what the available historical sources can tell us, and thus to indicate what can and cannot be expected from an historical reconstruction for this region. Before this task can be undertaken, however, a few words are needed regarding the chronology of the earlier periods, which is still controversial.

1. Chronology: King Lists, Date Lists, and Eponym Lists

Precisely calculable astronomical data, insofar as these can be tied to certain events, comprise the fixed points for the chronology of ancient Western Asia. Provisionally, there are only two such dates for Babylonia and Assyria: the total solar eclipse of May 28, 585, predicted by Thales of Miletus, which forced the Medes and the Lydians to break off a great battle, and the total solar eclipse of June 15, 763, reported in the eponym

---

1. For the early period, cf. H. J. Nissen, *The Early History of the Ancient Near East;* also vols. I-III of *The Cambridge Ancient History;* vols. 2-4 of the *Fischer-Weltgeschichte* (Frankfurt, 1965-1967): *Die altorientalische Reiche,* I-III; vols. I and II of the *Propylaen-Weltgeschichte* (Berlin, 1961-1962) (various authors).

Tiglath-Pileser III (745-727), founder of the Neo-Assyrian Empire, in his war chariot. Gypsum relief from Nimrud. *(Trustees of the British Museum)*

list of Bursagale, which precisely dates that portion of the Assyrian eponym canon which is complete back to 931.[2] From the Assyrian King List[3] we can still establish dates in Assyria with near exactitude back to about 1420. Babylonian chronology, which suffers from a number of gaps in the king lists, also profits from the Assyrian King List through synchronisms, which nonetheless leave a certain amount of room for play. The Assyrian King List is only incompletely preserved for the first half of the second millennium, and cannot provide entirely correct information at all points. Even in Assyria at that time dating was done

2. Cf. A. Ungnad, "Eponymen," *RLA* II (1938): 412-457, which of course now needs a great deal of supplementation; cf. also E. Weidner, "Die assyrischen Eponymen," *AfO* 13 (1939-1940): 308ff.; and C. Saporetti, *Gli Eponimi medioassiri* (Malibu, 1979).

3. Regarding this and what follows, cf. D. O. Edzard (A. "Sumerisch") and A. K. Grayson (B. "Akkadisch"), "Königlisten und Chroniken," *RLA* VI (1980): 77-135, where the texts are reproduced. The most recent position taken on the chronology of the Assyrian kingdom is by J. Boese and G. Wilhelm, "Assur-Dan I, Ninurta-apil-Ekur und die mittelassyrische Chronologie," *WZKM* 71 (1971): 19ff., with bibliography.

according to eponyms; unfortunately, we possess no eponym lists for this period, although such lists probably formed the basis for the great King List.[4]

The chronology of the remaining areas of Western Asia after about 1500 depends primarily upon that of Assyria. Yet this dependence makes possible only rather rare, tolerably exact numerical determinations, so long as further temporal data or synchronisms do not come into play from Egypt, as is sometimes the case with the Hittite kingdom and Syria-Palestine.[5] The numerous chronological references in the Old Testament create a particularly difficult problem as well.[6]

During the Old Babylonian period, it was customary to list simultaneously reigning monarchs one after the other (on the reasons for this practice, see below, XI.1). The same custom was employed in even earlier times, too, and has had extremely troublesome consequences for chronology. Thus we arrive at a margin of error of almost 150 years for Hammurabi's dynasty, after separating out useless assessments; the margin of error for still earlier times is occasionally even greater. For instance, we had long thought that for the time of Hammurabi's fourth successor, Ammi-ṣaduqa, traditional references to the Venus constellations, which are repeated every fifty-six or sixty-four years, radically limited the uncertainty. This assumption would have set Hammurabi's first year in 1728 according to a low chronology, 1792 according to a medial chronology, and 1848 according to a high chronology. After scholars had called into question the authenticity of the much later Venus references (which had been transmitted in omen texts), these came to be regarded by almost all modern astronomers as a later construct and thus lost all significance for chronology. Therefore, we had to renounce all exact dates prior to 1500, but could not at the same time resort to round, approximate numbers of the kind we have been accustomed to give for the early third millennium. This was because the exact length of each king's reign was almost always known for the period of the last Sumerian dynasty of Ur III and the following dynasties of Isin, Larsa, and Babylon, a situation completely different from

4. Cf. J. Hughes, *Secrets of the Times*, JSOT Supplement 66 (Sheffield, 1990).

5. Cf. E. Hornung, *Untersuchungen zur Chronologie und Geschichte des Neuen Reiches* (Wiesbaden, 1964); E. Bickermann, *Chronology of the Ancient World*, 2nd ed. (Ithaca, N.Y., 1980); R. W. Ehrich, ed., *Chronologies in Old World Archaeology*, 3rd ed., 2 vols. (Chicago, 1992).

6. Cf. most recently J. H. Hayes and P. K. Hooker, *A New Chronology for the Kings of Israel and Judah* (Atlanta, 1988).

that of the earlier period. Throughout this period, as had previously been the case in Babylon, dating was mostly done according to the names of the Sumerian years, which as a rule derived from an event of the previous year held to be of particular significance. These year names were assembled in date lists of years, of which large portions are extant;[7] they are the basis for the concluding section of the so-called Sumerian King List with its almost entirely exact numbers. There is presently no prospect that we will be able to construct a generally accepted absolute chronology for the Old Babylonian period and earlier periods. It is therefore expedient, in connection with the previous approaches, to establish either the low, the medial, or the high chronology in order to be able to date exactly within that chronology on the basis of king lists and date lists. I prefer the low chronology because it fits Hittite history best (or is only a little longer) and because valid reasons exist for the assumption that Yaḫdun-Lim and Zimri-Lim of Mari reigned after the end of the Twelfth Dynasty of Egypt.[8]

The dates deviate widely for the period of the Empire of Akkad, since the duration of the foreign rule by the Gutians which followed (see above, III.4a) is still disputed. For the time before Akkad, the Sumerian King List gives greatly exaggerated numbers which are of no use for chronology, and we are thrown back on estimates. Some kind of agreement with the chronology of the first dynasties of Egypt, which is admittedly still disputed, is necessary for the time of the invention of writing. Attempts have been made to establish dates more exactly with the help of the carbon 14 method, which measures the age of objects by ascertaining the level of radioactive isotopes. As a result of many methodological inadequacies, however, the results of these measurements deviate too widely to give reliable figures for the last five thousand years.[9]

7. Cf. A. Ungnad, "Datenlisten," *RLA* II (1936): 131-194; the multifarious corrections to the text of the date formulas and numerous additional dates have never again been assembled in a comprehensive form. On the Sumerian King List, see above, n. 3.

8. The Mari texts do not mention Egypt, which is almost incomprehensible in the time of the powerful Twelfth Dynasty.

9. On this, cf. B. Hrouda, and many collaborators, *Methoden der Archäologie: Eine Einführung in ihre naturwissenschaftlichen Techniken* (Munich, 1978). Other scientific methods treated in this work include the dendrochronological determination of age, archaeo-magnetism and magnetic dating, and thermoluminescence and obsidian dating.

2. Sources for Political History

Since the economy, society, and culture of ancient Western Asia will be treated in later chapters, only political history and the sources for this are at issue here. The following groups of sources are available in different degrees: (a) personal accounts of historical persons, primarily of kings and nobles, as well as their higher functionaries, in inscriptions, date formulas, and other forms of reports and letters; (b) accounts of events through other means, both contemporary and later (to these belong the lists of kings, eponyms, and dates, various types of chronicles [for all of these, see below, XI.1] and epic poems singing praises to kings [see below, XIII.3a], and further statements in the Old Testament and by ancient writers; outside of Israel, however, there was no historical writing in the ancient Orient in the strict sense of the term); (c) letters of officials and administrations, as well as many private letters (unfortunately, the letters are only rarely dated); (d) documents of all types, including political treaties (these are most often dated); (e) interpretations in the omen collections which are tied to political themes (see below, XI.5), primarily concerning conditions in the various countries, but references to incidents involving individual kings are also frequent; nevertheless, many of these statements are legendary; (f) references to historical events and mention of individual kings in literary works of various types; (g) oracular inquiries, prophecies, and comparable communications of various kinds.

The fruitfulness of this group of sources varies considerably according to the persons concerned, the time of composition, and the country of origin. Political and religious biases, as well as the frequent desire of rulers to laud themselves and other propagandistic influences, must be considered and evaluated. Here we can do no more than refer to these practices by way of examples of different kinds.[10]

10. Cf. R. Borger and W. Schramm, *Einleitung in die assyrischen Königsinschriften*, parts 1 and 2 (Leiden, 1961-1973); and in *RLA* VI (1980), the following articles: D. O. Edzard and A. K. Grayson, "Konigslisten und Chroniken," 77ff.; Edzard and J. Renger, "Königsinschriften," 59ff.; and P. Michalowski, "Königsbriefe," 51ff. (up to the Old Babylonian period).

3. The Early Sumerian Period and Early Dynastic Period

The Early Historical or Early Sumerian period began shortly before the invention of writing around 3200 in Babylonia, and is regarded to be the time of the earliest high civilization. It is divided into two main phases based on the development of writing and changes in architecture and art. The second of these phases, also known as the Jemdet Nasr period, may have lasted until 2800. There were as yet no royal inscriptions, and the numerous documents, mostly from Uruk, cannot be understood in their entirety. The Sumerian King List may contain some names that belong in this period, even though that may never be proven. The eight to ten "kings before the Flood" in this list, with Sumerian names and reigns extending up to 72,000 years, may in part be a later invention (cf. the comparable biblical genealogy in Genesis 5). That Eridu was the most ancient Sumerian city may nevertheless prove true.[11] On the problems of the Sumerians and the Semites, see above, III.1.

A period of relative stability began five hundred years after this early period and can be identified by its monumental architecture. It is called the Early Dynastic period in Babylonia, Assyria, and Mesopotamia and is divided into periods I, II, and III. Very brief royal inscriptions are attested for II, as well as extensive Sumerian inscriptions with reports of building activities, wars, and reforms, mostly since 2400 and stemming from Lagash, which encountered many conflicts with neighboring states after the reigns of Eannatum and Entemena (see below, VI.1, for the reforms of Uruinimgina [Urukagina] of Lagash). The King Lists for this time indicate frequent changes in sovereignty: a few historical reminiscences are contained in some Sumerian and Babylonian mythic poems, for example, on Enmerkar and Lugalbanda, Gilgamesh and Etana (see below, XIII.3.d, e). The Sumerian and individual Akkadian documents become widely understandable from period II on, and from period III on, overwhelmingly so. They mention many important personalities and are rich in many kinds of information from different cities. In spite of this, we know with certainty only a coincidental number of essential events. At the end of this period stands the conquering king Lugalzaggesi of Umma, who was ultimately defeated by Sargon of Akkad (see below).

11. In contrast to Ur(i), Unug (Uruk), Larsa, and other cities, Eridu had a Sumerian name. On the King List, see above, n. 3.

History begins in Syria with Early Dynastic III, which corresponds somewhat to the middle of the Early Bronze Age. The manifold reports on the kings of Ebla and other states — even Mesopotamia — contained in the documents, letters, and texts similar to state treaties from Ebla are to some extent conjectural, not least because many places and lands cannot yet be localized. Nor do we know yet whether Ebla at that time was the occasional capital of a realm which may have stretched as far as Assyria, or whether it was only a center of trade and culture. It has already been established that our previous conception of the history of the twenty-fourth century is in need of substantial correction, since heretofore unknown states have now come onto the historical scene.[12]

4. The Empire of Akkad and the Neo-Sumerian Period

During the Akkadian period, the sources, now largely in the Akkadian language, are abundant for the first demonstrable empire in history. The upstart Sharrukin — commonly known as Sargon[13] — bore arms as far as Anatolia and southwestern Iran by the middle of his long reign (ca. 2330-2274). His successors Rimush and Manishtushu were able to hold on to the core of the realm, which Naram-Sin (2250-2213) then, for a short time, expanded, primarily to the southeast. From these four kings we possess many inscriptions containing battle and campaign reports, though certainly these are only later copies that are not correct in every instance. To this may be added a rich saga-tradition from the Hittite Empire which embellishes the accounts considerably; individual pieces from this tradition were transcribed as late as the time of the Chaldean Empire. In these, as in many interpretations of omens, Sargon appears as the favorite of the gods and the ruler of good fortune, while Naram-Sin, despite his splendid beginnings, appears primarily as an ill-fated king. Even this multi-faceted tradition, however, fails to provide answers to many essential questions.[14]

12. The information in the books mentioned in ch. III, n. 7, has already become somewhat obsolete.

13. The nominal form Sargon, attested only once in the Old Testament for Sargon II of Assyria, is really a spelling error for Sargin, but it has nonetheless become accepted usage.

14. This topic has never been treated in a comprehensive fashion. For part of the Sargon tradition, cf. B. Lewis, *The Sargon Legend* (Cambridge, Mass., 1980).

Following the collapse of the Empire of Akkad and the expulsion of the Gutians (see above, p. 26) by Utu-ḫengal of Uruk, the Third Dynasty of Ur brought something of a renaissance of Sumerian culture. Despite many, primarily brief royal inscriptions, we know little of the political history of this period. That is because the kings of the Third Dynasty of Ur, just as most of the later kings of Babylonia, wrote of their victories in highly stereotypical and formulaic language without providing concrete facts, and otherwise only reported on their building projects. The year-date formulas say somewhat more, as do individual letters and notices from a later time. Shulgi (2046-1998), the most important of the dynasty, did not seek to establish an empire. On the cultic deification of the monarch, which for nearly three hundred years had been the most remarkable phenomenon of the period, see below, VI.2; on the bureaucracy attested through tens of thousands of documents, see below, VI.3.

The city-prince *(en-si),* Gudea of Lagash (approximately 2060-2035[15]), probably reigned simultaneously with Ur-Nammu (2064-2046), the founder of the Third Dynasty of Ur, from whom Gudea was loosely independent. Gudea's reign is attested through his many statues, sometimes featuring long inscriptions, and his peculiar building hymns (see below, XIII.2). He was apparently a man of great intellect and spirit who once more elevated the office of city-prince to high public regard, and made it the institution which had characterized Babylonia before the rise of the kings of Akkad, with their centralized administrations. Yet shortly after the end of Gudea's reign, Shulgi degraded the city-princes to the status of local governors. The city-princes nonetheless achieved renewed strength and importance as the central administration became increasingly weaker under the last king of the Dynasty of Ur, Ibbi-Sin (1980-1955), until Sumer was crushed between Elam and condottieri of Canaanite origin.

5. The Beginnings of Assyria and Its Trade Colonies

Because of a dearth of sources, very little is known of Assyria in the third millennium or what earlier inhabitants the Akkadians met there.

---

15. Gudea's temporal relationship to Ur-Nammu is disputed, and many begin Gudea's reign before that of Ur-Nammu.

Whether Assyria is mentioned in the Ebla texts is still disputed,[16] though individual documents and the inscription of a city prince are known from the Akkadian period. Assyria did belong to the Empire of Akkad at times, as well as to the Third Dynasty of Ur. From the nineteenth century we know of some royal inscriptions in the Assyrian language, primarily from the kings Ilushumma and Irishum I (about 1800). Our main sources for this period, however, are the many thousand Assyrian letters and documents from the trade colonies in Cappadocia, foremost of which was Kanish (modern Kultepe), the source of the most tablets by far.[17] There is scarcely any mention of historical events in these tablets, but a great deal can be learned from them on the subjects of economics, the social order, and many other matters.

A number of foreign usurpers followed the dynasty of Ilushumma, among whom Shamshi-Adad I (approximately 1750-1717) was the most significant (see below).

6. The Old Babylonian Period

The Old Babylonian period, from perhaps 1950 to 1530, was marked by unrest, but it was an age rich in new ideas as well. The often short-lived dynasties in the changing capital cities were primarily of Canaanite-Amorite origin.[18] Even in these cities, which were able to maintain relative stability for longer periods of time, albeit with fluctuating geographic parameters, the ruling families changed often. The ten successive generations in Babylon from Sumula'el, through Hammurabi (1729-1686), to Samsu-ditana (1816-1531), were an exceptional case; among the largely contemporary dynasties from Isin (1969-1732) and Larsa (1961-

16. The reason is the unconfirmed reading of a geographical designation for a land in the Eblaite writing style.

17. Cf. P. Garelli, *Les Assyriens en Cappadoce* (Paris 1963); and M. T. Larsen, *The Old Assyrian City-State and Its Colonies* (Copenhagen, 1976). Earlier, some scholars held the incorrect view that Assyria had formed an empire in this period.

18. Cf. D. O. Edzard, *Die zweite Zwischenzeit Babyloniens* (Wiesbaden, 1957); G. Buccellati, *The Amorites of the Ur III Period*. Kings who resided in immediate succession in the same capital city were brought together in the Babylonian king lists to form a dynasty, without their respective family origins having been taken into account.

1700; Rim-Sin, 1761-1700), the changes in the ruling families were more frequent.

Other important centers in Mesopotamia were Eshnunna on the Diyala and Mari on the middle Euphrates. In addition there were Halab (Aleppo) in Syria and Carchemish on the Euphrates. The previously mentioned usurper Shamshi-Adad, from the small city of Terqa, not far from Mari, marched as far as Assyria, so that from there he could conquer his homeland, along with Mari and northern Mesopotamia. Only after Shamshi-Adad's death was Hammurabi able to expand to the south as well as the northwest from his initially small land base, until he had subjugated all of Babylonia and parts of Assyria and Mesopotamia. Still, Hammurabi's modest empire-building did not long survive him, since southern Babylonia had already broken away under an independent Sealand dynasty in the time of Hammurabi's son Samsu-iluna (1686-1648). In any case, the center of Babylonia remained in the north, in contrast to the Isin-Larsa period. The First Dynasty of Babylon, already badly weakened by the Kassites (see below), was brought to an end by a Hittite incursion in 1531.

The sources for the Old Babylonian period are unusually numerous and manifold in comparison with the Neo-Sumerian period, though they are still very unevenly distributed and considerable gaps remain in our knowledge. The royal inscriptions in Babylonia had long been composed in Sumerian and were used primarily to report on building projects. Some Babylonian inscriptions from Hammurabi, Samsu-iluna, and some petty kings, as well as from Shamshi-Adad and his predecessor in Mari, Yaḫdun-Lim, offer somewhat more. Still, without the year-date formulas we would know nothing of many important events in this period.[19] As for Hammurabi, the historical introduction to his law stela is especially fertile (see below, X.1b). We also possess individual royal inscriptions from northern Syria (e.g., Ebla), for which the inscriptions of the Hittite king Hattusilis I (about 1550) contain further important supplementary information.

From numerous Babylonian cities as well as the kingdoms of Eshnunna (see above) and Mari we have hundreds and even thousands of legal and administrative documents of all kinds. These documents, with their date and oath formulas in which kings are named, along with other evidence, widen our knowledge of history. Similar documents

---

19. The sequence of years designated with date formulas often cannot be established, since the annual date lists from Mari and Eshnunna are still lacking.

from northern Syria are at present largely unpublished, with the exception of the archives of the city of Alalakh.[20]

To these documents must be added thousands of letters from private and public archives written almost exclusively in syllabic script. The private letters deal with subjects concerning mostly business or agriculture, but they also contain historical reports, for which, as a rule, the exact dating is absent. Only a small portion of the administrative correspondence of the kings of Isin and Larsa remains, but much more has been preserved from the time of Hammurabi and from his successor in Babylon, though the latter's records are fewer than are those of Hammurabi. Only through Hammurabi's correspondence and that of his highest officials do we know that his pronouncements of concern for the oppressed in the law stela and in his inscriptions are more than merely attractive figures of speech; even the common person and the inhabitants of conquered cities could appeal to the king when seeking justice.

The great palace archive of Mari provides far more comprehensive information than other sources regarding the patriarchal absolutism of this period. This archive contains primarily public correspondence from the time of Yaḫdun-Lim (before 1745), somewhat more from his nephew Zimri-Lim (1716-1695) and from the conqueror Shamshi-Adad I, who came out of Assyria and ruled between the latter two. A further difference between the Mari letters and those of Hammurabi's reign is that the Mari letters contain much information on foreign affairs, military campaigns, and treaties. Above all, however, the main characters in these letters come alive in a way which is highly unusual in the ancient Orient before the Sargonid period of the Neo-Assyrian Empire.[21] Thus, Shamshi-Adad appears as the educator of his sons: Ishme-Dagan I (1717-1677), who succeeded him in Assyria, and the much weaker Yasmaḫ-Adad, who resided in Mari as viceroy. The same is true of Zimri-Lim, along with the women of his court.

For the total picture of this period, the continued life of Sumerian literature (see below, XIII.1) is of even more significance than the emergence of an autonomous Babylonian literature (in many respects inde-

20. A great portion of the texts were published by D. J. Wiseman in *The Alalakh Tablets* (London, 1953). Many additions can be found in *JCS* 8 (1954): 1ff. and 13 (1959): 19ff., 50ff.

21. The letters and documents can be found primarily in the series *Archives royales de Mari*, which at present runs to twenty-six volumes, as well as in the French periodicals *Revue d'Assyriologie, Syria,* and *MARI.*

pendent of the Sumerian) and the introduction of new concepts in the realm of science (see below, XI.2). In comparison, Old Babylonian art, following the creative Akkadian era, is exceptionally modest.

7. The Ancient Orient between 1530 and 1000

The raid of the Hittite king Mursilis I on Babylon in 1531 was a political episode which brought the Hittites little gain, but in connection with other changes it held weighty consequences for Mesopotamia. The time between this incursion and 1400 is often called the "Dark Age" of Babylonian history. For this period there are scarcely any sources for Babylonia and Syria, outside of Hittite Anatolia, apart from later king lists, which are not always reliable. We can therefore only partially deduce, from the better documented political circumstances of the Amarna period (see below), the upheavals brought about by the Kassite invasion of Babylonia and by the invasions of the Hurrians in the north and west, as well as further Canaanite groups in Syria-Palestine. We learn almost nothing of the First Dynasty of the Sealands in southern Babylonia or of the early Kassite kings. The inscriptions of the later Kassite kings, composed in late Sumerian, are quite meager in terms of their historical contents.[22] After 1300, land-grant documents on boundary stones (Bab. *kudurru*) contain additional information on these kings, who had long since ceased to be regarded as foreign rulers. The Elamite king Shilhak-Inshushinak exploited the disorder in the last years of the Kassite dynasty (about 1677-1152) to conquer Babylonia. The Second Dynasty of Isin (approximately 1152-1020), with Nebuchadnezzar I (1120-1098) as the most significant king after Hammurabi, brought about a new political and cultural resurgence. Soon afterward, the Assyrian struggle with the Aramaeans (see below) brought serious reverses for the region. The sources, including Assyrian inscriptions and chronicles, give scant testimony to contemporary events, and then only to a few kings, as was the case with the Kassites. Far fewer letters and documents are preserved for this period than for the later years of the Kassite dynasties.[23]

22. Cf. J. A. Brinkman, *Materials and Studies for Kassite History,* I (Chicago, 1976). There are still unpublished documents from the early Kassite period.

23. Cf. J. A. Brinkman, *A Political History of Post-Kassite Babylonia, 1158-722 B.C.* (Rome, 1968), which also deals with the following.

North of Kassite Babylonia, the Mitannian kingdom (about 1460-1330; see above, III.3, 4) extended for a time from the Zagros to the Mediterranean, with the capital city of Wassukkanni (modern Tell Feheriya, near Ras el-ʿAin). Unfortunately, royal inscriptions are entirely lacking for this realm; for Saushtatar, the founder of the kingdom, a single seal remains. Through the archives at Tell el-Amarna (see below), a number of very long letters in the Babylonian and Hurrian languages have come down to us from Tushratta, the last completely independent king of Mitanni. Assyrian and Hittite inscriptions as well as treaties with Hittite kings also contain important information. Some archives of documents and correspondence have been found in provincial cities. The most important are the archives of the principality of Arrapkha (modern Kirkuk), especially those of Nuzi, which contain approximately four thousand tablets. Sumerian and Akkadian texts from the archives of Emar on the Euphrates (modern Meskene), whose contents are much more diverse, have recently been published.[24]

Even Assyria was for a long time incorporated into the Mitannian kingdom. The princes and kings of Assyria from Ashur-uballiṭ I (1354-1318) on regained their independence around 1350 and soon conquered the eastern portion of Mitanni. This was accomplished primarily under Adad-nirari I (1296-1264), Shalmaneser I (1264-1234), and Tukulti-Ninurta I (1234-1197), the last of whom temporarily occupied northern Babylonia and destroyed Babylon itself. A war epic vividly depicts the latter struggle (see below, XIII.3a). The murder of Tukulti-Ninurta I was followed by a period of decline, after which Tiglath-Pileser I (Ass. Tukulti-apal-Esharra; 1116-1077), after many struggles against the Aramaeans, created a great new empire stretching to the region of the Mediterranean. All of the above-named kings left behind many, often lengthy inscriptions with exhaustive war accounts. They were usually composed in a Babylonian dialect colored by Assyrian, which was regarded as elegant in Assyria. The documents and letters from Assyria and some of its provincial cities, dated as before according to eponyms, are less productive as historical materials. In this period, Shalmaneser I had already organized the first great deportations, and Tukulti-Ninurta I continued this policy.

24. D. Arnaud, *Emar VI. Recherches au pays d'Aštata 1-4* (Paris, 1985-1987). A comprehensive treatment of the archives of Nuzi, Arrapkha, and Kurrukhanni is still awaited, although many individual studies have been published, as well as the texts themselves.

Especially characteristic of Western Asia in the fourteenth and, to some extent, even the thirteenth century were the many forms of international correspondence and rather extensive treaties. These documents were written in the Babylonian, Hittite, and very seldom, Hurrian languages and stem from Asia Minor, Syria, and Egypt. The fourteenth century is called the Amarna Age after the archive found a century ago in Akhetaton, near el-Amarna, the capital city of the Egyptian sun king Amenophis IV/Akhenaton. The archive contains numerous letters written in a West Babylonian dialect, the diplomatic language of the time.[25] According to this diplomatic correspondence, the great states of that age — Egypt, Hatti, Mitanni, Babylonia, Assyria, and occasionally Alashia (Cyprus) — recognized each other as entitled to equal status and negotiated often and long in order to remove any grounds for war, until this system of states collapsed again after 1300. The petty states of Syria-Palestine — for example, Jerusalem, Gebal (Byblos), Ṣumur (Simyra), Halab (Aleppo), and Alalakh — were for the most part vassal states of Egypt, though in northern Syria they were subject first to Mitanni and later to Hatti. Local princes and condottieri occasionally attempted, however, to wrest away the territory from the great powers for themselves, and in so doing often made war upon one another. Their names were mostly Hurrian or Canaanite. In the highly mixed population of Syria, moreover, there were numerous class divisions (see below, VI.4c).

The archives of Ugarit and Hattusas also yield rich results for the thirteenth century. After the Sea Peoples stormed the Levant around 1200, a catastrophe which is still not clear in many of its details, all traditions were extinguished for a long time. For Palestine we are thrown back almost exclusively on the historical books of the Old Testament, which provide only incomplete information on the newly immigrated Israelite tribes and their more cultured opponents in the land. The few extant Phoenician inscriptions are rather unproductive. (For the very important archives of Emar, see above, n. 24.)

---

25. Besides the great edition of the Amarna tablets by J. A. Knudtzon, O. Weber, and E. Ebeling, *Die Amarna-Tafeln.* Vorderasiatische Bibliothek 2 (Leipzig, 1915), cf. A. F. Rainey, *El Amarna Tablets 359-379*, 2nd ed. AOAT 8 (1978); and J.-G. Heintz, *et al.*, *Index Documentaire d'el Amarna 1* (Wiesbaden, 1982). W. L. Moran, *The Amarna Letters* (Baltimore, 1992), provides a new English translation. Many additional studies are available which treat the cities and princes mentioned in the letters.

8. Western Asia from 1000 to 750 and the Rise of the Assyrian Empire

Before and after the turn of the millennium, the Aramaic tribes (see above, III.2b) brought about quite unstable circumstances. In Babylonia, only a few kings were able to establish themselves in the land and at the same time successfully defend their territories against the attacks of the Assyrians. The sources for this period are extremely scanty, and leave us in the dark on many questions.

The Assyrians were only a little better off in this regard, but they were able to defend their homeland against the Aramaeans. Syria-Palestine was left to itself: David of Israel was temporarily able to occupy Damascus, and perhaps even Aleppo, without fearing the intervention of the great powers. Royal inscriptions resumed after about 960 and soon became rich sources of information again. Supplementary information in official chronicles first appeared after 910. About this time Assyria again took the offensive, primarily against the Aramaic states in Mesopotamia, as we learn from the inscriptions, now composed predominantly in Assyrian. The Assyrians also fought with the Babylonians over border districts with mixed success. The reign of Ashurnasirpal II (884-859), marked by brutal but systematic military advances, represented the high point of the first great period of Assyrian expansion. During this king's tenure, he resettled great portions of those ethnic groups still intent on remaining autonomous, in an intensifying application of the policy the Assyrian kings had employed against rebellious subjects since the thirteenth century. Ashurnasirpal II's many inscriptions and his reliefs on the palace walls in Calah served primarily propagandistic purposes.

His son, Shalmaneser III (859-824), struck much further afield with the same methods, but Shalmaneser often overestimated his potential and suffered many reverses in Syria, where Damascus, Israel, and other states formed successful coalitions against him. Shalmaneser, too, left behind many long inscriptions and campaign reports in series of sculpted reliefs (see below, XIV.1).[26]

We hear much less from Shalmaneser III's successors, although Adad-nirari III (810-782) was the first to advance to the border of Egypt. The power of the governors of the larger provinces increased under him

26. Cf. Schramm in *Einleitung in die assyrischen Königsinschriften*.

and even more so under his much weaker successors. These governors, and their Syrian vassal-rulers, often set up stelas to themselves with their own inscriptions in Akkadian, Aramaic, and even hieroglyphic Luwian, and these contain important information.

The kingdom of Urartu in Armenia arose as an occasionally dangerous opponent of Assyria after around 850. The kings of this realm (Ispuinis, Menuas, and Argistis I; about 828-753) also expanded southward to Syria and left mostly Urartian inscriptions (see above, pp. 25ff.). In contrast, we have no written sources for northwestern Iran, where a new kingdom was emerging in Media, or for Elam in the south.

Syria-Palestine was unable to give rise to a great state encompassing the whole region, because the development of the region outside northern Syria was all too often disturbed by invasions by the great powers. Although Damascus was for a long time the leading state, it never became a political center. Other than Israel and Judah, we are only barely familiar with the history of the many smaller states, despite a number of inscriptions; these require their own treatment.

9. The Neo-Assyrian Empire: Its Zenith and Decline: Tiglath-Pileser III and the Sargonids

The usurper Tiglath-Pileser III (746-727), who may have been born in a collateral line of the ruling dynasty, was the actual founder of the Neo-Assyrian Empire. He decisively defeated Urartu in northern Syria, conquered Damascus, and reduced Babylon to a distinct type of vassal state. He reduced the size of the provinces in order to limit the power of the provincial governors, which had become excessive. His inscriptions, with their particularly dry stylization, are only partially extant. Letters from royal agents (e.g., in Urartu) and a single chronicle contain additional information. Records of Tiglath-Pileser III's son, Shalmaneser V (727-722), have been obscured for reasons which are not wholly known; he died during the siege of Samaria, the capital of Israel.

The ensuing period of the four great Sargonids, except for the later years of Ashurbanipal II, is much more richly attested in the sources, and in greater variety, than any other period in the history of Mesopotamia. Each king left behind numerous and often lengthy inscriptions, which both in style and in what they say or do not say bear the stamp of the royal personality (see below, XIII.2). A great body of correspondence, mostly from Nineveh and in the Assyrian and Babylonian languages, is extremely fruitful as well. Only the Old Babylonian archive from Mari (see above) is similarly informative with regard to the king and his functionaries. Among the texts preserved, the royal documents are particularly important.[27] Also included are oracular consultations of the gods Shamash and Adad by means of liver divination, as well as oracles from Ishtar of Arbela and royal prayers. The Old Testament, and occasionally Greek reports, are of supplementary significance. Finally should be mentioned the pictorial accounts on the palace walls of Dur-Sharrukin and Nineveh (see p. 234). We have only a few inscriptions from the successors of Ashurbanipal, some chronicles and groups of documents from Babylonia as well, which are important for dating. There is no comprehensive treatment of the Sargonide period.

The usurper Sargon II (Ass. Sharrukin; 722-705) completed the work of Tiglath-Pileser III. He defeated Urartu, pressed toward Cilicia and the Egyptian border, and even fought with Elam in Babylonia. At any rate, he did not always recognize Babylonia's borders. Sargon degraded most vassal states to the status of provinces. Out of his mistrust for the priests and citizens of the capital cities, he founded the new capital city of Dur-Sharrukin, but was unable to complete it. Sargon fell in battle in the east.[28]

Sargon II's highly gifted son, Sennacherib (Ass. Sin-aḫ-eriba; 705-681), was even less restrained, but achieved no permanent success, despite the total destruction of Babylon and an assault on Elam by sea. To his impressive technical accomplishments belong the great aqueduct of Jerwan in Assyria, much of which survives today. He transferred the capital city back to Nineveh, which was greatly expanded, but was murdered by his own sons for his persecution of the priests in neglected Calah. Although Sargon had been a patron of Assyrian art, it reached its zenith under Sennacherib.

Sennacherib's son Esarhaddon (Ass. Aššur-aḫ-iddin; 681-669) rebuilt Babylon and endeavored to settle the Assyrians' differences there,

27. Cf. J. N. Postgate, *Neo-Assyrian Royal Grants and Decrees.* Studia Pohl 1 (Rome, 1969); E. G. Klauber, *Politisch-religiöse Texte aus der Sargonidenzeit* (Leipzig, 1913), on the texts relating to liver divination.

28. Sennacherib allowed the theologians to affirm that the violent death of his father, and his failure to receive proper burial, had been a result of Sargon's sin in building his new capital city.

but he fell into difficulty with the Cimmerians east of Assyria (see pp. 27-28) and the Medes; his plight is expressed in numerous questions put to the gods. An alliance with the Scythians temporarily relieved the situation in the north. The ailing king was then able to conquer northern Egypt and died on a second Egyptian campaign. Prior to his death, Esarhaddon had determined that his successor, Ashurbanipal, must turn over northern Babylonia to his older brother, Shamash-shum-ukin.

After a further campaign to Egypt, Ashurbanipal (669-627) was forced to withdraw; later he turned primarily against Elam, which had supported Shamash-shum-ukin's bloodily suppressed revolt against him in 648. Following extensive warfare, the Elamite capital Susa was conquered and destroyed in 639. Ashurbanipal once again inspired artists to produce relief series with war and hunting scenes, and he encouraged scholars to collect the first great library in Nineveh; the extant remains have still not been completely edited.

Ashurbanipal's last years were darkened by a civil war in which his twin sons Sin-shar-ishkun (629-612) and Ashur-etel-ilāni (about 633-624) struggled with each other. The father spent his last years in Harran in northern Mesopotamia. This civil war weakened Assyria so badly that after futile initial attacks the Chaldean king Nabopolassar (see below), in conjunction with Cyaxares of Media (625-588), was able to conquer and completely destroy the Assyrian capital cities of Ashur, Calah, and, in 612, Nineveh. The epilogue ended in Harran in 609, after which the Assyrian Empire was partitioned between Babylonia and Media. The western provinces, which had long since lost their autonomy, were taken over without much struggle.[29]

10. The Neo-Babylonian Chaldean Empire (626-539)

During the period of the Neo-Assyrian Empire, Babylonia was ruled, often in rapid succession, by native kings or princes of smaller districts who were mostly of Aramaic origin and by Assyrian viceroys or governors. There was seldom rest in the land. In 626 the Chaldean prince of southern Babylonia, Nabopolassar, seized power and gradually estab-

29. For a conclusion to a controversial discussion over the last twenty-five years of the Assyrian Empire, cf. J. Reade, "The Accession of Sinsharishkun," *JCS* 23 (1970): 1ff.

lished himself throughout all of Babylonia. We only have exact knowledge of events during the Chaldean period for which the Babylonian Chronicle is well preserved, since the royal inscriptions, though numerous, are only partly comprehensive and depend upon Old Babylonian models, dealing in only select cases with politics and campaigns. The Old Testament and Greek historians provide some additional information.[30]

The most significant king of the dynasty was Nebuchadnezzar II (Nabû-kudurru-ussur; 605-562), who generally maintained peace with the Medes, frequently campaigned against Egypt, and in 597 and 586 conquered Jerusalem. After the destruction of the city and temple, many Jews were deported to Babylon, where they are even mentioned in cuneiform texts.[31] Nebuchadnezzar completed the high temple in Babylon (the "Tower of Babel") and set in place mighty fortifications.

After three brief interim regimes, Nabonidus (555-539), who came from the region around Harran, became king and sought to meet the Persian threat under Cyrus II which had been rising since 550.[32] Nabonidus thus attempted to establish a new center for the empire in western Arabia. Since Babylonia failed to support this religious but highly self-willed king, Cyrus was able to occupy Babylon almost without a struggle in 539 and, with that, to subjugate the entire realm. The great economic flowering of Babylonia was hardly impaired by these changes, and the administrative structure remained largely intact.

11. Persians, Macedonians, Greeks, and Parthians in Western Asia

While the Assyrian catastrophe of 612 left behind mostly ruins, so that only scant cultural traditions remained, changes in the rest of Western Asia took place only gradually. The region remained an economic unit

30. Because of the considerable gaps and manifold contradictions in the various traditions, the Chaldean Empire has not yet been treated in a monograph; no archive of political correspondence has been discovered.

31. Cf. B. Oded, *Mass Deportations and Deportees in the Neo-Assyrian Empire* (Wiesbaden, 1979); J. A. Brinkman, *Prelude to Empire: Babylonian Society and Politics, 747-626 B.C.* (Philadelphia, 1984). See below, p. 79.

32. Cf. P.-A. Beaulieu, *The Reign of Nabonidus, King of Babylon 556-539 B.C.* (New Haven, 1989); D. J. Wiseman, *Nebuchadrezzar and Babylon* (London, 1985).

under the Achaemenaean kings, but culturally the West broke with the Babylonians quite early. Aramaic was spoken almost everywhere and quickly became the administrative language in the West. Babylonian, Phoenician, and Hebrew continued to exist as written languages.

There were only minor revolts in Babylonia against Cyrus II (over Babylonia, from 539-529), Cambyses II (529-522), and Darius I (522-486). A wider revolt against Xerxes I (486-465) had severe political and economic consequences for the land. Outside of Nippur, only a few documents survive from Babylonia after 485; the land became visibly poorer. New and greater achievements came in astronomy alone (see below, XI.9).

Alexander the Great (336-323) wanted to make Babylon the capital of his world empire after his conquest of the Achaemenaean Empire, but he died too soon to accomplish this. Following the first clashes of the Diadochian rulers, Babylonia fell to the Seleucids, and after 312 dating was reckoned according to the rising Seleucid dynasty. Babylon, Borsippa, and Uruk subsequently became the primary centers of a mixed Babylonian-Hellenistic culture. From these cities come not only hundreds of cuneiform documents, but also a very large number of copies of earlier literary works, to which must be added some new texts in astronomy and other fields. After 150 the Parthians came to power in Mesopotamia. They nurtured astronomy for a good two hundred years longer, but the number of Babylonian documents diminished very rapidly. In the end, Hellenistic culture gained universal acceptance.

King Merodach-baladan of Babylonia (722-711) grants land to an official. Marble *kudurru* (boundary)-stone. *(Staatliche Museen, Berlin)*

CHAPTER VI

State and Society

1. The Monarchy

The greater and lesser states of ancient Western Asia were always ruled by princes or kings, who were themselves considered the representatives of the gods, or of the high god. The monarchy was usually hereditary, although a claim to the throne by the oldest son was not always recognized. In Elam, the younger brother normally succeeded before a son, so long as there was a brother in the line of succession. Still, usurpations by members of the royal family who had no legitimate claim to the throne were far more frequent than the sources would lead us to believe. In their inscriptions, usurpers stressed with particular intensity their legitimation through divine calling. Moreover, more than a few usurpers were exponents of power groups that were unsatisfied with the previous regime and expected a better representation of their concerns or interests from the new king. Yet only in exceptional cases can we demonstrate this in detail. Even when monarchs succeeded to the throne by legitimate means, they seldom enjoyed the absolute power which scholars often readily ascribe to the Oriental monarchies. In the early period there were often councils of elders who had to be consulted on important decisions. Later, priests and, above all, the military (cf. the intrigue recounted in 1 Kings 1–2) brought a strong degree of influence to bear on the throne. Besides these limitations, there were normative models against which the kings were measured. Next to service to the gods, great significance was frequently attached to provision for the poor and the weak. An expansive military policy was hardly seen as

63

an ideal in every case. Nevertheless, the monarch could only be freed from the duty to safeguard the independence of the land by an overwhelming superiority on the part of an enemy power. In individual cases, very different expressions could emerge in the monarchies of the ancient Orient, but only some indications of these can be given here.

The Sumerians in Babylonia distinguished between the city prince *(ensi)* and the king *(lugal)*, at least from the Early Dynastic period, and perhaps even earlier. The larger cities were the basic units for cult and administration, and in normal cases the office of *ensi* was hereditary. According to the testimony of some myths, the "assembly" *(ukkin)* of the elders assisted the *ensi*. The most powerful of the city princes at any given time stood above the rest as their king, with capital cities shifting accordingly. Yet, the monarchy in this form could also be hereditary over many generations. In the primarily Semitic northern part of the land, there may occasionally have been a king in his own right with his capital city in Kish. Since the god Enlil of Nippur was the one who installed kings in Middle Babylonia, the investiture ceremony may have taken place there. But according to the tradition of the Sumerian King List, Nippur itself was never the capital city. The responsibility for coordinating the irrigation and waterworks (see below, VII.3) and, as a rule, the defense of the land against external threat lay upon the king. Still, he was often unable to prevent wars between one city-state and another, even though there was usually more at stake in such instances than territorial changes. The institution of the *ensi* was first taken over from the Sumerians in the northern areas east of the Tigris, and in Assyria, but the practice of elevating one *ensi* to the superior position of king never developed in that region.

Over time, the tendencies toward centralization in Babylonia proved stronger than the tradition of the city princes. Although the local "divine states" (see below, XII.2) were not called into question, the Dynasty of Akkad and, after a short period of restoration, the Third Dynasty of Ur from Shulgi on, reduced the city princes to deposable officials. A partial restoration succeeded again in the Isin-Larsa period, until Hammurabi finally put an end to the ancient institution. The Akkadian loanword from *ensi, iššiakkum,* was then transformed into a word for "colon" (or "farmer") in the countryside.[1]

---

1. Cf. W. W. Hallo, *Early Mesopotamian Royal Titles* (New Haven, 1955); also D. O. Edzard, G. Szabo, E. Strommenger, and W. Nagel, "Herrscher," *RLA* IV (1975): 335ff.

As a counterweight to the possibility that the central power, which had grown so strong, would be abused, there emerged a religiously grounded sense of the ruler's responsibility for the welfare of all subjects, especially the socially weak. According to our sources, this sense was particularly pronounced during the reigns of Hammurabi and of Shamshi-Adad I of Mari and of Assyria. One may speak of a "patriarchal absolutism" under these kings, as well as many others in later centuries (see above, V.7).

After around 1500, there appear to have been only minimal institutional limitations on the powers of the kings of Babylonia and Assyria. Several of these kings surely felt compelled to expand certain privileges of the priesthood and the cities through decrees of exemption from various kinds of service *(andurāru)*, especially military obligations and similar duties. Esarhaddon found it necessary to have his peculiar law of royal succession (see above, V.9) approved by an assembly of nobles; perhaps that was merely an indication of his own weakness, conditioned by his sickliness.

For now we can say nothing with certainty concerning possible characteristics of the monarchy which may have been peculiar to Mesopotamia and Syria. The assumption that there was a limited, seven-year regnal period in Early Dynastic Ebla has not held up. The Sumerian King List strangely indicates that the foreign rulers of the Gutium Dynasty reigned no more than three to seven years each. However, it cannot be ascertained whether this information points to a temporally limited monarchy in western Iran prior to 2000, rather than the shifting tenures of regional governors.

In the years before 1500, Elam was apparently a confederacy of independent states. The Babylonians called the local lords kings, but the chief monarch, who was not absolutely required to reside in Susa, was termed strangely enough the "Great Minister" *(šukkallum)*. The reasons for this usage still need to be investigated. Later, however, Elam was ruled from the central power in Susa.

A vital source for the self-understanding of the kings of ancient Western Asia is found in the formulaic royal titles, which the kings included in their longer inscriptions. In general, purely secular titles such as "great, mighty king" stand next to others that stress the monarch's divine calling. Other titles, such as "king of the four boundaries of the world" (sometimes the four "corners of the world") found in Babylonia and Assyria, contain the claim to more extensive territories, for example, all of Mesopotamia. The formulaic titles of the petty kings are more modest, but these may also prove conclusive in many regards. Only minor indications can be given here regarding the problems of the formulaic titles in the various countries, their continuity, and their interchangeability.[2]

In the more lengthy formulaic titles, a statement of the king's intervention on behalf of the socially weak, particularly widows and orphans, is hardly ever lacking. The same is true of references to the king's commitment to justice in the land at the behest of the gods who installed him. Hammurabi was not the only one who saw his primary task as guaranteeing "that the strong does no injustice to the weak." On the contrary, he and many others as well took very seriously their greater social obligations in the framework of the social orders of their respective ages. At the same time, this sense of obligation has certainly been called into question in connection with other monarchs, primarily in Assyria. Indications of the social failure of kings, and the consequences of those failures, come often in the interpretations of omens, from which one can also deduce ethical norms (see below, XI.5). Generally accepted references to social reforms are more common, and concrete information about these can be gleaned from numerous law collections and legal decrees (see below, X.1). Still, such reforms became the primary theme of royal inscriptions only in the case of the social reformer Uruinimgina of Lagash (see above, V.3), who denounced the excessive withdrawals by his predecessors from temple properties and the exploitation of the populace through royal functionaries, and then went on to spell out exactly what was to be done in the future.[3] The deposing of this king by Lugalzaggesi of Umma after only an eight-year reign hindered the effective accomplishment of these reforms, which had also been determined in part by realistic political interests.

In addition to the kings, the ancient Oriental queens must be discussed briefly. Outside of South Arabia, where queens reigned frequently in the first millennium (cf. the biblical story of Solomon and

2. On the titulary formulas of various lands, cf. the comprehensive work of M.-J. Seux, *Épithètes royales, akkadiennes et sumériennes* (Paris, 1967), and his article, "Königtum B: II. and I. Jahrtausend," *RLA* VI (1980-1981): 140-173, which concerns the queens, revolts against kings, etc.

3. For an edition of the inscriptions, cf. H. Steible, *Die altsumerischen Bau- und Weihinschriften*, I: *Inschriften aus Lagaš*, ed. Steible and H. Behrens (Wiesbaden, 1982), 278-358.

the queen of Sheba), reigning queens were the rare exception. The tavern hostess Ku-Baba is said to have usurped the throne in Kish, not long before the Dynasty of Akkad. Even though only later reports on this subject are available, Ku-Baba was indeed an historical figure. Isolated instances of reigning queens occurred even in smaller states (as with Athaliah of Judah).

The queen as the consort of the king, on the other hand, normally had no function in the regime. Nevertheless, short inscriptions by queens are known in isolated cases, and it is certain that strong women often exercised considerable influence (in the Bible, cf. Bathsheba and Jezebel). Yet in most cases we only learn of such instances when letters serve as supplementary sources to the royal inscriptions. Zimri-Lim's consort Shibtum clearly held a strong position in Mari. Also, in Assyria queens frequently involved themselves in the struggles over royal succession (cf. 1 Kings 1–2). The Syrian-born wife of Sennacherib, Naqīya-Zakūtu, still possessed considerable influence during the first years of the reign of her grandson, Ashurbanipal, and was feared by the royal officials. That Sammu-ramat, the Semiramis of Greek literature, was temporarily regent after 810 cannot, however, be proven.[4] Finally, it may be mentioned in passing that in the Neo-Hittite Empire after 1400 queens were able to control important political functions and even received transcriptions of international correspondence.

2. The Divinization of the Monarch

Although the Egyptian pharaohs were respected and honored on account of their status as gods, the kings in Babylonia and Assyria were normally held to be mortals like any others. In exceptional cases, however, certain kings had themselves divinized out of hubris. Thus the Akkadian monarchs Naram-Sin (see above, V.4) and Sharkalisharri had the divine determinative set before their names in several inscriptions, thereby setting themselves in the position of the city god. Some kings of the Early Dynastic period in Sumer were posthumously divinized in

4. Cf. W. Schramm, "War Semiramis assyrische Regentin?" *Historia* 21 (1972): 513ff. W. Nagel interprets the legendary traditions regarding Ninos (probably = Tukulti-Ninurta I) in *Ninus und Semiramis in Sage und Geschichte: Iranische Staaten und Reiternomaden vor Darius* (Berlin, 1982).

mythic literature; these included Enmerkar, Lugalbanda, Dumuzi, and Gilgamesh. Inscriptions from these kings, however, are unknown.

Something fundamentally different is the so-called cultic divinization of the king. In Babylonia, this practice was employed by Sumerian and later Semitic kings as well, from the time Shulgi of Ur (see above, V.4) claimed it also on behalf of his father Ur-Nammu. Hammurabi put an end to the practice, although he and his successors were unable to prevent names such as "Ḫammurabi-ilī" — "Hammurabi is my god" — from being passed on. The basis for this type of divinization was not the power of the one venerated as the "god-king," but rather the cult of the "sacred marriage," in which the king represented Dumuzi, the god of fertility, and a high priestess represented Inanna (Ishtar), the goddess of love (see below, XII.5b). After completion of the ritual, the king was considered a god. Cultic structures similar to those of the traditional gods were erected for some of these kings. In royal Sumerian hymns, one pleaded for their intercession or actually praised them as gods of the upperworld (see below, XIII.5b). The fulfillment of other rituals by the king in the scope of his duties nowhere effected his ascension into the divine realm. One consequence of the divinization of the king between Shulgi and Rim-Sin was that individual Kassite kings set the divine determinative before their names. The Assyrian kings, however, never divinized themselves, even at the time of their greatest power, although they did transfer certain divine attributes to themselves and thus secularized those attributes. While the term "god-king" plays a substantial role in the archaeological interpretation of reliefs even after the time of Hammurabi, that terminology does not agree with the facts which can be plainly drawn from the sources.[5]

At present we are unable to determine whether there was already a type of monarchical divinization prior to the time of Akkad. On many pictorial reliefs, especially cylinder seals of the Early Sumerian period, one encounters the "man in the net robe," whom many take to be a god, others a king; he turns up mostly as the protector of the flocks or in cultic scenes, and he is often rendered more prominent through his size. Later it is generally a god who is portrayed as protector of the "holy flock" (see below, XIV.2).

Even more controversial is the interpretation of the discoveries in

---

5. The divinization of the king has still not been examined in a monograph. On the "sacral marriage," see below, ch. XII, n. 27, and XII.5b. All works on this topic, as well as the editions of the royal Sumerian hymns, deal with it, briefly or more extensively.

the so-called kings' graves of the royal cemetery in Early Dynastic Ur. The sacrifice of the royal followers and the abundant, costly (not only in terms of material) accessories in these graves, which find no comparison in later periods, are often taken as evidence for a belief in an afterlife together with the buried god-king. Others take these grave offerings as no more than the product of a sophisticated technology and highly developed artisanship. The latter interpretation, however, leaves much in the graves unexplained. The whole matter requires renewed, fundamental investigation.[6]

The usual Hittite designation for the death of a king — "he became God" — contains no apparent reference to the concept of a divinization of the king.

3. City, State, and Administration

Our knowledge of the realm of administration leaves much to be desired, despite the myriads of Sumerian and Akkadian documents and, for several periods, letters which deal with administration. In the Sumerian temple city of the early third millennium, the administration of state and temple probably coincided. Apparently, no royal palace corresponds to the extensive temple precincts in Uruk, the building of which demanded large multitudes of human laborers.[7] For the relationship between temple and palace in later cities, see below, XIV.1. Even in provincial cities, a palace (Sum. *é-gal*, "great house" > Akk. *ekallu*) later stood as an administrative center along with the temple, which was exceedingly rich on account of its considerable property holdings. The respective jurisdictions of each were clearly regulated at any given time. Prior to 700, the size of the cities varied between around 5½ square kilometers within the city walls (e.g., the "double city" of Uruk, the construction of which was never completely finished) and about 20 hectares. The later cities of Babylon and Nineveh were larger still. After

6. Cf. C. L. Woolley, *The Royal Cemetery*. Ur Excavations, II (New York, 1934); A. Moortgat, *Tammuz: Der Unsterblichkeitsglaube in der altorientalischen Bildkunst* (Berlin, 1949); idem, *Einführung in die Vorderasiatische Archäologie* (Darmstadt, 1971), 11ff.

7. W. von Soden introduces the manifold problems of the cities of ancient Western Asia and the possible numbers of their inhabitants very briefly, along with bibliography, in "Tempelstadt und Metropolis im Alten Orient," in *Die Stadt: Gestalt und Wandel bis zum industriellen Zeitalter*, ed. H. Stoob (Cologne, 1979), 37-82.

the era of the city princes, the mayor (Old Bab. *rabiānum*) was no doubt installed by the king and empowered with the necessary authority.

For all major periods, we possess an abundance of titles for office-holders of all types, from minister and governor down to the lowliest overseer. At the same time, we are unable to define with exactitude the corresponding administrative jurisdictions. Certainly these were often only loosely circumscribed, so that the ruler could install his functionaries according to his shifting needs. In this regard, the same designations were frequently applied to different offices in different periods. One holding high position in the royal court often discharged the duties of other high offices in the state as well.[8] Indeed, the king decided the extent of the authority of his functionaries from case to case.

Higher as well as middle and lower state officials could be called upon to oversee public works, or to serve as officers and soldiers in times of war. Whether designations of rank applied to the military alone must still be investigated (see below, VI.5). At least in campaign reports individual officers are rarely mentioned.

The earliest Sumerian documents attest to the *sukal*, Akk. *š/ sukkallu*, who often exercised the function of a minister, but who sometimes discharged his duties on a middle level. Conversely, "house-keepers" (Sum. *agrig*; Akk. *abarakku*) could also be the bearers of very high office in Assyria, and are often termed great-*abarakku*. From the Hurrian term *tertenn-* "follower," the Assyrian word *tu/artānu* developed, the designation of one of the highest ministers, the second after the king, who was also able to lead an army. Other high officials who could be installed in various governorships, and not only those of conquered districts, were the *šakkanakku* and the *šaknu*. The mayors of cities, who were required to discharge key functions, were usually designated *rabiānum*, "great one," in Old Babylonian; later, however, the term *haziānum/hazannu* generally prevailed.

Since administrative officials of all types had to master the art of writing, they were often simply called "scribes" (Sum. *dub-sar*; Akk. *tupšarru*), often with the addition of the area of work for which they were appointed. Particularly important areas of their employment, according to extant documents and letters, were the administration of the

8. The *rab šāqê* ("over-cupbearer") was one of the highest functionaries in the period of the Neo-Assyrian Empire, and often played a leading role in military campaigns [cf. Isaiah 36 = 2 Kings 18].

agricultural lands of the state and the temple. Among the primary obligations here were the surveying of the land, not only for official purposes but also for private landholders and tenants, and the discharge of oversight authority for livestock production, and for hunting and fishing. Further authorities were responsible for public works of all kinds, especially for the installation and maintenance of the great canals, which were so vital in the arid regions, and, where necessary, for the securing of the riverbanks against erosion. As late as the second millennium, workers were paid primarily in kind, and even later they received only partial payments in money. Silver and copper coins were not minted until the sixth century, after the model of Lydia. Until that time, metal had to be weighed out for each payment. Places to regulate and check the standardization of weights were initially found at the great temples; later these came under the jurisdiction of the city authorities as well. Tolls and other deductions from trade and commerce were brought in by tax collectors (Sum. *enku;* Akk. *mākisu*), although the institution of the tax tenant, working on the basis of his own reckoning, does not appear to have existed.[9]

The bureaucracy was already highly developed in Babylonia and Assyria at an early date. However, no comprehensive treatment which deals also with the determinative differences from period to period has yet been written. The greatest hindrance is perhaps to be found in the cities and petty states, where to date no substantial archives have been discovered. Numerous terms from Iranian and Greek administrative language are found in the documents of the later periods of the Achaemenaean and Seleucid Empires.

4. Society and Social Groups

Distinguishing the social groups in the lands and cities of ancient Western Asia is made extremely difficult by linguistic and technical considerations. Too seldom are the attested terms encountered in any significant context, nor were they used in the same sense in every period; only a few have been thoroughly investigated. Therefore, only selected

9. *CAD* and *AHw* afford citations and bibliography for all of the designated functionaries. Cf. also F. R. Kraus, *Staatliche Viehhaltung im altbabylonischen Lande Larsa* (Amsterdam, 1966).

terms will be discussed in the following treatment, in order to outline briefly the major issues.

a. Man, Wife, Marriage, Family, and Clan

In the ancient Orient the family was universally patriarchal in structure, although the rights of the father as head of the family were in no way unrestricted, especially in urban society. Within the family, these rights were sharply circumscribed, as is attested, for example, for the early patriarchal age in the Old Testament. Even the practice of polygamy had been completely done away with, so that the possibility was limited primarily to the upper class and the nobility, who could take slaves or other women as concubines.[10] Monogamy was generally accepted among the gods as well, and evidence is completely lacking for a harem in the royal courts of Babylonia. In Assyria, at least a few kings, perhaps under Hurrian influence, had separate houses for women, for which particular regulations were issued.[11] Similar practice obtained in many places in Syria.

Socially, the woman possessed a status similar to that of the man. While her husband was alive, she was completely free to engage in business, as long as she had his permission. When there was no man present, she could even run her own business, a fact which can be deduced from many letters and documents (see below, X.3). As a mother, she could claim under both divine and human law the respect of her adult children. Contempt for one's mother was no less a sin than a similar bearing toward one's father (a fact which is true of Hebrew law as well). Expulsion from the home and disinheritance threatened the child who said, "You are not my father . . ." or ". . . not my mother."

The marriage laws clearly show that the woman was to be purchased from her father at an early date, but the practice of marriage-by-purchase was overturned in the third millennium at the latest. That the woman nevertheless did not enjoy legal rights equal to those of a man is shown

10. It appears that a "second" wife was permitted in individual cases, e.g., for merchants, who had to spend a long time in a far distant land, although the marriage contract could exclude this possibility (see the Old Assyrian documents in *RA* 76 [1982]: 169ff.). Official state contracts of the fourteenth century occasionally support the presence of "consorts" at the courts of Syrian princes (cf. *UF* 6 [1974]: 116, l. 115).

11. Cf. E. F. Weidner, "Hof- und Harems-Erlasse assyrischer Könige aus dem 2. Jahrtausend v. Chr.," *AfO* 17 (1954-1956): 257ff.

with particular clarity by the laws on divorce, which put the childless wife at a sharp disadvantage. If a man respected his wife's rights to sustenance, he could expel her; of course, such measures could become quite expensive for him if children were involved. In addition, an expiatory fine was often demanded. On the other hand, a woman who broke away from her husband frequently risked heavy penalties, up to and including the death penalty; here there were many differences in the way individual cases were handled. A legal draft from Assyria around 1100 limited the rights of the wife in every aspect even more severely, although it is not known how much of that actually became law. Conversely, documents from about one to two hundred years earlier inform us that it had previously been the practice in Assyria to penalize the termination of a marriage by either man or woman with the same monetary fine, thus giving both equal treatment under the law.[12] In this light, the above-mentioned legal draft (see below, X.1c) sought to set back the rights of women significantly.

Conceiving and bearing children stood at the forefront of the marriage. Sons were preeminently desired over daughters, and were generally preferred as heirs (but see p. 195, n. 35). The eldest son often received a preferential portion of the inheritance. Still, girls were in no way disdained, at least as far as we can tell. Little is known of the principles by which children were raised, since the few references to the education of princes and the schooling of scribes cannot be taken as typical for all people. The strong bonding of children to their parents even found expression in that many gods were addressed as father or mother. Innumerable terra-cotta figurines, modeled primarily in miniature, depict a naked woman holding a child on her arm. Parents sold their children only in times of dire necessity, and such occurrences were counted among the worst omen interpretations.

There is rarely any mention of love among siblings. A Sumerian myth of Dumuzi (see below, XII.5b) narrates how his sister Belili descended into the underworld for him. In Elam and some districts of Asia Minor, a claim on the inheritance was often, though not always, accorded to the eldest brother before the children; this arrangement is termed a fratriarchate.[13]

---

12. Cf. C. Saporetti, *The Status of Women in the Middle Assyrian Period* (Malibu, 1979). Cf. also R. Westbrook, *Old Babylonian Marriage Law. AfO* Beiheft 23 (1988).

13. Cf. P. Koschaker, "Fratriarchat, Hausgemeinschaft und Mutterrecht in Keilin-schriftrechten," *ZA* 41 (1933): 90-183.

The institution of adoption had considerable significance in Babylonia and other regions. One adopted a child primarily, though not solely, when there was no male heir. The regulations varied from case to case, and from place to place. In Elam, one could also be adopted into "brotherhood" or "sisterhood"; through the latter means, even a concubine could come into the family. Adoptions for the sake of appearances played a great role in Nuzi, where they served to circumvent certain prohibitions on the acquisition of land.[14]

Next to the family in the narrow sense (Akk. *kimtu*) stood the extended family, or clan *(nišūtu)*, and the household community *(salātu)*, which included the slaves. In this connection the Sumerians appear to have known only the term *im-ri-a*, though the reasons for this still need to be investigated. For the Babylonians and Assyrians, these three communities comprised the life support of a person, and the members felt themselves jointly responsible before the gods for the guilt of all the other members. Particular legal ordinances for the clan and household community are not extant, though the household economy is occasionally mentioned in letters.[15]

b. Free Persons and Slaves

The designation "free" refers here to citizens of the cities and to farmers and shepherds. The ancient Semitic languages know the term "free" only in the sense of "free of debts" (i.e., freed from certain obligations), rather than in the full sense of the words for "free" in the Indo-European languages, simply because the concept of "the free" did not exist as an ideal model. Thus, one understood under "liberation" only the release from particular taxes and obligations to service. The members of particularly dependent groups were also "free" in comparison with the

14. Cf. G. Wilhelm, *Grundzüge der Geschichte und Kultur der Hurriter* (Darmstadt, 1982), 66ff.

15. Cf. Å. Sjöberg, *Zu einigen Verwandtschaftbezeichnungen im Sumerischen.* Heidelberger Studien zum Alten Orient (Wiesbaden, 1967), 201ff.; cf. also E. Ebeling, "Familie," *RLA* III (1957): 9ff.; and J. Bottéro, "Küche," *RLA* VI (1981): 277ff.; see further F. M. Fales, "La structura della parentela," in *L'Alba della civiltà*, ed. S. Moscati, I:180ff.; E. Cassin, "Structures familiales et pouvoirs de la femme," *RA* 63 (1969): 121ff.; I. J. Gelb, "Household and Family in Early Mesopotamia," in *State and Temple Economy*, I (Löwen, 1979): 1-98.

"slaves." If we understand this correctly, slaves belonged either to individuals or temples, but never to the state, as often in imperial Rome. For this reason, too, we hear nothing of slave revolts. Even in the courts of the nobility there were never such large masses of slaves as to allow the nobles to recruit armies of slaves. Nor, by all appearances, were slaves ever handed over to their masters without retaining any rights, even though the regulations treating these two classes often differed in detail (there have been no comprehensive studies on this). According to Old Babylonian documents and letters, slaves were able, though certainly only with the permission of their masters, to be active in business. In order to make their flight more difficult, they were frequently required to bear marks of their slavery. One such mark was a half-shorn head. The authorities were responsible for seizing runaway slaves and leading them back to their masters. The theft of slaves was often punished severely, and particular ordinances applied to palace slaves.[16]

That a great many slaves fell into slavery through warfare is indicated even by the cuneiform word-signs for male slave and female slave: ligatures of a man or woman and mountainous land. The documents teach us, however, that slaves were frequently bought and sold; if a slave suffered an epilepsy attack (Akk. *bennu*) within one hundred days of purchase, the seller had to take the slave back. At the same time, slaves were often manumitted in an arrangement by which a certain tie to the house of the previous owner could remain in place, but not necessarily. Freed slaves were frequently adopted, while in other cases they had to purchase their freedom. Particular problems arose when female slaves bore children to their masters; these women could not thereafter be sold at leisure, and manumission was not unusual in such cases. The father decided the status of the children, but when there were already children by a legitimate marriage their rights had to be respected first.

The mistreatment of slaves was certainly not infrequent, but as members of the *salātu* (the household community) in Babylonia (see above) they were bearably treated under normal circumstances. The words for male slave and female slave, Sum. *ìr* and *géme*, Akk. *(w)ardu* and *amtu,* were simultaneously designations for male servant and

16. Cf. I. Mendelsohn, *Slavery in the Ancient Near East* (New York, 1949); I. J. Gelb, "Definition and Discussion of Slavery and Serfdom," *UF* 11 (1979): 283ff., with bibliography; I. Cardellini, *Die biblischen 'Sklaven'-Gesetze im Lichte des keilschriftlichen Sklavenrechts* (Königstein, 1981); G. Ries, "Lastenfreiheit," *RLA* VI (1983): 508ff.

female servant. These terms were also employed as self-appellations by free citizens as well as by members of the upper class in prayers before the gods. Thus nothing derogatory was attached to the words for slave. In what was, of course, a satirical and hyperbolic usage, the "Dialogue between Master and Slave" from the early first millennium (see also p. 223) shows that slaves occasionally were permitted to speak candidly over and against their masters.

I am aware of no conclusive evidence for the ascent of slaves to prominent positions. To be sure, no one would have called attention to the possibility of his or her origin in the slave class.

c. Sedentary and Nonsedentary (Nomads and Seminomads)

Ancient Oriental society was often more or less unstable, including even the great cities. This situation was owed not only to warlike confrontations between states and larger migratory movements, but also to the close proximity of sedentary and nonsedentary populations as well as the generally short-lived marginal groups which existed in most areas. Almost all of our written sources stem from the cities and villages of the settled peoples, and even in those places they are available in sufficient breadth only for relatively brief periods. In between lie often longer periods for which we know almost nothing. For wide reaches of Syria and Mesopotamia, sources are almost always lacking. Far-reaching conclusions concerning those regions which we are reasonably able to survey can therefore be drawn only with great caution.

A brief introduction to terminology is necessary. Nomads are wandering shepherds who migrate with their herds through districts which are not suitable for regular agriculture. With the term Bedouin, borrowed from the Arabic, we designate today only camel-nomads, who traverse vast stretches of desert by means of the dromedary, whose capabilities are vastly superior to those of the ass. Many nomadic (i.e., Bedouin) tribes or clans occasionally pursue agriculture in addition to animal husbandry on the fringes of the settled land, where it appears feasible to them. In such cases we speak of seminomads (semi-Bedouin) or transhumancy. According to the Old Testament, the patriarchs are typical representatives of seminomadic life. As a rule, nomads fall upon the settled land only for the sake of plunder, since they have no desire at all to become sedentary. Conversely, seminomads can more easily make the transition to settled life. At the same time, individuals or groups who must flee the cities find it easier to attach themselves to seminomads than to full nomads. Exactly such persons, who have changed from one group to the other, often become elements of disruption as condottieri, who with a sufficient following can effect considerable changes.

M. B. Rowton has studied these relationships with particular intensity during recent years and has treated various aspects in a series of essays. Rowton writes of a "dimorphic structure" in ancient Western Asia and terms those making the transition from "urban society" to "enclosed nomadism" (seminomadism) and vice versa "parasocials."[17] Powerful states were generally able to protect themselves against such troublemakers; or they could try to take them into their service, for example, as officers or leaders of raiding forces or in the building of canals. Passing through such social stations, more than a few individuals rose to positions of princes or kings and as "town-dwellers" founded dynasties. Such was frequently the case in Babylonia, for example, in the centuries following the last Sumerian kingdom of the Third Dynasty of Ur (see above, III.2) and then again after 1000, in the time of the incursions by the Aramaean tribes. In the Old Babylonian documents, those elements not fully integrated into urban society were called *Martu* (Akk. *Amurru*)-people or "westerners," since they came primarily from the west. They served as occasion demanded as workers on public projects or as soldiers.[18] Even the hired workers (Akk. *agru*) brought in for the harvest by the landowners or tenant farmers stemmed in part from this class of people. Slaves were used more rarely in harvesting the crops.

There is still no unanimous opinion concerning the class of persons designated by the Akkadian term *muškēnum*, literally, "the one prostrating himself." These are mentioned only rarely and in strange circumstances in the Old Babylonian laws, letters, and omen interpretations.[19] Wherever the

---

17. The final essay of M. B. Rowton on this topic, in which the earlier contributions are cited, is "Dimorphic Structure and the Parasocial Element," *JNES* 36 (1977): 181ff.

18. Cf. J.-R. Kupper, *Les nomades en Mésopotamie au temps de rois de Mari* (Paris, 1957), 147ff.; G. Buccellati, *The Amorites of the Ur III Period*; R. Harris, *Ancient Sippar* (Istanbul, 1975), 94ff.

19. Cf. F. R. Kraus, *Vom mesopotamischen Menschen . . . und seiner Welt* (Amsterdam, 1973); also *"muškēnu,"* *CAD*, X/2 (1977): 272ff., with bibliography. A new, broader investigation of the term is necessary.

muškēnum stands opposite the *awīlum,* the "free man" or "citizen," his status is clearly subordinated, and for exactly this reason the laws contained many particular prescriptions for his protection. Members of this class were often in the service of the palace. In Syria there are some instances of the *muškēnum* class as early as the Amarna Age. Otherwise, after about 1500 the texts apply the word in the sense of "the poor." It is in this sense that the term made its way into Hebrew, Aramaic, and Arabic, as well as, much later, the Romance languages — French *mesquin* and Italian *meschino.*

There were different designations for groups of foreign origin who were not fully assimilated, which naturally often formed elements of unrest. Such was the case as early as the Old Babylonian and even before, but above all in the Amarna Age in Syria and Nuzi. Among these terms, the word *ḫapiru,* the basic meaning of which still has not been clarified, has been frequently discussed. This word appears in ancient Egyptian and in Ugaritic as *'pr,* and sounds similar to Hebrew *'ibrî,* "Hebrew," although *ḫapiru* is certainly not to be equated with *'ibrî.* It is impossible to speak in only a few sentences about these and similar, less widespread group designations, since these frequently denote different types of groups, depending on the place and time.[20] Most importantly, however, the fate of Syrian city-states was decisively determined in part by the non- or only partially integrated fringe groups such as the Ḫapiru.

Particular kinds of fringe groups arose in the Hittite Empire. They appeared in Assyria as well, on a small scale after 1300, but after 900 in ever widening circles through deportations and resettlements (see above, V.8), which were officially called "uprootings" and primarily affected the upper classes of enemy lands. The Chaldean king Nebuchadnezzar II renewed this practice, deporting a substantial portion of the Jews to Babylonia after 600. However, the destination of the resettlements was by no means limited to the core region of the empire; often it was to be found in provinces far removed from the homelands of the affected peoples. Certainly, only some of the deportees were enslaved; a great many more were put to work on public projects, and others were incorporated into the army if qualified. Craftsmen were able to carry on with their professions primarily when their skills were in frequent

20. Cf. J. Bottéro, "Ḫabiru," *RLA* IV (1972): 14-27; O. Loretz, *Habiru-Hebräer.* Beihefte zur Zeitschrift für die alttestamentliche Wissenschaft 160 (1984); M. Greenberg, *The Hab/piru* (New Haven, 155). The cuneiform writings permit readings with *b* and *p;* in Egypt and Ugarit the term was written *'pr.*

demand, as in the case of many types of artistic skills. In most cases, the assimilation of resettled peoples was encouraged. Much remains to be gleaned from the documents concerning this, but there are only a few studies on the subject.

The Assyrians gave as the number of those deported in the thirteenth century the round figures 14,400 and 28,800; later such numbers were certainly overstated, and six-figure citations are not rare. Here it must be asked how the transport of such masses of humanity could have been accomplished over such great distances. Assyrian reliefs often show women and children in wagons, with the men on foot.

All in all, the Aramaeans (see above, V.8) comprised by far the greatest part of those deported from the petty states of Mesopotamia and Syria. Since considerable numbers of Aramaean groups had already come to Babylonia and Assyria by infiltrating the plains, the deported Aramaeans had little if any difficulty being assimilated. The development of particular fringe classes similar to those found in Babylonia and Syria in the second millennium probably never took place in Assyria and the cities of Babylonia in the first millennium, since our sources report conflicts between groups of inhabitants of different ethnic origin. The fifth-century documents from Achaemenaean Nippur mention many particular groups, but these can scarcely be arranged in different social classes.[21]

d. The Great Temples: Feudal Tenure and Feudalism

Among the Sumerians ownership of land was rare, since the land belonged to the great temples which formed the basis of the city-states, yet were not identical with them. Nevertheless, the city princes and other members of the aristocracy no doubt undertook to build private land holdings with some frequency, and texts from Lagash in the 24th century expressly condemn this practice.[22] No kind of feudalism was able to develop under these circumstances. Comprehensive stone documents recording numerous royal land purchases outside the Sumerian districts

21. Cf. M. W. Stolper, *Management and Politics in Later Achaemenid Babylonia: New Texts of the Murašû Archive* (diss., University of Michigan, 1974); M. D. Coogan, *West Semitic Personal Names in the Murašû Documents* (Missoula, 1976).

22. For the so-called "Reform texts of King Uruinimgina" which address social ills, see above, section 1.

first become extant during the time of the Semitic kings of Akkad (see above, V.4).[23] Since it is possible that many functionaries also engaged in such purchases, the beginnings of feudalism may have emerged at that time, but these would scarcely have survived the foreign rule of the Gutians which followed, especially in the Akkadian north. In the following centuries down to about 1500, the sources make no reference to any kind of feudalism; rather, a bourgeois society is the rule.[24]

The irruptions of the Hittites and Hurrians into Asia Minor and Syria-Mesopotamia, as well as of the Kassites into Babylonia, and the formation of states by these same peoples, led to radically altered relationships. In all of the states founded or occupied by these peoples, there frequently arose small seigneurial classes with privileges similar to those found elsewhere among the nobility, bearing particular obligations over and against the princes. The members of these classes were generally allotted lands, which were increased either through additional purchases or by further gifts in cases when particular services were rendered. Smaller or larger groups of agricultural workers or tenants on the estates often became dependent upon the landlords. One can therefore speak of a genuine feudal system in all of these states, although within the cities the status of the citizenry and the priesthood frequently showed little change. Of course, this system developed differences in particulars wherever it arose. Our sources provide good insight into the feudal system primarily in the east Tigris principality of Arrapkha (see above, V.8), as well as in Babylonia and, in Syria, at Ugarit. For other Syrian cities and for Assyria the sources are less fruitful, and they are completely lacking for Mesopotamia. We have few documents from the Hittite Empire during this period, and many questions still require clarification.

The liberation from Kassite domination after 1150 and the liquidation of most of the Hurrian states by the Hittites and Assyrians apparently had little effect on the feudal system in this region. In Assyria proper a native feudal nobility increasingly gained prominence, which was opposed in the great cities by a highly self-assured citizenry. The kings sought to play the different groups off against each other and at

23. Cf. I. J. Gelb, "Old Akkadian Stone Tablet from Sippar," *RSO* 32 (1957): 83ff., which also treats the obelisk of Manishtushu.

24. Large, private land holdings, even if they existed, played no role at that time. Apparently there was not even a hereditary, urban patrician class. Cf. further Harris, *Ancient Sippar*; B. Kienast, *"ilku," RLA* V (1976): 52ff. Many issues in this regard are given variant interpretations and thus require further study.

the same time to strengthen the power of the central government, with varying degrees of success. But they had to pay equal attention to both the landowners and the citizenry. The incursions by the Aramaean tribes into Babylonia after around 1000 led to ever-increasing losses in the estates of the landed aristocracy, whose importance was thereby starkly reduced. The natural social development thus led away from feudalism and enhanced primarily the power and prestige of the great temples. According to the testimony of the sources, the temples held and managed extensive properties outside the cities. Through these holdings, the great temples were transformed into gigantic economic concerns during the Chaldean and Achaemenaean periods, although their activities still have not been comprehensively treated. The temples could confer upon the citizens many more or less lucrative temple offices, such as performance of certain handicrafts in the temple precincts or sharing in sacrificial services. Such benefits came to be treated as company stocks, particularly in the period of Seleucid rule (see below, XII.5e).

The end of the Neo-Assyrian Empire led to the destruction of most of the Assyrian cities and to immense losses in human life, and was coupled with the dissolution of all earlier forms of order as well. In Babylonia, however, the previous order remained largely in place following its incorporation into the Achaemenaean Empire, while the Iranian feudal system was gradually transferred to Babylonia. The documentary archive of the great trade and banking house of Murashû in Nippur, which stems from the fifth century, attests to this transition in manifold ways. Still, too many terms in these documents are insufficiently understood.[25]

Within the middle class were found the artisan, trade, and scribal classes. The scribal class controlled the administrative apparatus and was partially organized along the lines of a guild in later times.[26] At the same time, closed social castes are nowhere recognizable. Specific studies still have much to clarify on these subjects.

The written sources, which stem mostly from the cities, reveal very little about the social relationships in villages. The agricultural and administrative estate of Puzrish-Dagan comprises a special case. Myri-

---

25. Cf. Stolper; G. Cardascia, "Lehenwesen in der Perserzeit," *RLA* VI (1983): 547ff.

26. Cf. D. B. Weisberg, *Guild Structure and Allegiance in Early Achaemenid Mesopotamia* (New Haven, 1967); H. M. Kümmel, *Familie, Beruf, und Amt in spätbabylonischen Uruk* (Berlin, 1979). Comprehensive treatments of the subject are still lacking.

ads of documents from the time of the Third Dynasty of Ur are known from this site in the vicinity of Nippur. Nonetheless, this mass of documents has yet to be studied systematically.

5. The Army and Warfare

As in the rest of human history, military operations of all kinds, from setting and repelling small ambushes up to great wars, dominated the history of the ancient Orient. The primary weapons available to the individual soldier, such as axes, war clubs (usually from the thighbones of large animals), swords, spears, and bows and arrows, scarcely vary. After the fourth millennium, different types of bronze joined the materials already in use: stone, wood, and reed; after 1400 the Hittites introduced wrought iron, but iron never completely replaced bronze weaponry, owing to the difficulty of working the iron and to the richer abundance of copper in many regions. Defensive weapons included small round set shields and different types of armor, in later times even for horses, along with helmets and shields. Protective armor for horses, which sometimes included protection for the neck, consisted of scales or rings of metal sewn onto leather or strong cloth material. Among the technical terminology there are many shifting terms.[27]

For a long time, battles were fought on foot either in closed or open order. Illustrations depict the phalanx, which the Sumerians had used for hand-to-hand combat since about 2500. Against this formation the Semites employed nets, which were thrown out by special commandos to entangle the long spears approaching, thereby rendering parts of the phalanx ineffective.[28] The Akkadian kings abandoned the rigid phalanx. We possess a large number of battle illustrations for the time after 900. These come from Assyria and show no closed battle formations. Still, the Akkadian words for the battle ranks (*sidru, sidirtu*) indicate a thoroughly methodical arrangement of the units. The sources give no information about the military training of the troops.

Similarly, the sources provide only the most unsatisfactory infor-

27. Cf. E. Salonen, *Die Waffen der alten Mesopotamier* (Helsinki, 1965), with bibliography and illustrations.
28. The partially preserved depiction of a battle on the so-called vulture stela of King Eannatum of Lagash is particularly characteristic of the phalanx style of warfare.

mation on the strength of the military forces on large campaigns. In Old Babylonian letters from Mari we read that various coalitions generally fielded formations thirty thousand strong. The armies of individual states were sufficient for more extensive operations only in rare cases.[29] The Assyrians, in fact, often give highly overstated numbers for the enemy dead and captured. These numbers often reach six figures, and in a king's later inscriptions are frequently much higher than in the initial campaign reports. Such reports, however, are to be taken at face value no more than the boast of Shalmaneser III that he led an army of 120,000 to Syria in his fourteenth year.[30]

Still, even after critical evaluation of the numerical assertions, we should not doubt that great masses of troops were committed to individual battles, and that massive armies were provisioned and marched across hundreds of kilometers, as from Assyria to Syria. Even when requisitions were recklessly carried out, this very fact presupposes a well-thought-out organization and the preparation of usable routes. Wherever possible, the armies divided and marched overland by different routes. Otherwise, individual details, such as the employment of commandos for special kinds of work, can rarely be gleaned from the sources.

Of the division of the armies above the level of the smaller units, which are often represented by the numbers ten, fifty, and one hundred, we know little. The larger units presumably were formed according to the respective needs of the situation. Only the beginnings of a hierarchy of higher ranks of service existed even in Assyria.[31]

The majority of soldiers were generally called up only according to the circumstances; often that could mean year after year. There were, however, always greater or lesser units which stood in perennial service

29. Even far distant lands occasionally sent auxiliary troops; for example, at the time of Zimri-Lim of Mari, Elam sent troops to Eshnunna and even traded with Mari.

30. In the age of the great wars of conquest, the Assyrians probably kept large troop formations in provinces far removed from Assyria, so that they could be quickly brought into service in the spring.

31. Cf. E. Salonen, "Heer," *RLA* IV (1975): 244ff., with bibliography. A special training program must have been necessary for higher-ranking officers in order to procure for them the knowledge of leading troops accumulated over generations, though as far as I know no textual evidence for this exists. Cf. also F. Malbran-Labat, *L'Armée et l'organisation militaire de l'Assyrie* (Geneva, 1982); J. M. Sasson, *The Military Establishments at Mari.* Studia Pohl 3 (Rome, 1969).

to the king, and which simultaneously served as cadres for the formation of larger units. These permanent units were never very large, as can be gathered from Sargon of Akkad, who considered it noteworthy that 5,400 men always stood at his disposal, provisioned in the palace. Comparable numbers from later times are unavailable. Insofar as conquered regions became provinces of the empire in the Neo-Assyrian period, the imperial governors had under their command military units which served the fortifications and were probably settled in the vicinity. From time to time, these units were transformed into the private armies of the governors and made possible revolts against the central administration.

The infantry formed the core of the armies, as everywhere else. More recent texts distinguish the lance-bearers and the shield-bearers from the archers. The engineers achieved considerable significance as bridge-builders and road-builders, primarily in the armies of the Assyrians. According to both pictures and texts, cumbersome battle chariots, drawn by onagers and using round, flat wheels, were in use among the Sumerians. But chariotry did not emerge as a decisive weapon until the Hurrians and Hittites first introduced masses of light, spoke-wheeled chariots drawn by teams of horses. Charioteers were primarily the vassals of the kings, and thus the upper class of the feudal states in the period following 1500 (cf. the Canaanite *maryannu*). Racehorses, which had undergone an intensive training program, were used to pull the chariots.[32] The original chariots carried only a warrior and a driver; later a shield-bearer was added. Riders were used to carry messages from an early date, though cavalry with a military function did not exist prior to 900, and thereafter primarily in Assyria, where they were developed to defend against attacks by mounted Iranians. About the same time, the domestication of camels in Arabia made possible the use of camel riders in battle. Assyrian reliefs depict numerous clashes with camel riders.[33] We are told nothing, however, of camel riders on the (two-humped) Bactrian camels introduced from Central Asia by way of Iran.

32. Cf. A. Salonen, *Die Landfahrzeuge des alten Mesopotamien* (Helsinki, 1951); W. Nagel, *Der mesopotamische Streitwagen und seine Entwicklung im ostmediterranen Bereich* (Berlin, 1966); W. Farber, M. A. Littauer, and J. H. Crouwel, "Kampfwagen," *RLA* V (1980): 336ff. Cf. also Crouwel, *Wheeled Vehicles and Ridden Animals in the Ancient Near East* (Leiden, 1979).

33. Cf. E. Strommenger–M. Hirmer, *Fünf Jahrtausende Mesopotamien* (Munich, 1962), esp. pl. 242-43.

In preparing for war, the Assyrians employed spies and agents, which we learn from numerous letters. The *dayyālu* even appear as a separate category of troop. Propaganda, designed to intimidate by word and picture, also played a very large role (see below).

Siege warfare developed early on as a special category of warfare. An outer wall (Akk. *šalḫû*) was often built in front of a fortification wall furnished with towers (Akk. *dūru*), and complicated gate designs were intended to impede penetration by the enemy. Abutment to a river was often sought. In mountainous regions, the mountain fortifications were elaborately improved. For their part, the attackers employed wall breakers with heavy battering rams and erected siege ramps wherever possible; these were meant to come as close as possible to the crest of the wall. From the Old Babylonian period we are familiar with many mathematical problems with their respective solutions, which were designed to drill the students in calculations which would be required in the preparation of siege fortifications. In some cases, the courses of great rivers were redirected in order to make both walls and buildings to collapse by means of masses of water.[34]

Boats were provided and, where possible, bridges were built in order to cross rivers. The individual soldiers used inflated sheepskins to reach the riverbank walls. That the art of swimming was then unknown is shown by the complete lack of words for "to swim" in the languages (other than Egyptian).

Sennacherib was, so far as is known, the first to undertake crossing the bays of the Persian Gulf with a naval flotilla. He did this around 700 with warships built by Greeks. Otherwise, we can draw little from the sources regarding possible maritime wars conducted by coastal states such as Elam or the Mediterranean countries. In any case, these could only be carried out in coastal regions.

The reasons for which wars were fought in the ancient Orient, and the desired goals of those wars, were just as multifarious as elsewhere in the history of the world, and yet in principle the same: on the one hand, defense against real or feared encroachments by others, and on the other, the attempt to subjugate and exploit others and, where they resisted, to wipe them out entirely. People were persuaded that warfare fulfilled the will of the gods, either to restore violated rights or to expand

---

34. Cf. H. Waschow, *4000 Jahre Kampf um die Mauer: Der Festungskrieg der Pioniere* (Bottrop, 1938); E. Ebeling, "Festung," *RLA* III (1957): 50ff.

present dominions. Nevertheless, the desire to live in peace was everywhere a living hope, so far as it was considered possible. Peoples who occupied economically rich districts were repeatedly compelled to defend themselves against attacks and encroachments from less well-endowed peoples. In order to make territorial defense easier, the tendency developed to protect one's homeland by means of a buffer zone of conquered territories. By this means, attacks could be detected in good time. The desire to expand these security zones frequently led to policies of unbridled conquest, as for example by the Akkadian kings of Babylonia and later by the Assyrians, as well as by many other kings. It must be said, however, that others restrained themselves and set only limited goals. Among these were Hammurabi of Babylon and his older contemporary, Shamshi-Adad I of Assyria,[35] along with many others.

Everywhere the making of war involved the application of especially barbaric methods, particularly when the situation either suggested or enhanced that possibility. Nevertheless, boasting of the atrocities and even exaggerating them, as was done by the Assyrians in word and picture, was not the usual practice. Rather, the Assyrians publicized their atrocities as a type of propaganda, so that peoples would submit to them without combat on account of their horrifying illustrations. That there was always humaneness alongside barbarism did not appear to them to be worth mentioning, and was therefore forgotten, then as now.

35. Shamshi-Adad I of Assyria briefly instructed his son Yasmaḫ-Adad to treat the inhabitants of subjugated territories in such a way that they would freely recognize the king without force.

CHAPTER VII

Nutrition and Agriculture

Agriculture will be understood here in the broadest sense of the term, including also the activities of gathering and collecting, especially fishing and hunting. We do not know whether any type of forest management was practiced in the partially wooded mountain regions; some allusions to the care of forests found in myths could be interpreted in this direction.

The conditions for farming, gardening, and livestock production are often quite diverse, depending upon the natural circumstances (see above, ch. II). Only a separate monograph could present this subject in detail, and that has yet to be written. The written sources at our disposal for certain periods of Babylonian history are overflowing with information, and they are also very rich for Assyria as well as for parts of Mesopotamia and northern Syria. The manifold possibilities of pollen analysis have been used very little until now, and we may still expect important conclusions to be provided by increased use of the methods of natural science.[1]

Collecting and gathering in the technical sense generally played only a very subordinate role in the nutritional scheme of the ancient Orient. Mushrooms are only rarely mentioned,[2] and for many wild plants, fruits, berries, and so forth we may simply not know the terminology. "Honey" (Sum. *làl*, Akk. *dišpu*) in Babylonia seldom referred

---

1. Cf. B. Hrouda, *et al., Methoden der Archäologie.*
2. Cf. *"kam'atu,* 'Truffle,'" *CAD,* VIII [K] (1971), 120; *"kamūnu B,"* *CAD,* VIII, 133.

Inlaid friezes depicting bulls (top) and various dairy activities (bottom), including milking and the preparation and storage of butter. Temple of Ninḥursag, Tell el-Ubaid (3rd millennium). (*University Museum, University of Pennsylvania*)

to bee honey, and certainly syrup made from dates is far more frequent. Bee-keeping was significant only in Asia Minor.[3] The gathering and collecting of herbs for healing was widely practiced (see below, XI.8). With respect to animals, there is evidence that people ate both turtles and grasshoppers (locusts), and that they gathered the eggs of turtles and of several kinds of birds.

1. Fishing and Fowling; Hunting

Fishing was practiced by professional fishermen[4] and played a highly significant role in nutrition wherever a body of water was not too far distant. Still, we scarcely know anything of fishing in the Mediterranean and in the great salt seas. At the same time, abundant sources are available for Babylonia between about 2500 and 1500 and again in the later period. These show that one must distinguish between freshwater fishing and fishing in the saltwater lagoons and in the Persian Gulf. Unfortunately, many Sumerian and Akkadian expressions and terms for fish found in economic documents cannot yet be clearly interpreted. The implements for fishing were primarily nets, either set or thrown, as well as fishing spears, harpoons, and baskets. Rods were used less frequently, perhaps because of the many large fish. Normally people fished from the riverbank or from boats; on the sea they used sailing ships. Baskets were generally used to carry the catches. Among the many types of river fish, carp (Cyprinidae) were the most common. Large amounts of salt were needed for preservation, and there were even some means of preservation using spices. Fish were often depicted in art, individually or as the inhabitants of rivers and lagoons, and they play a role in some myths (see below, XIII.3e, on the myth of Adapa).

The economic significance of fowling was certainly much less than that of fishing. Nevertheless, fowlers (Sum. *mušen-dù*; Akk. *us/šandû*) are frequently mentioned in cuneiform texts. Nets and snares were the primary means of catching birds, but people are also depicted shooting

---

3. The governor Shamash-reshu-ussur, on the middle Euphrates, bragged in the eighth century of having introduced bee-keeping; cf. E. Ebeling, "Biene," *RLA* II (1938): 25.

4. Cf. A. Salonen, *Die Fischerei im alten Mesopotamien* (Helsinki, 1970); the fisherman was called *šu-kua* in Sumerian, and in Akkadian, *bā'eru*, "catcher," or *šuḫaddāku*.

at birds. Decoys were often employed, and hunting falcons were used, though primarily on royal hunts. Our inadequate knowledge of the ancient names of birds makes the determination of the preferred types of hunted birds all the more difficult.[5] That birds were regarded not only as a source of meat and eggs is shown by some texts which attempt to reproduce birdcalls (see below, XI.7). For domesticated birds, see below, section 2d.

Hunting had two primary functions: it served to provide meat for eating as well as furs for clothing and bones for the production of various articles, and it served to defend against predators as well as against the varmints that plagued the fields and gardens. Early on, hunting gained significance by means of a third function which was scarcely less important than the other two, namely as a sport which brought pleasure. Here it served as an arena where manly strength could be proven before others. The princes, with their retinues, and the feudal lords generally reserved for themselves the right to hunt for its own sake, simply because the animals which were hunted did not exist in sufficient quantity to permit the sport to all. Those who hunted, however, joyously represented their deeds as fulfilling the commandment of the gods of the hunt, especially Ninurta, the Nimrod of the Bible.

By both written and pictorial accounts, the hunts of the Assyrian kings from Tiglath-pileser I on are especially well attested. The reliefs depict the pursuit of lions and other predators, as well as gazelles, ibexes, stags, wild horses, and elephants. The king hunted from a chariot or on horseback, and large dogs were set loose on the chase. Hunting is mentioned less frequently in the letters, as in those from Mari. Documents often record articles which were made of the skins or body parts of game animals, but they contain no references which would permit us to draw conclusions concerning the economic significance of hunting expeditions. In fact, hunting made a significant contribution to the nutrition of the populace only in the mountain districts, but we possess only a very few reports from these areas.[6]

---

5. Cf. A. Salonen, *Vögel und Vogelfang im alten Mesopotamien* (Helsinki, 1973).
6. Cf. A. Salonen, *Jagd und Jagdtiere im alten Mesopotamien* (Helsinki, 1976); W. Heimpel and L. Trümpelmann, "Jagd," *RLA* V (1977): 234ff.

2. Animal Husbandry

Animal husbandry is one of the main categories of agriculture, but it is not limited to the service of agriculture. For example, all animals were regarded as possible sources for omens. Here we will treat animal husbandry as a whole.

a. Dogs, Cats, and Mongooses

The dog (Sum. *ur-gi₇*; Semitic *kalbu*) was one of the earliest domestic animals and served primarily to protect herds and dwellings against enemies. Despite the fact that many dogs roamed freely in the cities, the dog in the ancient Orient was at all times generally bound to a single master and was cared for by him. Of course, the dog was also a carrion eater, and in the villages it provided the same service as hyenas and jackals. As far as we can tell, there were only two main breeds of dog: large greyhounds which were used primarily in hunting, and very strong dogs (on the order of Danes and mastiffs), which in the ancient Orient were more than a match for the generally smaller wolves and for that reason were especially suitable as herd dogs. The sources distinguish numerous sub-breeds, but we can only partially identify these. The dog was often the companion of gods of therapeutics. Although the expression "vicious dog" occurred, "dog" as derogatory term was little used.[7]

The house cat (Sum. *sa-a*; Akk. *šurānu*) was universally kept as a mouse- and rat-catcher, but played no further role of any significance, and was only rarely depicted (in contrast to the artistic treatment given dogs).[8] As mousers, cats had, as at present, an important competitor in southern Asia in the larger and stronger mongoose (Sum. *nin-kilim*; Akk. *šikkû*), which also had the critical function of a snake-killer and is often mentioned in texts.[9] As with the cat, we learn almost nothing of the mongoose from Syria and Asia Minor.

---

7. Cf. W. Heimpel and U. Seidl, "Hund," *RLA* IV (1975): 494ff.
8. Cf. W. Heimpel and U. Seidl, "Katze," *RLA* V (1980): 488ff.
9. Cf. B. Landsberger and I. Krumbiegel, *Die Faune des alten Mesopotamien* (Leipzig, 1934), 110ff. Snakes and wild animals are treated there as well. For the depiction of animals, cf. E. D. van Buren, *The Fauna of Ancient Mesopotamia as Represented in Art.* AnOr 18 (1939).

b. Equids and Camels

Although the subject of horse breeding is frequently treated in the documents, many uncertainties remain.[10] The interpretation of pictures is often disputed, but above all, the various words for equids, insofar as they do not permit us to draw more precise meanings from them, came in the course of time to designate several different species, without allowing us to distinguish these clearly in every case. The domestication of equids and camels was by all accounts difficult, dragging on for centuries and requiring many fresh starts.

The first to be domesticated was the ass (Sum. *anše;* Semitic *ḥimāru;* the she-ass, Sum. *ème;* Akk. *atānu*), which had wide-ranging economic uses and even made possible transport over great distances, as long as sufficient water was available. Documents, letters, and literature everywhere treat the ass in manifold ways, but characterize neither it, nor camels, nor sheep as (especially) stupid. The ass was also ridden, as it still is in Arab lands, and could carry considerable loads when fitted with the proper harness. Ass's milk was drunk only rarely. Asses were affordable, not merely for the well-to-do.

The onager *(equus hemionus)* was not only frequently stubborn like the ass, it was also disposed to bite and kick. As early as the third millennium the onager was employed to pull wagons, but it had to be firmly restrained. Only the foals of the onager could be tamed, the adults never. According to bones found in Syria, there must have been a further species of equid which became extinct very early, and which was used like the onager. What the Semites named these animals is still unclear; in Ebla in the third millennium the words *kūdanum* and *agalum* could be used for this species, but in contemporary Akkadian and even later these terms specified other equids. In Babylonia, as distinct from Mari and Assyria, these terms were only applied in literary contexts. At present, it is impossible to demonstrate the use of the onager in agriculture, and basic studies of these equids are still lacking.

Many scholars even speak of mules as early as the third millennium

---

10. Cf. A. Salonen, *Hippologica Accadica* (Helsinki, 1955), on all the equids; F. Hančar, *Das Pferd in prähistorischer und früher historischer Zeit* (Vienna, 1956); I. G. Khlopin, "Das Pferd in Vorderasien," *Orientalia Lovaniensia* 13 (1982): 1ff. In Sumerian the horse was called "mountain ass" *(anše-kur-ra);* Akk. *sisû* (cf. Heb. *sûs*) is a loanword of uncertain origin (cf. *AHw,* 1051-52).

in the Orient, but they do not take into consideration that this would presuppose horse breeding alongside the domestication of asses, since mules as a rule are sterile. Regarding horses, we encounter only rare mentions of them in Sumerian texts from the period around 2000, and in Old Babylonian and Assyrian texts such references are infrequent. It is therefore doubtful whether mules are really mentioned in the Mari texts. Even after the middle of the second millennium, mules were introduced only in limited ways, primarily to draw wagons; that is because mules were more costly than asses, on account of the expense involved in crossing horses and asses. Horse breeding itself was nurtured in the Hurrian states, among the Hittites, and a little later in Assyria, as indicated by Hittite and Assyrian training instructions.[11] Horses, however, were always in the service of the kings, princes, and great landowners, as well as the army (see above, VI.5). After about 900, important centers of horse breeding were to be found in Armenia and northwest Iran, where the export of horses was an important economic factor. Horse breeding also played a large role in Syria-Palestine in the first millennium, and the Assyrians claim to have taken away thousands of horses as spoil during their campaigns there. White horses were considered particularly valuable and were frequently given as gifts to the temples (cf. the horses at the temple in Jerusalem, 2 Kings 23:11).[12]

Camel breeding was carried out primarily in Arabia by Bedouin or seminomads (see above, VI.4c) after about 1100. About the same time, the two-humped Bactrian camel was being bred in northern Iran. Many camels came into Assyria and other lands as tribute and through purchases, and were generally used as beasts of burden. Centers for the breeding of dromedaries must also have existed after about 700 in southern Babylonia, a fact which is born out by tribute lists and several reliefs. The Old Testament is an important source for the keeping of camels in Syria-Palestine. See above, VI.5, for the Arabs' use of camels as mounts in war.[13]

11. Cf. A. Kammenhuber, *Hippologia Hethitica* (Wiesbaden, 1961); E. Ebeling, *Bruchstücke einer mittelassyrischen Vorschriftensammlung für die Akklimatisierung und Trainierung von Wagenpferden* (Berlin, 1951).

12. Persons guilty of breaches of contract were sometimes penalized by being required to produce a gift of a (certainly very costly) grey or white horse.

13. The comprehensive and somewhat controversial literature on the domestication of the camel is synopsized in W. Heimpel, "Kamel," *RLA* V (1980): 330ff. It is an anachronism when Genesis ascribes camels to the ancestors of Israel (Genesis 12:16; 24:10 and *passim*; 30:43; 31:17, 34; 32:7, 15).

c. Cattle, Sheep, Goats, and Pigs

The beginnings of cattle breeding in the Orient, like the beginnings of agriculture, reach back into the sixth millennium. Only settled farmers could raise cattle, and only where the cultivable ground was sufficient for both fields and pasturage, because the cattle herder had to be able to keep the animals out of the fields. The sources attest a developed practice of cattle breeding in the third millennium. That is especially true for Syria. In Ebla one often finds remarkably high numbers of cattle listed in documents (e.g., one listing 11,788). One must ask where persons could have pastured so many beasts.[14] Later tallies of spoils occasionally run to five figures, but these may be considerably overstated. If I perceive it correctly, much smaller numbers are cited as a rule in Babylonia. According to one Old Babylonian letter, one head of cattle cost as much as thirty sheep, but despite this was not viewed as all that expensive.

Because of their aggressiveness, bulls were generally used only for breeding purposes. Oxen had to plow, harrow, pull farm wagons, and carry out the threshing (see below, section 3b). Yet they seldom served to pull loads on main thoroughfares. There were also fattened cattle which were destined for sacrificial slaughter or for the tables of the princes. Cows served almost entirely for breeding purposes and to provide milk. Information on age is especially frequent for cattle. There were special cattle herders and feeders for the larger herds, and these often stood in the service of the temples and had to keep the stalls (only for mothers?) in order. Whether manure was widely used as fertilizer is not known. Dried cow piles were an important source of fuel in Babylonia, where wood was scarce. Covers and even shoes were produced from the tanned hides, and many objects were made from cattle horn.

Bulls are frequently depicted, and cows somewhat less often, and these on reliefs with the milker or with the calf. The bull was ascribed to the moon god and the weather gods (see below, XII.2, on this and the horned crown). The difficult, but auspicious, birth of a calf with the

14. Cf. D. O. Edzard, *Archivi reali di Ebla*, II: *Verwaltungstexte verschiedenen Inhalts* (Rome, 1981), no. 25. There is no monograph on the breeding of cattle; for plowing oxen, cf. A. Salonen, *Agricultura Mesopotamica* (Helsinki, 1968), 376ff. Spans of four oxen are mentioned with particular frequency, but spans of two, six, and eight were employed as well. Cf. F. R. Kraus, *Staatliche Viehhaltung im altbabylonischen Lande Larsa* (Amsterdam, 1966).

help of the moon god as portrayed in the myths was a favorite theme for incantations in Babylonian rites to aid in birth (see below, XII.6). Even kings occasionally laid claim to the divine epithet "bull."

The sheep was the most important domestic animal for sedentary farmers as well as for nomads, since it was easily satisfied and could be repeatedly driven to other pasturage. The great temples, just as the royal palaces and some individuals, often controlled extensive flocks; in Ebla, six-figure numbers are given for the total holdings of sheep (see above). The sheep gave milk, could be sheared regularly, and was the most important source of meat. The manure served as fertilizer, and the hides and horns could be put to manifold uses. The shepherd was considered the archetype of the herdsman. The kings thought of him when they designated themselves the shepherds of their people. At the same time, herdsman (Sum. *sipa;* Akk. *rē'û*) was also a widely used divine epithet. Large dogs (see above, section 2a) served to protect the flocks. In documents, letters, and other sources, so many thousands of references to sheep are found that, even by limiting one's study to certain periods, a comprehensive treatment of sheep breeding could be prepared only with great difficulty.

The sheep was the animal most commonly used in sacrifice. Divination by means of examining the innards of the sacrificial beast, especially liver divination, was performed almost exclusively on sheep (see below, XI.5). However, while the sheep was the sacred animal of the goddess Inanna (Ishtar) (see below, XII.3), artistic representations are relatively infrequent, and then primarily in miniature.

In comparison with sheep breeding, the keeping of goats played only a subordinate role in the Orient. Nonetheless, goats are frequently discussed in documents and letters. Besides goat's milk, goat's hair found manifold applications, and he-goats are mentioned quite frequently.

Whenever butter is mentioned in the texts, what is generally meant is a specially prepared type of cream — primarily from sheep — and not the butter that we know. Cheese is discussed so remarkably seldom that it cannot have had any great significance for nutrition; but particular studies here are lacking.[15]

---

15. Butter (Sum. *ì-nun-na,* Akk. *ḫimētu*) is mentioned in every period. However, cheese (Sum. *ga-àra;* Akk. *eqīdu* or *gubnatu*) receives rare notice in Akkadian texts, but is frequently found in Neo-Sumerian documents. A further Akkadian word for a type of cheese may still be unrecognized.

Pork was not generally prohibited as unclean in Babylonia and Assyria, in contrast to Israel, and pork as meat was used just as widely as was pork lard, although its consumption was not as common as that of mutton. In documents from the first millennium, however, the hog is mentioned so seldom that we can only conclude that by this time there must have been only a minimal consumption of pork. How hogs were kept has yet to be studied.

d. Poultry

As far as we can tell, the raising of poultry began much later than livestock domestication. Geese were first kept in Babylonia toward the end of the third millennium, and ducks were introduced sometime early in the second millennium. In both cases, the meat as well as the eggs was sought. Neither geese nor ducks are mentioned in the letters and documents in the earlier period; and any mention of eggs is quite rare prior to the first millennium, the most frequent, however, being of ostrich eggs, which were certainly collected in the arable steppe along with other eggs. It is therefore clear that poultry raising had no essential economic significance in the second millennium.

Various kinds of wild hen, as for example the francolin, are identified as game birds as early as the second millennium. The domestic hen was no doubt introduced from India in the first millennium and is often depicted in the later period, but it cannot be identified with certainty in texts.[16] Sacrificial birds in the Neo-Babylonian period were primarily ducks and doves, and less frequently geese. The bird keeper often dealt in these. In Israel, only doves were known as sacrificial birds, and the poor could bring these in place of sheep. The Old Testament does not mention ducks, geese, or hens, and eggs as well as young birds were apparently gathered from the nests of wild birds (cf. Deuteronomy 14:11-20; 22:6-7).

16. An Akkadian word for the domestic chicken is unknown. Important studies of the keeping of fowl are found in A. Salonen, *Vögel und Vogelfang im alten Mesopotamien*, under *kurkû*, "goose" (216-17), and *paspasu* and *ūsu*, "duck" (237ff., 288ff.). *Tarlugallu*, "cock" (154-55), probably refers to the domestic rooster only in isolated cases.

3. Farming and Gardening

a. Requirements

The plains and mountain slopes which were suitable for farming in Western Asia were subject to manifold changes with regard to their extent and quality; of these changes we can comprehend only a very small portion. The arable regions were especially widespread during the rainy fourth millennium (see above, ch. II), and a considerable proportion of these was certainly still forested at that time, although the clearing of the forests had long since been under way. Here we can treat only the historical period, which began about 3000 in Babylonia and in other districts considerably later. In this period, people were no longer helpless in the face of short- or longer-term climatic fluctuations, but they still had only very limited possibilities of counteracting the loss of farmland through too much or — more often! — too little water, or through the salination of the soil. In this climate, the hilly districts where rain-based agriculture was possible (see above, ch. II) were greatly favored in comparison with those districts which were completely dependent upon artificial irrigation and draining projects. The boundaries of both zones in those districts of Mesopotamia which abutted the mountains were subject to considerable fluctuations. Even in rain-based agricultural districts one could in no way always count on completely sufficient quantities of rainfall. In addition, the rainfall usually was unevenly distributed over the year. The small watercourses, which were so important for farming, were found only in a few places outside of the hill country, such as in the region of the spring-fed sources of the Habur. But even in the mountains, not all streams were perennial. It was only rather seldom that all of the natural requirements for abundant harvests from good soil were on hand.[17]

In the rain-poor regions, agriculture was only possible where rivers could be diverted into canals, which could then repeatedly branch out until they reached the fields. The canals could thus bring the water as far as the slope of the land permitted. The maintenance of the main canals was a concern of the state; the upkeep of the smaller canals lay upon the field owners and tenants (see above, VI.3). The canals carried

17. In the *Tübinger Atlas des Vorderen Orients* (Wiesbaden, 1977–), which is still in the process of publication, one can find important maps on agriculture.

sufficient water for agriculture only for part of the year, and they were always threatened with silting up. The danger for the fields, by contrast, lay in the salination of the soil, especially by saltpeter. When the salt level could not be reduced through drainage, very good land could become unproductive. Agriculture in Babylonia, which was never carried out throughout the whole land, thus demanded much work and careful planning, yet with these it also brought good harvests.

The possibilities for intensive cultivation in Assyria were as good as those in Mesopotamia in the vicinity of the great rivers, and in vast reaches of the plains and the hill country — so good, in fact, that surpluses could often be exported. Apart from the rivers, the land was dominated by steppe, as in much of Arabia, and south of the Euphrates, by desert. At the same time, there were fertile districts in the hilly lands of western and eastern Arabia.

b. Methods

The circumstances depicted above not only made agriculture very difficult in extensive areas, they also compelled the inhabitants to think through an appropriate policy of soil management at an early period and to improve their tools repeatedly. Plows with copper-covered plowshares and, even before 3000, bronze plowshares replaced hoes and spades; even harrows may have been used at an early date. The introduction of the sowing plow with a built-in funnel for the seeds, which only lightly broke the surface of the ground and which was used in addition to the ground-breaking plow, cannot be dated with certainty. (Some Assyrian kings did boast that they had introduced new plows.) When the seeds fell into the furrows cut by the plow, much less seed was lost on the ground — which, whether dry or irrigated, was often very hard — than was the case with hand-sowing. On hard ground, clumps of earth had to be "shattered" in Old Babylonian times, even after harrowing. From the period around 2000 we possess a Sumerian teaching poem on farming which still cannot be entirely understood.[18] The poem describes the process from irrigation to the particular tasks

18. Cf. Salonen, *Agricultura Mesopotamica*, 202ff., on the Sumerian agricultural didactic poem; also A. Deimel and B. Meissner, "Ackerbau," "Ackerbauwirtschaft," *RLA* I (1928): 16ff.; and K. Butz, "Landwirtschaft," *RLA* VI (1983-1984): 470ff.

and confirms what can be deduced from documents, namely, that the respective plots of land in Babylonia required much less seed than is the case for comparable units today: 6 m. of furrows required about 8 g. of seed; an area 6 m. wide required only 8 furrows, perhaps to protect the soil, and the direction of the furrows was altered regularly. This standard, however, should certainly not be generalized.

Every year following the harvest, certainly under normal circumstances, the ground had to be broken up, in the extremely short timespan in early summer between the receding of the floodwaters which had been allowed to flow over the fields and the drying of the ground to the hardness of stone. Sowing came in late autumn, harvest in early spring.[19] On good soil, Babylonia had generally rich harvests, which in a good year could bring an increase of sixty- or a hundredfold. There are unfortunately still many meteorological uncertainties which make an evaluation of the ubiquitous numerical citations in letters and documents more difficult, and which until now have hindered such an evaluation. Grain was cut with a sickle. The erection of sheaves or sheds for drying the grain, or the turning of the sheaves, is only mentioned in isolated cases. Animals were normally driven over the carefully smoothed threshing-floor to "tread out" (Akk. *diāšum*), or thresh, the grain. It is uncertain whether threshing sledges were used. After the threshing, winnowing was important to separate the grain from the chaff, and this could only be done under windy conditions. Additional workers always had to be hired for harvesttime, since harvesting as well as cultivation stood under a certain amount of time pressure (see above, VI.4c). After the harvest, the grain was either stored in storehouses near the fields or transported away, wherever possible, on the waterways. The amount of grain was measured, not weighed. There was no more than scant protection from vermin in the grain, though cats and mongooses were used to control mice.

In areas where farming was dependent on rainfall and in the mountains, working the land was organized differently in many respects. However, only for Assyria and Old Babylonian Mari do we have abundant sources for this, as well as for some cities in northern Syria, and specialized

19. On the seasons for sowing and harvesting in connection with the autumnal and spring sowing, cf. Salonen, *Agricultura Mesopotamica*, 190ff. There are numerous, varied problems regarding details on account of the month calendar, which varied from place to place.

studies of this subject are still lacking. Even in such districts, people often employed artificial irrigation. After 700, Sennacherib of Assyria built a canal 50 km. long, as well as other water projects. This canal crossed a valley on a broad aqueduct 280 m. long and diverted water from the River Gomel into the Hoser, in order to bring more water into Assyria (see above, V.9). Nonetheless, the Urartians were the master canal-builders; considerable portions of their great projects still remain.

c. Types of Grain; Flax, Sesame, and Peas

Barley, emmer, wheat, and millet are attested as types of grain in the ancient Orient; rye and oats were not cultivated, and there were sub-species of the main types. Yet the significance that each of these had for nutrition was not everywhere the same. In part these variations were at least a result of the different qualities of the respective soils. The interpretive problems are exacerbated by the fact that some words could specify a particular type of grain as well as grain in general, and that linguistic usage in Assyria diverges somewhat from that in Babylonia.[20]

The Babylonian words *še'u* as well as *uṭṭatu, kunāšu,* and *kibtu* corresponded to the Sumerian words *še* ("barley," "grain"), *zíz* ("emmer"), and *gig* ("wheat"). Barley was the grain primarily preferred for human use in Babylonia and in the third millennium in northern Syria (Ebla). Bread, all manner of groats, flour, and the regular form of beer were produced from barley.[21] The main part of all wages was also paid in barley, which served widely as a means of payment. Bread made from barley (Sum. *ninda;* Akk. *ak[a]lu*) was the staple diet, and appears as such along with water even in poetic works. *Uṭṭatu* also signified a "single grain," and was, with a weight of about $\frac{1}{22}$ g., the smallest unit of weight. From emmer, and even more often from wheat, fine baked goods and groats were made which were more expensive, and also a sweet beer. Exact numbers cannot be given, even provisionally, for the proportion of emmer and wheat in use, and it is impossible to elaborate upon the innumerable specific citations in letters and documents. Then

20. Cf. F. Hrozný, *Das Getreide im alten Babylonien* (Vienna, 1913); R. C. Thompson, *A Dictionary of Assyrian Botany* (London, 1949), 89ff.

21. In addition to the work of Hrozný, cf. W. Röllig, *Das Bier im alten Mesopotamien* (Berlin, 1970).

as now in the Orient, breads of all types may have been baked primarily in flat cakes. No doubt bread was baked mostly at home: bakers, in contrast to millers and cooks, are mentioned only rarely.

In Assyria also the cultivation and use of barley were primary, and we seldom hear of baking with wheat. The same was no doubt true of Asia Minor in the second millennium. In the Hittite texts the usage is similar to that in the Babylonian word lists: a remarkable number of types of breads — perhaps even pastries? — are named. In Israel, on the other hand, barley served predominantly as food for livestock, if the references in the Old Testament have been correctly interpreted.

Millet (Akk. *duḫnu*), which grows in poor soil and has a poor yield, is frequently named only in isolated groups of texts, such as those from Nuzi, and in Neo-Babylonian documents.

Oil was extracted from oil-rich sesame seeds by pressing in Babylonia and in those parts of Mesopotamia where olive trees did not flourish. The word "sesame" goes back to the Akkadian word *šamaššammu*, or to an even older word. The Akkadian word *šamnu*, just as the Sumerian word *ì*, designated fatty oils of all sorts; however, the most widely used types of animal fats had their own specific words. Sesame must have been cultivated extensively, at least in some districts, since oil-presses (Akk. *ṣāḫitu*) are mentioned quite frequently. In mountainous districts, among other places, olive oil was preferred if it was available. Sennacherib may have been the first to introduce the olive tree into Assyria. Oil was also used in personal hygiene. Apparently flax was cultivated for linen and linseed oil less in Babylonia and Assyria than in Palestine.

Among the protein-rich legumes, peas (Sum. *gú-gal*; Akk. *ḫallūru*) were cultivated, occasionally even in fields, and trade lists sometimes cite remarkably large quantities of them. The meaning of other Sumerian and Akkadian words for legumes is disputed. In Palestine, lentils were apparently eaten in preference to peas. Whether forage crops such as lupines or types of clover were sown is unknown, but crop surpluses were important export items for regions of intensive agricultural cultivation (see below, IX.5).

d. Gardens and Groves: Date Palms, Fruit Trees, Vegetables

Within the cities, as well as in front of their gates and in the villages, wherever water was available, were gardens and groves of all sizes. These were primarily groves of trees, since only trees provide vegetables and herbs with the necessary shade. References to gardens and their respective yields are found in documents, letters, and other texts from Babylonia and Assyria in overwhelming abundance, but great and manifold difficulties hinder their proper interpretation, and the subject still has not been treated comprehensively.[22]

Among those trees cultivated in groves, the date palm had by far the greatest significance in Babylonia and in those parts of Mesopotamia in which it grew; only for this tree have specialized studies been undertaken.[23] The words for palm tree and date (Sum. *gišimmar;* Akk. *gišimmaru; zulum[b]; suluppu*) stem no doubt from the Proto-Euphratic language. In order to bear fruit, the date palm required ample quantities of water, and in Mesopotamia the northern boundary for this tree lay around the 35th parallel. Date palms were not cultivated at all in Assyria or Syria-Palestine (but cf. Jericho, "the city of palms"). The pollination of palm trees could only succeed with human assistance, as is often depicted. Thus, the cultivation of date palms required a great deal of labor. In Babylonia, dates were one of the most important food sources. Dates were eaten fresh or dried, or they could be prepared in different ways, and date syrup replaced honey. Palm wood was also used in a variety of applications, as were the panicles and fronds, although the wood itself was of little worth as a building material. In case of an abundant harvest, dates could also be exported.

Among the fruit trees, the most important — and not just in Babylonia — were the fig, the pomegranate, and the apple tree, since they were widely eaten. Far more rarely mentioned were pear and quince trees, and some other fruit trees which as yet have not been identified. Citrus fruit most likely was not known at this time. Pistachio and carob-bean trees were widespread, not only in gardens, as were olive trees (outside of Babylonia), whose fruit was generally pressed into oil. Besides these, ornamental trees and those yielding timber were certainly planted in gardens, although these were found in far greater numbers in the mountain forests.

Extensive groves of trees also were found in Babylonia, primarily

22. Cf. E. Ebeling, "Garten," *RLA* III (1959): 147-150.
23. Cf. B. Landsberger, *The Date Palm and Its By-products according to the Cuneiform Sources* (Graz, 1967); D. Cocquerillat, *Palmeraies et cultures de l'Eanna d'Uruk* (Berlin, 1968).

as the property of the temple. In Assyria, from the time of Tiglath-Pileser I, the kings laid out great parks with many kinds of fruit- and timber-bearing trees, as well as olive trees in later times. These parks were described in the inscriptions, with numerous specific references regarding the trees. They were often even used as zoos, and many types of imported trees were planted there. In some cases these parks (Ass. *kirimaḫḫu*) had earlier been forests.

In the gardens, beds were laid within the shadow of the trees for all kinds of vegetable seedlings and herbs, and these were carefully tended and watered. We can only interpret a small portion of the numerous names of garden plants of all kinds which have come down to us from Babylonia and Assyria, and that because of frequent comparisons with Aramaic plant names. Whether flowers were cultivated for their own sake is not known, but many poetic statements suggest that. Herbs, or parts of them, were in wide use for medicinal purposes (see below, XI.8). How many medicinal herbs were raised in the gardens or along the edges of the fields cannot be said. The high frequency with which the gardener (Akk. *nukaribbu*) is mentioned in the texts is a further sign of the great significance of horticulture in the ancient Orient.

CHAPTER VIII

Artisanry

1. The Term; Organization and Instruction; The School

There is no term for "artisanry" in the ancient Orient. There is, of course, the pre-Sumerian word *ummia*, or the Akkadian *ummiānum/ ummânu*, whose meaning runs in the direction of "specialist." This word is attested in Ebla in the third millennium and (later) designates specific artisans, scholars, and artists, as well as moneylenders (see below, IX.4) — in other words, always people with specialized schooling. *Ummânūtu* is the "skill" which the artisan learns, as well as his "learning" or "erudition"; in the latter sense it is related to *ṭupšarrūtu* (see below). Numerous designations for artisans are pre-Sumerian and go back at least as far as the fourth millennium.[1]

Ummia/ummânu designates the master artisan. The apprentices working under the journeyman readily called him, as their comrade, the "big brother." The apprentices concluded a contract of indenture with the master artisan, who demanded a complete apprenticeship from them and set down the necessary payment. Such contracts have been preserved at Nuzi and stem from the Middle and Neo-Babylonian periods.[2] Since the

---

1. For this entire chapter, cf. E. Salonen, *Über das Erwerbsleben im alten Mesopotamien: Untersuchungen zu den akkadischen Berufsnamen*, Part I (Helsinki, 1970).

2. Cf. M. San Nicolò, *Der neubabylonische Lehrvertrag in rechtsvergleichender Betrachtung* (Munich, 1950); and supplementally, E. Salonen, *Über das Erwerbsleben im alten Mesopotamien*, 29ff.; also the Code of Hammurabi § 188f., according to which the apprentice could be taken up into the house of the master as his foster child; H. P. H. Petschow, "Lehrverträge," *RLA* VI (1983): 556ff.

Seated on a low footstool, a woman spins wool; in her left hand she holds a spindle, in her right a card containing thread. Stone relief, Susa. *(Louvre)*

knowledge of a craft was not fixed in writing, such knowledge could only be mediated by means of an intensive oral and practical apprenticeship.

Even the scribal school was organized along the lines of a trade guild. The master artisan and the "big brother" instructed the pupils under strict discipline in writing and reckoning, in Sumerian and in the requisite professional knowledge of that time, and above all else in terminology. Many scribes only needed to write letters and documents; but those who wanted to transcribe literary works had to undergo a learned education at another place. The documents to be transcribed were generally dictated. Stone inscriptions were no doubt prepared by stone masons working from copies written in clay.[3] Even

3. Writing errors indicate that, without possessing any knowledge of cuneiform, stonemasons often carved into stone inscriptions originally written on clay tablets. On the scribe as an administrative official, see above, VI.3; concerning the school or "tab-

scholars often called themselves merely "scribes" (Sum. *dub-sar;* Akk. *ṭupšarru*).

2. Spinning, Weaving, Sewing, and Embroidery

Spinning and weaving were predominantly, though not exclusively, the work of women in the ancient Orient, just as they were later. Ordinarily the women took care of the carding and unraveling of the wool, as well as of most of the spinning, which could be handled with only a spindle and was therefore not a skilled profession. As far as I can tell, male wool spinners are never mentioned, and female spinners (Bab. *ṭāmītu*) are mentioned only in isolated texts, though they are occasionally depicted artistically.

The situation was entirely different with weaving. After a certain period of apprenticeship, weavers (Akk. *i/ušparu*) became specialized in particular types of weaving, such as the weaving of linen or of colored material. They worked while seated upon weaving stools, whose parts are often known only from lexical lists. Female weavers are frequently mentioned. Materials of all types, coarse as well as extremely fine, were woven. Cloth was widely exported, as is shown by Old Assyrian trade documents, which distinguish many and various types of cloth. Pigments included alum, crimson, and other substances, which still cannot be identified precisely. In later times, colors and bleaches were procured from specialists. Male and female washers alike were considered skilled workers, and were generally called fullers (Sum. *azlag;* Akk. *ašlāku*).

The sewing of clothing was no doubt left to the women, and it was not considered a skilled craft, as is seen from the fact that there is no Akkadian word for tailor, and one for the repair or jobbing tailor (Akk. *mukabbû*) occurs only in late texts. This is quite strange, since extremely artistic and ornate vestments were produced for kings, statues of gods, high priests, and others, and this work demanded the utmost ability. It is possible that many weavers were also tailors. Neo-Babylonian texts often mention tailors of mourning garments (Akk. *šaqqāya*).

---

let-house," Sum. *é-dub-ba,* see below, XIII.4c, d. In Old Babylonian Sippar, women also served as scribes. The god of the scribes was Nabû (see below, XII.3b). No monograph has yet been written on what was certainly the most multi-faceted profession of the ancient Orient. See below, section 6.

Statues and reliefs are a bountiful source for the adornment of garments. The ornamented robes of state of the Assyrian kings, which are so rich even in mythological scenes, and which we know from the painstakingly exact representations in the reliefs, were presumably embroidered. Yet words for embroidery and the artistic embroiderer are no better known than a word for the producer of artificially fringed hems.[4]

The sack makers (Akk. *sabsû, sabsinnu*) and the rug tyers (Akk. *kāṣiru;* Nuzi *mardatuḫlu*) were considered as having specific professions, although the *kāṣiru,* of course, worked together with the weavers and shared in other textile work as well. The production of rugs and tapestries is especially richly attested in Old Babylonian Mari and in Nuzi, although the technique of tying carpets was probably developed after 1500.[5] The weaving of cloth certainly occupied a great many people in all periods and was thus a particularly important branch of the economy. A specialty of Syria, and particularly of the Phoenicians, was the production of purple cloth, since purple snails were to be found only off the Phoenician coast. The name Canaan was surely derived from the designation for purple cloth attested in the Nuzi documents: *kinaḫḫu.*[6]

3. The Preparation of Hides: Leather

Skins of all kinds were the earliest clothing worn by people and also served to carry water and other liquids. The so-called shaggy robe found in Sumerian reliefs was a stylization of a robe of skins. The tanning of the skins to make leather, after the hair had been removed with the aid of oak apples, tree bark, alum, and other substances, was probably attempted very early, but the process had to be carried out gradually so that a sufficient firmness and water resistance could be attained. Since the remains of leather can only be preserved in completely dry ground, there is scarcely any chance of conducting a chemical analysis of ancient leather.

4. Cf. H. Waetzoldt and E. Strommenger, "Kleidung," *RLA* VI (1983): 18ff.; and Waetzoldt, "Leinen," *RLA* VI: 583ff. The cuneiform texts mention a great many types of cloth, but we are able to identify only a few of these.

5. Cf. W. Mayer, "*Mardatu* 'Teppich,'" *UF* 9 (1977): 173ff.

6. Cf. B. Landsberger, "Über Farben in Sumerisch-Akkadischen," *JCS* 21 (1969): 139ff. (on dyed wools, see pp. 155ff.).

In most cases, the ancient languages do not distinguish between hide, skin, and the different types of leather (cf. Sum. *kuš;* Akk. *mašku;* Aram. *gildā* and *ṣallā;* Heb. *ʿōr*). The Akkadian word *dušû,* however, designated only raw, untanned leather. In addition, there was only one (pre-Sumerian) word for leatherworker (Sum. *ašgab;* Akk. *aškapu;* Aram. *aškāpā*); shoemakers and harness makers were not differentiated, and a particular word for tanner (Akk. *rēsinu*) only appeared very late. The apprenticeship to a leatherworker must have been especially intensive, although a specialization in a certain category of leather work was unavoidable.

One of the main tasks of the leatherworker was the production of sandals and, later, other types of shoes such as boots (Akk. *s/šuḫuppatu*). The word for shoe (Akk. *šēnu*) is itself found in Proto-Semitic. Shoes were doubtless prepared predominantly from the especially firm cuts of cowhide, as far as the availability of cattle would permit. Goat's leather, however, may have been used for the leg of the boot covering the lower leg. Sinews and tendons served as laces and thread. Statuary, reliefs, and clay models, especially from those periods when floor-length robes were not customary, show us how sandals and boots looked.[7] There is no evidence yet for stockings, though leggings and garters were occasionally used.

The use of different types of leather, or perhaps untanned hides on occasion, was multifaceted. Belts of leather were used along with cloth belts, but leather was of particular importance for equipping soldiers. Leather straps and insets were necessary primarily for helmets and armor (which hardly ever consisted entirely of bronze or iron), and, together with metal sheeting, for shields of all kinds. Here one could presumably nail or sew two or three layers of leather together. At least in the first millennium, bowcases (Akk. *šalṭu;* Heb. *šeleṭ*), like many quivers, were made from leather. Finally, leather was needed for the war chariot and especially the bridle, along with cords and lines, as well as for numerous kinds of tools.

Leather was not used in Babylonia for the purpose of writing until the later period, and then only sporadically. Even in Syria-Palestine leather was only used for writing here and there prior to the Persian period, and then only under Egyptian influence.

7. Cf. M. Stol, "Leder(industrie)," *RLA* VI (1983): 527ff.; A. Salonen, *Die Fussbekleidung der alten Mesopotamier* (Helsinki, 1969).

In Babylonia in the early second millennium, doors consisting of as many as ten oxhides were produced, but these were no doubt an exception, since the word "door" normally had the determinative for wood.[8] A comprehensive treatment of the production and application of leather in the ancient Orient is still needed.

4. The Use of Reeds: Basketry

Reeds (Bot. *Phragmites communis*) that grew in abundance along the waterways and in the marshes and thickets had a far greater economic significance in the treeless plains of Western Asia than in the forested lands. They were used not only for baskets of all sorts, the shafts of arrows, spears, and light structures and fences, but also in manifold ways in boat- and shipbuilding, in the making of doors and reed furniture, and above all for huts and shelters for humans and animals in the countryside.

Accordingly, the reed worker — the Akkadian word *atkuppu* derives from a pre-Sumerian culture — was required to possess a variety of skills, especially since he was at the same time a weaver of mats who had to work with all materials suitable for weaving, including bulrushes and esparto grass. Only sporadic references to the Akkadian *sābiku* and *musabbiktu* — the male and female weavers of reeds — are found alongside those to the *atkuppu*. In view of the multiple tasks of the *atkuppu*, there must have been narrower specializations, at least in the cities: one certainly did not need the skills of the *atkuppu* merely for light reed and plaiting work. In other places he worked alongside cabinet makers, shipwrights, and armor makers. In the later periods, artisanry in the service of the temple was so lucrative that it came to be treated as a benefice. It has not been determined whether certain objects made of reeds, including mats, were exported.[9]

In great building projects, such as the high, terraced temples (Akk. *ziqqurratu*), layers of reed mats were laid at intervals between the layers of bricks, and thickly plaited reed lines were drawn as guy-lines. We do not know whether this was the task of the *atkuppu* as well. Reed mats

8. Cf. A. Salonen, *Die Türen des alten Mesopotamien* (Helsinki, 1961); the determinative for wood was applied frequently to doors.

9. For the use of reeds and bulrushes, cf. *ibid.*, and various passages in the books of A. Salonen cited in nn. 10-14 below.

were widely used for roofs; the carbonized remains of these mats and lines are still frequently preserved.

5. Woodwork: Carpentry, Joining, and Furniture Making

The conditions for preparing and using wood in the richly forested mountain regions were fundamentally different from those in sparsely wooded Babylonia. The occasional house and longer bridges could be built of wood only in wooded regions. Still, numerous objects as large as wagons and ships were made primarily of wood, regardless of whether the quality of the available wood was suitable for those objects. Therefore, the Babylonian lexical lists of wood objects are considerably larger than those for objects made of copper, clay, or leather. Since only in desert regions did wood survive as anything more than carbonized remains, we must draw our knowledge of woodworking almost entirely from the ancient texts, which survive in great abundance for all of Mesopotamia and northern Syria. For some objects reliefs, paintings, and models of clay or stone provide illustration and thereby make possible the interpretation of the various descriptions.[10] Thus, we can interpret the terminology preserved in cuneiform for the most important types of wood, but for many other words we can offer only suggestions, and we often cannot say whether we are dealing with native or imported wood.

A great many wooden objects no doubt were produced at home without involving the services of skilled artisans, but other kinds of woodwork, as well as many types of carpentry, demanded the skill of a trained craftsman. Given the breadth of work required, it is strange that no linguistic distinction was made between carpenters and joiners. Indeed, the same pre-Sumerian word was used for all types of woodwork. It appeared in Sumerian as *nagar,* in Akkadian as *na[g]gāru/nangāru,* in Aramaic as *naggārā,* and in Arabic as *naǧǧār.*[11] Through the addition of genitives, wheelwrights, shipwrights, and other craftsmen could be distinguished more exactly. Very little is known yet of the tools used by the carpenters and joiners, although these certainly would have been numerous.

10. A throne from Urartu, for example, is depicted with great exactitude on an Assyrian relief. Cf. A. Salonen, *Die Möbel des alten Mesopotamien und sumerisch-akkadischen Quellen* (Helsinki, 1963), which includes Syria and Urartu as well.

11. Cf. A. Salonen, *Die Hausgeräte der alten Mesopotamier,* Part I (Helsinki, 1965).

Whether and to what degree carpenters were needed for the building of simple, single-story houses is unknown; certainly they would have been called upon to cut the timbers properly for the flat roof and, where necessary, the doors. Moreover, saws would hardly have been available to everyone. A high degree of skill was demanded of these artisans for the building of temples and palaces as well. For these projects, valuable building woods, including all kinds of cypress, cedar, beech, and others, were imported, the primary source being Syria. For the great palatial doors, beams had to be cut and joined with exactitude. The simplest homes, however, may have had doors with only wooden frames, onto which mats on wooden bars were fastened.[12] Which other parts of a house might be made from wood certainly varied greatly, depending on the quantity and quality of the available wood. The texts, especially the letters and documents, have not yet been systematically studied in connection with these questions.

The great tree trunks from Syria and other forested regions were floated downriver on rafts bound together with strong lines of plaited reeds. For other loads ships had to be built, predominantly of wood, but also with the manifold application of lighter reeds and bulrushes. Both carpenters and "sailors" appear in the texts as shipbuilders, the latter primarily for those ships which only traveled downstream and which were dismantled on arrival (because one could only sail upstream in light currents, and then only for short stretches). Ships intended for longer-term use and for the coastal trade had to be constructed with far greater care, and they were sealed more permanently. In warfare, ships first became important in the eighth century, when the Assyrians began to wage war against Elam across the bays of the Persian Gulf. For this purpose, Greek shipwrights certainly had to be brought in to help. In Assyria itself, however, the shipbuilders of Sennacherib succeeded in constructing rafts which were able to transport stone blocks weighing up to 30 tons on the fast-flowing Tigris. These blocks were held in place by cords once the rafts had embarked.[13]

From the earliest times, the four-wheeled transport wagon (Sum.

12. Cf. Salonen, *Die Türen des alten Mesopotamien;* E. Heinrich and D. O. Edzard, "Haus," *RLA* IV (1973): 176ff.

13. Cf. A. Salonen, *Die Wasserfahrzeuge in Babylonien.* Studia orientalia 8/4 (Helsinki, 1939), which includes warships; *idem, Nautica Babyloniaca.* Studia orientalia 11/1 (Helsinki, 1942); M.-C. de Graeve, *The Ships of the Ancient Near East (c. 2000-500 B.C.)* (Louvain, 1981).

mar-gíd-da; Akk. *ereqqu*) stood alongside the light, two-wheeled chariot (Sum. *gigir;* Akk. *narkabtu;* Heb. *merkabâ*), which was used for battle and individual journeys. These vehicles could only be built by skilled craftsmen, who curiously remained firm in using the cumbersome flat wheels which felt every bump in the road. Not until after 1500 did predominantly six-spoked wheels, and later eight- or even ten-spoked wheels, gradually begin to prevail. The other parts of the wagon, built from different materials, also came to be better constructed.[14] Nevertheless, riding animals continued to be more comfortable for longer journeys. From an early date, wagons and chariots were often carefully modeled in art, although the small clay models, which are quite numerous, were only coarsely formed.

Furniture-making was highly developed, especially for palaces and temples, and often involved metal sheathing. Urartu was the leading producer of these goods after 800.[15] As far as we can see, no cabinets were built, and we cannot tell in what measure protective varnishes were prepared from the oil and pastes which are frequently mentioned in documents. Wares made from wood were no doubt frequently painted, and this was done by the producer himself, since a profession of painting does not seem to have existed. Only cloth dyers *(ṣāpû, muṣappiu)* are mentioned with any frequency.

6. Mud and Clay: Bricks, Ceramics, and Miniature Sculpture

Although mineralogists distinguish between clay and iron-bearing mud, in archaeology one always speaks of mud-bricks without reference to the respective material, and of clay vessels, figures, and tablets. In the contemporary languages, Sum. *imi,* Akk. *ṭīd/ṭu,* and Heb. *ḥomer* all stand for both clay and mud.

The mass production of bricks in the ancient Orient did not stand on equal footing with the crafts; the profession of "brickmaker" (Akk. *lābinu*) is found rather seldom. The monumental building projects of

14. Cf. A Salonen, *Die Landfahrzeuge des alten Mesopotamien* (Helsinki, 1951); M. A. Littauer and J. H. Crouwel, *Wheeled Vehicles and Ridden Animals in the Ancient Near East* (Leiden, 1979).

15. Cf. A. Salonen, *Die Möbel des alten Mesopotamien;* R. D. Barnett, "The Excavations of the British Museum at Toprak Kale near Van," *Iraq* 12 (1950): 1ff.; 16 (1954): 3ff.

early Sumerian Uruk may have used several million small tiles with the dimensions of 18×8×8 cm.; by contrast, Nebuchadnezzar II's great buildings in Babylon would have needed hundreds of thousands of large bricks (approximately 33×33×10 cm.). After preparing the requisite amount of mud, one put it into a wooden form and then removed each brick when it had dried. The number of bricks which were then baked in ovens was much smaller, but still considerable, and these then had to be smoothed off and polished. Besides the thousands of brickmakers and workers were those who organized the work. It was their responsibility to supervise the inscribing and stamping of a portion of the bricks. After approximately 1400, though primarily in later Assyria, brick reliefs of occasionally gigantic proportions were produced from embossed, often colorfully glazed bricks. The glazing substance was frequently designated as (artificial) lapis lazuli. Many bricks were covered with asphalt, predominantly for use in foundation walls and courts. Finally, an appropriately durable mortar had to be mixed in corresponding quantities.

The invention of air-dried as well as burned brick in the ancient Orient probably took place in Babylonia-Assyria in the fourth millennium. Other countries then borrowed this technology from Mesopotamia.[16]

The making of pottery is much older than the production of brick, and the creations of pottery — with or without decoration — exhibit far more variety in all lands than is found in brickmaking. As late as the fourth millennium, everyday pottery was made without the aid of a potter's wheel and was very coarse. Even without the potter's wheel, however, a finely painted or inscribed cultic or decorative pottery could be produced. The subsequent introduction of a slowly rotating potter's wheel, later followed by wheels that revolved more rapidly, made possible the creation of ever new, occasionally very thin-walled vessels with spouts, handles, covers, and even reliefs. Exactly what these potter's wheels looked like, and how they functioned, is still unknown, as is the Akkadian word for this device. Unfortunately, we know very little as well of what must have been a wide variety of the types of pottery ovens (Sum. *udun;* Akk. *utūnu*).

The pre-Sumerian word for potter appears in Sumerian as *baḫar,*

---

16. Cf. A. Salonen, *Die Ziegeleien im alten Mesopotamien* (Helsinki, 1972); H. Gasche, "Lehm als Baumaterial," *RLA* VI (1983): 55off.

in Akkadian as *paḫāru,* in Aramaic as *paḫḫārā,* and in Arabic as *faḫḫār.*
We may suppose, in view of the great number of types of pottery vessels
that are found all over the Near East, that potters had to specialize in
particular varieties, and that not all were able to produce decorated
pottery. Historically it is remarkable that following the great period of
prehistoric painted ceramic ware (e.g., Tell Halaf, Samarra), after 3000
there was only temporarily a painted ware of any quality, primarily in
the Jemdet Nasr period and shortly thereafter, but not again until the
time of the Mitannian kingdom. Later, an enameled and glazed ceramic
ware took the place of the painted ware, primarily in Assyria, and this
new style of ceramic found innovative forms of portraying old pictorial
motifs.[17] However, although inscribed pottery was widespread, found
in almost every period, only rarely did it feature simple pictorial depictions. For smaller vessels, sinter was often used in place of clay. Huge
vessels capable of holding up to 250 l. were produced predominantly in
Urartu, perhaps for storing wine. Unfortunately, since the study of
pottery is so strictly limited to sketching the profiles of innumerable
vessels, a great deal of technical information remains unknown.[18]

Many other vessels as well as a great number of models of all kinds
were also prepared from clay. The cuneiform scribes also had to work
with clay; they had to form their tablets themselves, and in addition to
drying them, they were also required to fire them (see further, X.2). The
widely varying quality of preservation of the ancient clay tablets was
determined to a great degree by the choice of clays, which was not always
made with the care that we might wish, even for literary texts.

Finally, by far the greatest portion of miniature sculptures was also
produced from clay. Because stone was always much more difficult to
work, and the metal figurines, aside from those made of gold, were
always more or less subject to rapid corrosion, clay was the preferred
medium for miniature sculpture even in areas where good stone was
available. Terra-cottas, however, were rarely made piece by piece. In
almost all cases, clay forms were produced and then fired with particular

17. Cf. A. Salonen, *Die Hausgeräte der alten Mesopotamier,* Part II: *Gefässe* (Helsinki, 1966); also A. L. Oppenheim and H. Kuhne, "Glas," *RLA* III (1969): 407ff.; Oppenheim, R. H. Brill, and A. von Saldern, *Glass and Glassmaking in Ancient Mesopotamia*
(Corning, N.Y., 1970).

18. In view of the massive ceramic finds in every excavation, no one has yet been
able to undertake a comprehensive treatment of ceramics in the ancient Orient. For
certain aspects, cf. B. Hrouda, *et al., Methoden der Archäologie,* 139ff.

care. For complete, three-dimensional figures, two forms were required for each. In early times, terra-cotta figurines were often painted; in later periods they were often overlaid with colorful glazes in the same manner as vessels. On the terra-cotta figures and depictions, see below, XIV.2.

7. Stone for Devices, Monumental and Miniature Sculpture, and Buildings

Despite its hardness, stone was worked at a very early period, and was used in a greater variety of ways than clay and metal. As early as the fourth millennium, people were not only gathering individual stones of all kinds, but they were also breaking stones of lesser hardness, such as limestone, wherever possible. By the third millennium, people were able to break off blocks of hard stone with the help of bore-holes and wood swollen by water. From there, workers could turn these blocks into larger and smaller sculptures through toilsome, tedious work with hammer, chisel, and all sorts of polishing techniques. Quarries for statues of dolerite and diorite probably were located in Oman. Other types of stone were imported from the mountains of Iran, Asia Minor, and Syria. For the most part, unworked blocks were transported to the work sites. The considerable residue from the working of the larger blocks was available for use as stone implements and vessels, and above all for the myriads of cylinder seals and stone beads. The limestone found occasionally in rocky outcroppings in alluvial regions could also be used for these purposes, but it was less suitable. Small stone objects were no doubt frequently exported. For the place of stones in mythology, see below, XIII.3d, e.

Among those artisans involved in the preparation of stone, only the cutter of seals (Sum. *bur-gul;* Akk. *pa/urkullu*) appears in the documents with any frequency. The Sumerian loanwords *zadimmu,* "stone-worker," and *alamgû,* "picture carver," are just as infrequently attested as *urrāku* and *ēṣiru,* "sculptor" (only in Assyria?). Obviously, the carving of reliefs in Babylonia dramatically decreased in significance after about 1600, while in Assyria it was perpetuated by court servants. On the stone carvings, as well as cylinder and stamp seals as works of art, see below, XIV.1.

While stone knives, even those made from fine black obsidian, were only occasionally produced after 3000, stone vessels remained in

115

use, not least as mortars and millstones of different sizes made from whatever material might be available. We are familiar with a great many lists of magical stones from Babylonia and Assyria, mostly in the form of pearls. These begin, as a rule, with lapis lazuli, which was imported from the east and was especially in demand. For use in jewelry one often finds agate, jasper, carnelian, rock crystals, and other semi-precious stones. The actual precious stones, such as emeralds, are found only in the later periods, and then rarely.[19]

As building material, broken limestone was rather seldom used in Babylonia in any substantial quantity; it appears primarily in early Sumerian Uruk in a very large limestone temple foundation and in the "stone building,"[20] as well as for stone graves in the so-called royal cemetery of Early Dynastic Ur (see above, VI.2). For the most part, the stone blocks at these sites were not cut square. By contrast, stone was used much more often in Assyria and Syria for buildings of various kinds, and sometimes even for great, stone sarcophagi. In both regions, just as in Asia Minor, great rows of monoliths cut from limestone were erected in palaces, along with massive statues of mixed-form creatures having the bodies of bulls (Ass. *aladlammû;* note the winged bulls of Sargon II). Such monoliths reached weights of up to 30 tons at Dur-Sharrukin and Nineveh. The quarries from which the huge blocks were hewn are generally known. There the limestone is very soft when it is cut from the earth, but it becomes very hard when exposed to the air (see below, p. 234).

In many Syrian cities as well as Asia Minor, building was done with rough quarry stones, though sometimes ashlar blocks were used as well. The construction of stone walls was perfected in the fortress complexes and temples of Urartu after 800.

19. Cf. R. C. Thompson, *A Dictionary of Assyrian Chemistry and Geology* (Oxford, 1936); Landsberger, *JCS* 21 (1969): 139ff.; G. G. Boson, "Edelstein (Halbedelstein)," *RLA* II (1938): 266ff.; D. O. Edzard and M. Tosi, "Jaspis," *RLA* V (1980): 269-270; "Kalkstein," *RLA* V: 323ff.; "Karneol," *RLA* V 448ff.; and W. Röllig, G. Herrmann, and P. R. S. Moorey, "Lapislazuli," *RLA* VI (1983): 488ff.

20. Cf. E. Heinrich and U. Seidl, *Die Tempel und Heiligtümer im alten Mesopotamien: Typologie, Morphologie, und Geschichte* (Berlin, 1982), 35ff.

8. The Smelting and Refining of Metals

The beginnings of metalworking lie in Western Asia as early as the fifth millennium, but it was not until the fourth and especially the third millennium that metalworking first attained considerable economic significance. The prerequisite for exploitation of the ores which could be found on the earth's surface or in a few gorges, especially in Asia Minor, was the ability to smelt metals and to regulate appropriately the sometimes very high temperatures needed for smelting. Moreover, the different techniques of metalworking — the pouring, the hammering of the still soft metals, and refining — could only be acquired gradually. It was learned very early that several metals were useful only when alloyed with others. In pure form copper, silver, and gold are rather malleable, and are generally found as alloyed ores. During the alloying process, the quite dissimilar melting points of the respective metals had to be carefully observed. Often attempts to create alloys no doubt succeeded in spite of such factors and sometimes, perhaps, even by accident. We are told nothing of the mistakes. It is particularly frustrating that we are insufficiently informed of the copper alloys in use in the ancient Orient. Besides the use of a copper-tin alloy, which was standard in later times, there was also a copper-arsenic alloy with its own peculiar technical problems in use in areas where no tin was available. There are cuneiform texts from which one can deduce the various alloy proportions, but these have still not been systematically studied. Nor have analyses of metal artifacts been sufficiently performed. There is, therefore, much work to do before we can hope for a satisfactory understanding of these problems.[21] The same is true of our lexical work, which still cannot clarify the linguistic usage of such frequently used words as Sum. *an-na* and Akk. *annaku*, "tin" and probably also "arsenic." Some words, in fact, could designate more than one type of metal.

The most general word for "metalworker" is Sum. *tibira*, Bab. *qurqurru*, and Ass. *tabiru*. More frequently used, however, are Sum.

21. Cf. Thompson, *A Dictionary of Assyrian Chemistry and Geology,* 58ff.; H. Limet, *Le travail du métal au pays de Sumer au temps de la IIIe Dynastie d'Ur* (Paris, 1960); C. Zaccagnini, "La terminologia akkadica del rame e del bronzo nel I millennio," *OrAnt* 10 (1971): 123ff.; cf. also F. Schachermeyr, "Eisen," *RLA* II (1938): 316ff.; W. F. Leemans, H. Otten, J. Boese, and U. Rüss, "Gold," *RLA* III (1969): 345ff.; W. Röllig and J. D. Muhly, "Kupfer," *RLA* VI (1983): 345ff., with extensive bibliography; H. Waetzoldt and H. G. Bachmann, "Zinn- und Arsenbronzen in den Texten aus Ebla und aus dem Mesopotamien des 3. Jahrtausends," *OrAnt* 23 (1984): 1ff.

simug and Akk. *nappāḫu,* "smith" (literally, "blower" of the bellows *[nappaḫ[t]u]* for the smelting oven, Sum. *dinig;* Akk. *kūru*). Since copper, with its chief alloy bronze, was by far the most-used metal down into the second millennium, one finds the above-mentioned terms most frequently in connection with these metals. Besides these, we often find the *nappāḫ ḫurāṣi,* "goldsmith," who also processed silver and other metals for jewelry and valuable utensils. After the end of the second millennium, the *nappāḫ parzilli,* the "ironsmith" or "blacksmith," was added to these, involved primarily in the production of weapons. To be sure, iron from meteors was known in eastern Asia Minor as early as the beginning of the second millennium and was valued there more than gold. The working of iron on a larger scale, however, first became possible when the Hittites succeeded in smelting some form of iron ore and in producing it in appropriate alloys for the respective applications. Nevertheless, bronze continued to be employed even in later times for many useful objects. Even with gold, which had to be imported from distant regions and was often scarce and extremely expensive, there were alloys of varying fineness. The Ebla texts speak of remarkably large quantities of gold in Syria in the third millennium, though many today are skeptical of the figures given in these texts.

The number of vessels made completely or in large part of bronze or other copper alloys — utensils, tools, nails, and other objects — was very large.[22] Later, iron was often preferred primarily for cutting and striking tools on account of its greater hardness. Bronze was widely used for artistic works, and especially for larger sculptures for which gold and silver were too expensive (see below, XIV.2). The kingdom of Urartu was a center of metal artwork between 900 and 650, where new techniques continued to be developed. Figurines of deities made of bronze have been found in great number especially in Syro-Phoenicia. Naturally, very little has come down to us in the form of vessels or sculptures of precious metals, or with precious metal overlays, since again and again enemies and thieves carried these off and melted them down. Occasionally, objects of precious metals have been preserved in graves which escaped the tomb-robbers. The best example of such a find is the royal cemetery of Ur from the Early Dynastic period (see above, VI.2). The production of artistic works from a variety of materials may have required a number of artisans working in concert.

22. Cf. A. Salonen, *Die Hausgeräte der alten Mesopotamier,* Part II, 249ff.

CHAPTER IX

Trade and Commerce

1. Roads and Highways

Improved streets with brick or stone pavement, and frequently with drainage, were generally found only in the cities. Prior to the Achaemenaean period, the primary connections in both the plains and the hills were, with perhaps some exceptions, overland routes or tracks. These were tolerably passable in the dry season, when they could be as firm as a paved road. Since the cuneiform texts often speak of the maintenance (Akk. *šutēšuru*) of roads, we may assume that something was done to keep the particularly well-traveled connections passable and to firm up difficult places, not least of all for the movement of armies, so that during the rainy season the downpours would not make them impassable. Small rivulets and shallow rivers were bridged where possible, and larger rivers were crossed at fords or on ferryboats. The Habur, for instance, had two great fords between the joining of the headwaters and the mouth; these were used for the main east-west roads down into the modern period. The Assyrians even built pontoon bridges at suitable places; for these they used separate, round coracles made from leather-covered wickerwork or boats of papyrus reeds, as frequently depicted on reliefs.[1] Ferry-lines may have facilitated the crossing of powerfully flowing rivers. According to the texts, individual permanent bridges had already been built across the Euphrates in some Babylonian cities early in the second millennium, but stone bridges in

---

1. Cf. A. Salonen, *Die Wasserfahrzeuge in Babylonien* (Helsinki, 1939), pl. XVIIIff.

Babylon and Nineveh are first attested with certainty for the period after 700. The Bible, however, never mentions bridges.[2]

The situation in the mountains was completely different. Here, the building of roads by cutting through obstacles and shoring up other places was not possible in many localities. Moreover, wooden bridges over raging streams and lesser gorges had to be rebuilt repeatedly because of frequent destruction by floods, and these bridges were supplemented by bridges of lighter construction meant only for pedestrians and pack animals. The Assyrian kings reported on bridges of tree trunks and the building of roads even in the higher mountain ranges after 1100, but the sources still do not permit more exact assertions about the details.

2. Water Routes

The state of the roads just depicted, which only with difficulty permitted the use of heavy wagons over longer stretches, forced traders to transport goods in bulk by water routes wherever possible. This was true even when the rivers, on account of the rate of descent, could only be used to transport goods downstream. Thus, the water routes acquired an overwhelming importance in long-distance commerce and, where such routes were available, a monopoly on the transport of heavy goods such as long tree trunks and huge stone blocks. In the alluvial regions, the extensive system of rivers was supplemented by the great canals. The emergence of trade centers apart from the rivers and canals was scarcely possible in the river valleys. Ships could also be towed over land for short stretches.[3] Where necessary the banks of the rivers were secured, and the retaining walls required frequent repairs. The river courses themselves had to be dredged in areas where the current was weak, but such activity was only possible in times of peace. Lighter ships and boats were propelled by rudders, while heavy transport vessels and rafts were pushed along with poles; still, sails could often be employed in both

2. Besides the old word *titurru*, there emerged in Babylonia after 700 the term *gišru*, which was also taken over into Aramaic and Arabic, and which originally designated a felled tree. More exact studies based on the remains of ancient bridges are still required.

3. Those charged with such towing (Akk. *šaddidu*) are mentioned frequently.

Assyrian trading vessels dragging or carrying logs in the sea. Alabaster relief from Khorsabad, 721-705. (Louvre)

cases. Rudders were necessary for steering precisely when a ship could be carried along on the current. The mountain rivers were never passable for more than short distances. The great inland lakes were particularly important for shipping, primarily those which lay in northwestern Iran and Armenia (especially Urmia and Van).

The seas did not form insurmountable barriers to commerce in the Near East. Even early on there were no limits on the coastal shipping trade in the eastern Mediterranean, as the settlement of Crete in the fourth millennium shows; Cyprus, too, was settled by people from the mainland not much later. Nevertheless, sailing on the open seas made far higher demands on the shipbuilders and on the seafarers,[4] who had to maintain their orientation out of sight of land. For this reason, seafaring was only pursued by the inhabitants of the coastal cities. In Babylonia, river shipping ended in Ur. From there, goods were loaded onto vessels which could navigate the bays and lagoons and were then transported as far as the islands of Failaka and Bahrain (Akk. Tilmun). As far as we can tell, shipping in the Persian Gulf was in the hands of the Elamites, who traveled to the coast of Oman and as far as the mouth of the Indus. The route around the Arabian peninsula and into the Red Sea must have been navigated by about 3000, since in the period when writing was invented there were connections between Babylonia and Egypt which did not run overland by way of Syria. There is as yet no known attestation of the circumnavigation of Arabia in the subsequent period down to the time of the Achaemenaean Empire.

The connection between Byblos (Gebal) and Egypt by way of the Mediterranean must have existed at least on occasion as early as the third millennium. In the second millennium, shipping in the eastern Mediterranean lay predominantly in the hands of the Cretans, who were later replaced by Phoenicians and, in the first millennium, increasingly by the Greeks. Neither the Hittites nor the Assyrian conquerors of Syria ever became seafarers in that region. Scarcely anything is known about Greek shipping in the Black Sea, or of any shipping in the Caspian Sea, though it certainly existed.

Great centers of trade often remained in place for extensive periods. That was especially true of many port cities, but it has also been found for many inland centers, including Aleppo, Nineveh, and several

---

4. Cf. M.-C. de Graeve, *The Ships of the Ancient Near East (c. 2000-300 B.C.)* (Louvain, 1981).

others. Others were unable to survive great catastrophes and achieved considerable significance only for a time.

3. Basic Terms of Trade: Buying and Selling, Money

By "trade" in the wider sense we understand the exchange of goods of all sorts, including humans (slaves), real estate, and immovable stock, on a local level as well as over longer distances between different lands, without considering whether the goods were paid for with money or whether other goods were the basis of exchange. Our sources for trade in the ancient Orient are, first of all, documents of all kinds, business contracts as well as manifests of wares, and trade letters, which we possess in many thousands from the region of Mesopotamia, and references to trade of every kind in literary texts and official inscriptions. In addition to particular depictions found in the course of excavations, archaeological sources include objects that certainly, or at least in all probability, came from far away, as well as coins and other objects used as a means of payment. In view of the immense abundance of sources, there are no immediate prospects for a systematic study of these, and apart from some more or less summary presentations, comprehensive treatments exist for only subcategories.[5] The proportion of business proceedings that was documented was particularly high in most of the cuneiform cultures, though the number of such documents from the Hittite kingdom and Urartu is small. We naturally know almost nothing of businesses which traded in kind without documents.

The phase of trade in the ancient Orient which involved pure barter had been supplanted by the middle of third millennium at the latest. In Babylonia, where metal was scarce, buying and selling were conducted on the basis of grain exchanges. One might even speak of a "grain standard" there. Sheep may also have served as a standard of value for trading goods. As the supply of metals, especially copper and silver, increased in the land in the third millennium, trade was con-

5. Cf. W. F. Leemans, *Foreign Trade in the Old Babylonian Period* (Leiden, 1960), and his article on "Handel," *RLA* IV (1973): 76ff.; cf. also J. Krecher, C. Wilcke, K. Hecker, G. Cardascia, H. P. H. Petschow, R. Haase, and B. Kienast, "Kauf," *RLA* V (1980): 490ff.; G. Pettinato, *"Il commercio con l'estero della Mesopotamia meridionale nel 3 millennio av. Cr. alla luce delle fonti letterarie e lessicale sumeriche,"* *Mesopotamia* 7 (Turin, 1972): 43-166; see below, n. 9.

ducted first on the basis of copper and later on the basis of silver. In this process, metal pieces which had to be weighed by the buyer in the presence of the seller came to serve as the means of payment. The verb for "to weigh" or "weigh out" (Sum. *lá;* Akk. *šaqālu*) became the normal word for "to pay." Normally a person used metal pieces with an established standard weight, but the loss of weight through constant use as well as the filing down of the pieces with fraudulent intent necessitated repeated weighings. There was a sort of "Bureau of Standards" for the control of the weights: in Assyria the office was known as the *bīt ḫiburne.* It is amazing that none of the peoples involved in intensive trade over so many centuries in the ancient Orient ever thought to stamp these metal pieces so as to make their loss of metal visible. Such stamped (or minted) pieces of metal would have greatly facilitated all procedures of payment. It was a small country, Lydia in Asia Minor, which produced the first coins stamped on both sides, about 600. From Lydia, the institution of stamped coinage rapidly triumphed throughout the Mediterranean world.

In practical terms, however, the transition to a money economy was achieved much earlier. In view of the low value of copper, which made it unsuitable for large payments, a shift was made in the Old Babylonian period to a kind of silver standard. Though silver was at that time too scarce in Babylonia to serve as a universal means of payment, the same was even more true of gold. Where laws and documents nevertheless demand most payments in silver, this often meant only that barley, livestock, and wares of all kinds had to be traded in direct proportion to the requisite payment in silver. The word for silver, Akk. *kaspu* (Heb. *kesep*), thereby became the word for money itself, even though money later occasionally came to be reckoned in terms of gold as well. Whether the monetary economy came to predominate as early as the second millennium, or whether the barter system continued to dominate as it had before, depended on the highly variable economic relationships in any given area.[6]

6. Cf. C. Zaccagnini, "La circolazione dei beni," *L'Alba della Civiltà*, II: 423ff., with extensive bibliography.

4. The Organization of Trade: The Merchant

Valid assertions concerning the organization of trade cannot be made for the entire ancient Orient. The political and economic conditions were too variable. The size of the political entities concerned played a decisive role in overland trade over great distances, since the crossing of borders always brought particular problems for the participants. In the third millennium, smaller or medium-sized state territories were primarily involved, so that most of the overland trade was subject to the shifting circumstances of foreign policy. Customs fees and duties of all kinds could be exacted, and the level of these was seldom firmly established. Once formed, the empires, especially the Empire of Akkad, were too short-lived and too unstable to alter the conditions of foreign trade decisively. In the course of military campaigns, moreover, much was confiscated which otherwise would of necessity have been purchased. It is therefore highly unlikely that merchants, who had to conduct their business entirely at their own expense, would have been able to undertake any great ventures under these circumstances. The risks for life and limb, as well as for the wares, were simply too high. On the other hand, the princes who controlled overland trade among the Sumerians, according to our documents, were able to conclude treaties with neighboring princes concerning the protection of trade. Such treaties dealt with permitting trade across a number of boundaries, as well as with trade between neighboring lands. The failure to keep to the terms of such a trade agreement, which normally were in the interests of all parties, could lead to war. Thus, a local ruler would not easily have refused protection of the caravans as negotiated. From time to time, merchants who assert their claims before the king appear in poems about the imperial kings of Akkad.

The kingdom of the Third Dynasty of Ur opened many new possibilities for trade between eastern Arabia and Syria. In the following period, however, the political instability of a world characterized by petty states with frequently changing borders and treaties brought increasing difficulties for trade. Thus, a state monopoly on trade was no longer claimed, especially in the time of Hammurabi, and private trading houses gained greater latitude. Still, these merchants had to reckon with conscious trade restrictions in dealing with opposing states, and trade wars became a political tool. In the period of the Kassites and Hittites, correspondence shows an upsurge in state-sponsored trade.

The great empires which followed, as, for example, the Hittite Empire, were able to establish entirely new trade relationships, if only for a time, and they also made possible a wide-ranging domestic trade. After around 880, the Neo-Assyrian Empire united ever-greater portions of Western Asia within its boundaries. Following its demise, the short interlude of the Chaldean and Median Empires gave way to the much vaster Achaemenaean Empire. At this time, a domestic trade emerged which was carried out entirely by private trading firms over vast distances. Yet this phenomenon receives strangely little attestation in the contemporary documents and therefore cannot be properly described, any more than is possible for the remaining foreign trade. For these reasons, a comprehensive treatment is lacking.

We know very little with regard to the details of trade on the waterways; it is to be supposed that ships only rarely ventured alone across great distances. The great rafts put together from beams of cedar and cypress may also have been used primarily for heavy trade goods. Shipping in the Mediterranean cannot be discussed here.

Overland commerce carried out over vast distances was based almost completely on caravan traffic, first with asses and, after 1100, increasingly with camels as pack animals. The caravan alone offered protection against attacks from the occasional bandits and, where such dangers existed, from wild animals. Moreover, only caravans could contain the transport costs within bearable limits. Strangely enough, few words are found in the languages of the ancient Orient which could chiefly be used for caravan. Sum. *kaskal* and Akk. *ḫarrānu* are primarily words for "highway," "street," or "journey"; therefore when the subject is commercial travel it is often unclear whether these words are being used in the sense of "caravan."[7] The caravans were tied to particular caravan routes, which remained in approximately the same places for millennia without interruption. In the mountains there were often only a few viable passes, and watering places were rarely found in the steppes at necessarily short intervals. With regard to camel caravans, these watering places could lie at considerably greater distances from one another than had been the case with the ass caravans in earlier times. The rivers had no more than a few passable fords, and crossing them on boats was only possible where these were available. When the rivers

7. Cf. D. O. Edzard and I. Eph'al, "Karawane," *RLA* V (1980): 414ff.; see below, n. 8.

were in flood stage, either from snow and ice or from great heat, night treks were impossible and crossings had to be kept to a minimum. Interruptions occasioned by the weather often could not be financed. Experienced caravan leaders were just as essential as were guides who could negotiate with people of different languages. Nevertheless, very little can be gleaned from the sources concerning specifics.

Because of the paucity of sources, the question must remain unanswered as to whether on the long trade routes from eastern Iran or southern Arabia to Mesopotamia the caravans formed at the beginning of the treks remained together — for several weeks, if necessary — until they reached the destination of the wares, or whether after a certain distance the wares were transferred to newly formed caravans for further transport. The latter is more likely, since with every extension of the length of the journey difficulties in communication and other problems must have emerged. Foreign caravan leaders must have been necessary in any case.

After 1850 the caravan traffic between Assyria and its trade colonies in eastern Asia Minor, centered at Kanish (see above, V.5), present a special case. This trade was carried out without lengthy interruptions for 100 to 120 years, from the time of Ilushumma until perhaps the early years of Ishme-Dagan I, and is profusely documented by thousands of documents and letters from Kanish.[8] It was apparently operated by small trading firms in close connection with the administration in Ashur and Kanish, who received customs fees and duties at rates which for the most part were firmly and precisely established. The same is true of the princes through whose districts the caravan routes passed. Only occasional reports exist of disturbances of this traffic through attacks along the way. The Assyrians dwelt outside the walled city of Kanish in their own quarter, which was called *kārum,* as were the authorities. The precise route of this caravan traffic, and whether there were possible alternate routes along certain stretches, is unknown. The duration of the 1000 km. journey is presumed to have been about two months, including days of rest.

The Akkadian *tamkārum* (Sum. *dam-gàr*) played a central role in the development of the caravan trade in Babylonia as well as Assyria.

---

8. Cf. P. Garelli, *Les Assyriens en Cappadoce* (Paris, 1963); M. T. Larsen, *Old Assyrian Caravan Procedures* (Copenhagen, 1967); K. R. Veenhof, *Aspects of Old Assyrian Trade and Its Terminology* (Leiden, 1972).

The *tamkārum* acquired both public and private functions, although the respective allocation of these varied according to time and place, and he appears in the texts often without being named. The *tamkārum* was at once a type of trade and business overseer, a merchant and trader in his own right, as well as a financier (Akk. *ummiānum;* see above, VIII.1), since there were no banks.[9] Unfortunately, no modern word exists which is appropriate for all of his various functions. Prior to the Akkadian era the *tamkārum* appears only rarely in Ebla, but frequently in Sumerian documents, and certainly in public functions in most cases. Nothing much had changed in this regard until the Third Dynasty of Ur, although private businesses run by the *dam-gàr* do exist. In the Old Babylonian period, the laws of Hammurabi, along with documents and letters, show the manifold undertakings of the *tamkārum.* Just as important, although of a somewhat different nature, were his services in the Assyrian trade colonies in eastern Asia Minor. After 1500 he appears more rarely in many groups of documents, though from time to time he also organized the import of slaves. Yet, comprehensive treatments of this matter are still lacking. Nor can the place and function of the frequently mentioned chief *tamkārum* (Akk. *wakil tamkārī*) be determined with certainty. The number of servants attached to a *tamkārum* varied, but it must certainly have been very high.

5. The Merchandise

It is seldom possible to give exact figures for the quantity of trade goods, including slaves and animals, as well as their places of origin and their destinations, despite the abundance of documents. Moreover, we rarely find the indications of origins for particular wares which would permit conclusions regarding those lists of wares where no origin is given. In many cases, wares could be imported but did not have to be. Even foreign designations — of plants, animals, and many other objects, for example — do not point implicitly to foreign origin, since such plants certainly were often introduced and then cultivated in the new land

9. Cf. W. F. Leemans, *The Old Babylonian Merchant: His Business and His Social Position* (Leiden, 1950); R. Harris, *Ancient Sippar*, 71ff. (with lists of *tamkāru*-overseers); see *Iraq* 39 (1977) for numerous essays on the *tamkāru* and on trade (see above, n. 5); cf. *AHw*, 1314-15 on *tamkāru* and *tamkārūtu.*

itself. Even in Babylonia, where metals originally had to be imported, metal could be produced domestically by melting down older objects for reuse in a variety of ways. In the case of such materials, foreign origin can frequently only be presumed. The same is true of metal, stone, ivory, and many other items that have been found in excavations. Even more difficult, and often unanswerable, is the question as to whether in lands with highly developed manufacturing technology (such as Babylonia, Assyria, and numerous districts of Syria, Asia Minor, and Iran) the predominant imports were of raw materials and only rarely of finished goods and objects of art. Sometimes the foreign origin of such wares is easily recognized, but most often we cannot detect it. One must presume that the exports from Babylonia, aside from grain and dates, were overwhelmingly of finished goods, although proof of this is not easily adduced from the documents. We will therefore do well if we only make exact pronouncements in those cases where they can be justified from the sources, and otherwise content ourselves with summary observations.

We are extremely well-informed on the trade between Assyria and its trading colonies in eastern Asia Minor (see above), since a great many of the pertinent letters deal solely or predominantly with trade goods. Ashur imported tin or arsenic (Ass. *annukum*), which was indispensable for the production of bronze, from northwestern Iran and exported these metals to their trade colonies and to the south. Many types of cloth, which came in part from Babylonia, also made their way to Asia Minor. For its part, Asia Minor exported primarily copper, of which several varieties were distinguished, both as metal and in the form of many types of copper utensils. Gold and silver were less export wares than monetary standards. The Old Assyrian documents provide, in addition, an important source for trade inside Asia Minor.

Ebla, in northern Syria, was also a center of the metal trade in the third millennium; some texts from there mention strikingly large quantities of gold, which certainly could not have been found in that region. Syria was the predominant supplier of timber for Babylonia, as long as the Euphrates' water route was open. Copper came into Babylonia primarily from Asia Minor, Cyprus, and eastern Arabia, as far as we can ascertain, and gold came from Egypt, at least at the time of the Kassites,[10]

10. Cf. W. F. Leemans, H. Otten, J. Boese, and U. Rüss, "Gold," *RLA* III (1969): 504ff.

though Egypt had no trade connections with Mesopotamia in the Old Babylonian period. The import of stone from eastern Arabia has already been discussed (see above, VIII.7). The richly bubbling asphalt sources along the middle Euphrates made exports beyond Babylonia possible, though overland transport was undoubtedly difficult. Among smaller wares, which were often transported over long distances, essences and fragrances of all sorts must be mentioned.

Grain, with which Babylonia especially was able to pay for part of the raw materials which it lacked, stood in the foreground of the trade in foodstuffs. Naturally, there were considerable fluctuations in this form of trade for climatic and political reasons. Babylonia produced only sesame oil domestically and had to import the highly desirable olive oil from the west. Furthermore, wine had to be imported for the upper class from parts of northern Mesopotamia on the fringe of the mountains, from northern Syria, and, not last of all, from Cilicia, in addition to the popularly consumed beer. The distribution of wine is often discussed in the Old Babylonian documents from Mari. Meat could always be dried for transport, though this practice is attested primarily for fish. We learn little, however, of the trade in salt, which certainly was significant. In simple form, salt was acquired from the salt deposits along many rivers.

Commerce in animals first began to play a significant role after about 1400, when horses began to be imported in large numbers from Asia Minor, Armenia, and northern Iran. Later, dromedaries, along with Bactrian camels from Iran, were added. In addition, there were specialty imports of exotic animals of all kinds. Finally, the slave trade, which supplemented the massive procurement of slaves in wartime, must not be forgotten. Many slaves came from Iran to Babylonia in the age of Hammurabi. During the time of the later empires, however, there was little need for a trade in slaves.

CHAPTER X

Law

1. Legal Prescriptions and Law Codes

a. Basic Terminology and General Aspects of Law: Sumerian Laws

There was no universal term for "law" in the ancient Orient. Sum. *di* or Akk. *dīnu* designates the legal case, the legal decision, and the process itself. *Nì-si-sá = mīšaru* refers to justice as the highest good, which is supplemented by *nì-gi-na = kittu:* "constancy," "integrity." All of the gods were responsible for the protection of law and justice, but the sun god, Utu (Shamash), was preeminent in this regard. In the strict sense, there is no merely secular law, but only religious law, so that decisions pertaining to trade may have carried far less weight than more central legal tenets. Upon the earth, the king holds responsibility for the law; he is the chief justice *(di-ku₅ = dayyānu),* the final court of appeal, and, where necessary, the lawgiver. Hammurabi termed his individual laws *dīnat mīšarim* ("cases of justice").

Whether all the common law precepts which determined practice were proclaimed by a king sometime in the distant past is unknown. Certainly, however, there were legal prescriptions for centuries before the first law codes were promulgated around 2000. None of these collections of laws is a "code" in the sense of the Code of Justinian, even though this term has become established in our usage. Even the Code of Hammurabi treats only a small portion of the legal material; it is a collection of reform laws that were probably appended to long-established legal cases. In this

131

Fragment of the Lipit-Ishtar law code, dealing with boat rental, orchards, and slaves. Nippur, about 1850. *(University Museum, University of Pennsylvania)*

respect, none of the legal collections is systematically ordered; cases of penal, civil, trade, and work law alternate with one another. Most of the laws are formulated casuistically and begin in Sumerian with *tukumbi*, "if," in Akkadian with *šumma*, and in Hittite with *takku*.[1] Thus, "If a man has committed robbery, he will be killed." By contrast, the apodictic formulation typical of religious laws (as, for example, the Ten Commandments) is a rare exception: for example, "A prostitute is not permitted to veil herself; her head must remain bare." The tariff cases found in Old Babylonian laws are similarly formulated.

In most of the earlier collections of laws up through Hammurabi's, a prologue in the style of a royal inscription precedes the body, which contains the legal cases. This prologue is preserved only in the laws of Eshnunna — and there only briefly — but in a style different from that of the laws it mentions the king's success in war. Except for the laws of Eshnunna, we also find epilogues with curses against those who should lay their hands on the law stela (to deface or alter it). The epilogue to Hammurabi's laws is much longer than anywhere else; that of Ur-Nammu, which must have been brief, is broken in the extant copy. Furthermore, the later copies omit parts of the prologue and epilogue. One does find in the laws themselves occasional verbatim correlations between two or more collections. Still, taken as a whole, each collection comprises a new, independent legal work.

The Babylonians termed proclamations of legal prescriptions which often altered earlier regulations *mīšaram šakānum* and the individual decisions *ṣimdatum*.[2] A new king usually promulgated such presciptions as a means of introducing himself at the beginning of his reign, often accompanying them with proclamations of a reduction in work (contrast this with the attitude of Solomon's successor in 1 Kings 12). Documents and letters make frequent reference to a *ṣimdatum*, and three of these are still partially available to us (see below). In the later period, the term *ṣimdatum* is no longer known, although there must have been comparable proclamations in Assyria. No such act of lawgiving is known from any later king in Babylonia, and the same is true for the states of Syria and Asia Minor. For Elam, see below.

1. For all of the legal collections, cf. J. Klíma, H. Petschow, G. Cardascia, and V. Korošec, "Gesetze," *RLA* III (1966): 243-297, with extensive bibliography.

2. On these and other juridical terms see the relevant articles in *AHw* and *CAD*; see also below, n. 8.

The oldest known collection of Sumerian laws stems from the founder of the Third Dynasty of Ur, Ur-Nammu. Approximately forty short paragraphs deal with punishable acts; as a rule, physical wounds were punished by monetary fines, and more serious crimes, such as murder and robbery, were punished by death. By contrast, the more comprehensive, though much more poorly preserved collection of the laws of Lipit-Ishtar of Isin, as far as it is extant, deals primarily with cases of marriage, family, and property law.[3] According to § 28, a man may take an additional wife if his first becomes infirm, but he must provide for both of them. Tablets of school children from the first millennium dealing with regulations of family law, among them one furnished with an Akkadian translation, show just how far the state had gone by that time in intervening in this area (see above, VI.4a), even protecting slaves from excessive caprice. None of these laws refers anywhere to judges.[4]

b. The Laws of Eshnunna and the Code of Hammurabi: Legal Edicts

As far as we know, Dadusha of Eshnunna was the first to promulgate laws in the Babylonian language. In 1735 he published a corpus of sixty paragraphs which is almost completely preserved; it begins with the establishment of tariffs and then addresses ships and grain, family and slaves, physical wounds, animals, and the building of houses without any strict arrangement of the material. Nowhere is a judge mentioned, though the palace is mentioned once as the court of judgment. It is remarkable here that the death penalty is prescribed only five times, though in two further instances the king must decide whether to pronounce it. Similar to the Sumerian laws, mutilations, beatings, and banishments are never demanded. As with Hammurabi, a marriage can only be constituted by means of a marriage contract.[5] These laws have

3. W. H. P. Römer and H. Lutzmann offer the most recent partial translations with appropriate citations in *Texte aus der Umwelt des Alten Testaments,* ed. O. Kaiser (Gütersloh, 1982), 1:17ff. Our understanding of these ordinances in many instances still leaves much to be desired.

4. Cf. Klima, *RLA* III: 250ff.

5. The most recent translation, with an extensive bibliography, is by R. Borger in *Texte aus der Umwelt des Alten Testaments,* ed. Kaiser, 1:32ff.

not yet been compared with the largely unpublished documents from Eshnunna.

The Code of Hammurabi towers above all previously mentioned law codes. The lone original stela on which this code was inscribed survives, along with fragments of many copies from contemporary and later Babylonia and Assyria. The text itself served as a literary standard for the schools. Seven columns of the front side of the stela were chiseled out after it was carried off to Susa, and these can be reconstructed only partially from the clay tablets onto which the laws were copied. The approximately two hundred cases are numbered as 282 paragraphs.[6] The penal law contained in the concluding laws formulated around 1695 is much harsher than in the older laws. The death penalty is frequently threatened, in particular cases in a sharpened form; in addition, mutilations according to the *lex talionis* (the law of "an eye for an eye") are frequently prescribed, along with beatings. The rigid application of such analogies could even lead to the death of the innocent.[7] The reason for the often much harsher penalties and fines can only be that Hammurabi held the traditional, less stringent penal code to be inadequate for deterring crime in an empire newly acquired through conquest. We do not know to what extent the law was carried out. The king laid high expectations upon the judges for investigating and judging their cases; they had to convict the suspected perpetrators by summoning witnesses. Careless conduct of judicial duties led to removal from office or to high fines (§ 5), and Hammurabi nowhere tolerated caprice. Just when the king himself or a governor could be invoked as the highest court of appeal is not made precisely clear; according to the letters it was not a rare occurrence.

It is not possible here to go into the details of family, slave, prop-

6. The numbering of the paragraphs established by the first editors does not correspond to the Babylonian divisions, which do not regard the various subcases as separate laws. Thus, e.g., for the Babylonians § § 9-13 of the Code of Hammurabi comprised only one law. The most recent translations of the Code with citations of pertinent literature are by R. Borger, in *Texte aus der Umwelt des Alten Testaments,* ed. Kaiser, 1:39ff.; and A. Finet, *Le Code de Hammurapi* (Paris, 1983), with a brief commentary and index.

7. § § 229-230 of the Code of Hammurabi require the execution of a master builder who through negligent workmanship causes the death of the man for whom he was building the structure; if the master builder had caused the death of the man's son, the builder's own son should die in his stead.

erty, and business law, though we have referred to some of these things above. The many studies on the Code of Hammurabi in the last ninety years have revealed the strange fact that in the hundreds of legal documents from the time following the proclamation of these laws, various regulations other than those one would expect from the Code are frequently encountered. Only in part of the documents is the validity of the Code confirmed. From this we must conclude that the reforms were only partially carried out and that often, in the cities, various forms of the common law could not be changed. That is true not least of all for the laws directed specifically at the *muškēnum* (see above, VI.4c). Moreover, some of the laws were completely unrealistic: for example, the monetary fine established for a failed operation was far higher than the fee the surgeon would have received had the operation succeeded (§§ 215ff.). A comprehensive presentation of the law which was actually applied in Hammurabi's reign remains to be written.

Of the legal regulations (see above) which are mentioned in the texts, only one precept from the beginning of the reign of Hammurabi's fourth successor, Ammi-ṣaduqa, is in large part preserved; only very small parts are known from a further edict from Samsu-iluna and perhaps one from a third king, which agree for the most part with that of Ammi-ṣaduqa.[8] These contain only the prescriptions for individual penalties in connection with the economic and social regulations on which account the edicts were issued. For his part, Ammi-ṣaduqa distinguishes repeatedly between the population groups of the Akkadians and the Amorites and declares invalid any documents which run contrary to his stipulations. These edicts still give us numerous problems.

From the period in Babylonia following the Old Babylonian era, we know only a Neo-Babylonian fragment which may be from the seventh century, along with regulations on marriage and slave law, and on controversial questions of property rights. In contrast to earlier periods, apodictic laws are more frequent in these laws or legal drafts

8. On these and other edicts, as well as many juridical, social, and economic questions in connection with them, cf. F. R. Kraus, *Ein Edikt des Königs Ammi-ṣaduqa von Babylon* (Leiden, 1958), and by the same author, incorporating further studies by other scholars, the highly detailed *Königliche Verfügungen in altbabylonischer Zeit* (Leiden, 1984).

than are the casuistic. How comprehensive the whole law corpus was cannot at present be determined.[9]

c. Laws in Asia Minor and Assyria

We do not know whether legal regulations which can be deduced from the Old Assyrian documents and letters from Anatolia are based on the written laws of the Assyrians or those of local rulers. In three small fragments one can see mostly the vestiges of laws, though they might also be merely a kind of merchant statute. The Hittites in Anatolia began to compile collections of laws as early as the sixteenth century. These are significant because the death penalty is prescribed in very few cases, and restitution of debt is set above retribution (as is the case in Hebrew law). This is not the place, however, to go into greater depth regarding these laws.[11]

Soon after regaining their independence under Ashur-uballit I, the Assyrians began to write down individual regulations, although nothing is left of the pertinent tablets. About twenty mostly fragmentary pieces of a compilation of three law tablets from the time of Tiglath-Pileser I have been discovered, as well as a tablet with provisions regarding the maintenance of order in the palace, particularly in the king's harem.[12] This last tablet occasionally names the king from whom the legislation stems: the earliest is Ashur-uballit I, the latest Tiglath-Pileser I. On the first tablet of laws, which is almost completely preserved, the woman is the center of concern. The second, which likewise has eight columns, deals with property rights, while the third, which was written by a

9. Cf. Borger, in *Texte aus der Umwelt des Alten Testaments*, ed. Kaiser, 1:92ff., with bibliography.

10. Cf. G. Eisser and J. Lewy, *Die altassyrischen Rechtsurkunden vom Kültepe*, I (Leipzig, 1930), 334ff.; and further, B. Kienast, *Das altassyrische Kaufvertragsrecht* (Wiesbaden, 1984). Finally, I am indebted to H. Hecker for important additional insights.

11. Cf. most recently E. von Schüler, in *Texte aus der Umwelt des Alten Testaments*, ed. Kaiser, 1:96ff.

12. For the most recent treatment of these laws cf. Borger, in *Texte aus der Umwelt des Alten Testaments*, ed. Kaiser, 1:80ff. (only Tablet 1); and G. Cardascia, *Les lois assyriennes* (Paris, 1969), with bibliography; on these decrees, see E. F. Weidner, "Hof- und Harems-Erlasse assyrischer Könige aus dem 2. Jahrtausend v. Chr.," *AfO* 17 (1954-1956): 257ff.

different hand, gives laws dealing with slaves, livestock, and goods. Specific laws generally fall outside the general scope of these tablets. Nor has it been completely explained whether all laws were regarded as in force, or whether parts of them should be looked upon rather as drafts for a new structure of lawgiving and a new ordering of legal material.

Changes in the face of the legal praxis discernible in the earlier documents present many enactments, primarily for women, which are absolutely degrading, as has already been shown in an example in VI.4a. In no other ancient Oriental law is the status of a woman as low as it is in these Middle Assyrian laws. Nor do we find a penalty system so harsh and brutal as that found in the contemporary palace ordinances. The husband himself is frequently permitted to inflict harsh punishment upon his wife; at least in such cases, no one else who had taken part in the crime would come off better or worse than the wife, as, for example, in the case of adultery. Similarly, only both together can be freed from punishment. Besides the death penalty, beatings up to one hundred blows, forced labor, and manifold mutilations were prescribed, often in combination. Ordeals often served as a means of proof for the judges (see below). In criminal law, as in property and case law, the concern for justice and differentiation according to the particular circumstances can be recognized, and the possibility of a renunciation of punishment also existed. How the often contradictory administration of these laws was carried out can be discerned only in part. The vast majority of the extant Middle Assyrian documents stem from the time before Tiglath-Pileser I, and a codification of law in Assyria from the first millennium is unknown.

2. Documents and Other Legal Sources: Legal Praxis

We possess legal documents and contracts in the Sumerian, Babylonian, and Assyrian languages from the wider area extending from northern Syria to Elam representing many periods and in extremely large numbers. These are supplemented in many ways by public correspondence and business letters and, much more rarely, by other types of texts. Legal documents and business correspondence from the Hittite kingdom and Urartu are almost entirely lacking. The testimony of the content of the documents and letters regarding particular legal materials cannot be treated here: they are simply too diverse. Something must be said, however, concerning the structure of the documents and how much they can tell us. Furthermore, we must limit ourselves to the laws of private contracts, which comprise by far the greatest mass of these documents; for the documents of the legal process, see below. Contracts are so numerous because the basic principle in force was that all large-volume business transactions and all agreements of any importance had to be written out in the presence of witnesses. Indeed, the laws declare invalid a marriage without a marriage contract, even when the partners had long since consummated it.

Documents were often enclosed in sealed clay "envelopes," in order to protect the text against the possibility of destruction or from unauthorized alterations made by one of the parties. The text was often completely repeated, or at least reproduced in its major parts, on the outside of the clay shell. If it later became necessary to read the text in its entirety again, this envelope had to be shattered and became worthless. Many documents and letters have been found still in their envelopes. Documents were baked more often than were letters, but they could also be air dried. No doubt duplicates were often written for two or more contract partners, but these have seldom come down to us. It was often prescribed for clay certificates of debt that after the debt had been repaid, the original certificate had to be destroyed; but thousands of these documents have been preserved to this day.

Purchasing, hiring, tenancy, and the exchange of goods, plots of ground, fields, houses, animals, and persons are among the principal themes of the documents. Slaves were purchased, for example, and harvest-workers were hired. To these were added sureties, liabilities, deeds of partnership, gifts, deposits, and, primarily in the later period, the sale of benefices (see above, VI.4d), as well as the debt certificates already mentioned, sometimes with the giving of a surety. In spite of the demand for written contracts, marriage and adoption contracts are noticeably scarce, as are disputes over inheritances. Many types of contracts which are even less well-attested must be added to these.

At all times and everywhere, there were locally differentiated, widely established formulas for certain types of documents, as, for example, certificates of obligation or bills of sale for land, while more flexibility existed for other types of documents. Only specialized studies would be able to describe these in detail. Generally, the documents begin with the designation and more precise characterization of the matter with which it is concerned: for example, the amount of barley, or the dimensions and location of the piece of ground. In other documents, the partners taking part in the business venture are named first; in these cases, the father's name is found in place of the family name (which was not in use). The various types of "conversational" documents are not rare either. In these, the one partner brings his offer or demand, and the other gives answer to this or grants his request, or he may demand the bringing of witnesses. In such cases, it was necessary to specify the sum which the one partner had to pay to the other. Where offers of some kind were made, it had to be stressed that these had been put forth voluntarily. Quite frequently, any subsequent challenging of the contract had to be expressly excluded and a dissolution of the contract forbidden. High penalties were often threatened for anyone breaking the agreement. Still other extreme demands were added, especially in later Assyria, even where the disputed sum was small. Thus, for example, one man was made to lick up 1 l. of kress seeds which he had allowed to be strewn along the road (see below, XII.5d). In most cases, a shorter or longer list of witnesses follows, sometimes with the addition of the rolled or pressed impressions of their respective seals. Many Neo-Babylonian documents also contain curse formulas. Finally, in late documents and sometimes even earlier, the place is often given, or at least the exact date was stated with the appropriate standard designation of the year — using the date formulas, the eponym, or the regnal year of the king. These are sometimes followed by particular concluding clauses. In Nuzi, superscriptions designating the type of document are particularly frequent.

In view of the limited number and uneven distribution of the legal collections, as well as their limited value as witnesses to actual legal praxis, the legal documents, in connection with the letters dealing with the same themes, are the richest source for the study of ancient Oriental law and the activity of the judges. Despite their often modest numbers, the documents from Syria, the Hurrian districts, and Elam are especially important for us: by far the greatest proportion of them are written in the Babylonian language. Among the archives discovered in Syria, only those from Ugarit (about 1400-1200) and Alalakh (1700-1200) have been published in large part, but the juridical materials have only begun to be evaluated.[13] Here, the king seems to have exercised direct influence over private legal agreements with particular frequency. Documents

---

13. The journal *Ugarit-Forschungen* contains many additional contributions.

pertaining to feudal law are rather richly attested in Assyria, Babylonia, and especially in the principality of Arrapkha, where the archive of Nuzi — by far the largest of this period — was found.[14] Certain legal institutions which are unattested in neighboring lands played a very large role in Nuzi. Among these were adoption for the sake of appearances (mentioned above, VI.4a), the purpose of which was to circumvent conventional law, and the furnishing of a security deposit in the *titennūtu*.

Elamite law reveals other completely different peculiarities, which are attested by about five hundred documents from Susa during the period 1720-1500. These documents, which are written in Babylonian, contain a simultaneous interworking of divine and temporal law to which we are otherwise unaccustomed; this is found, for example, in the many sales contracts, in debt law, and so forth. Many terms of the documents have not yet been sufficiently explained. The cutting off of hand and tongue is often threatened, along with monetary fines, as a penalty for breaches of contract.[15]

3. Judges and the Judiciary

The *di-ku₅*, "judge" (Akk. *dayyānu*), appears as a profession already in the Early Dynastic period, often, for example, in Ebla and in Lagash, and occasionally alongside the city prince *(ensi)*. In the somewhat later legal documents he emerges with particular frequency as a member of the majority, since in legal matters more faith was put in a council. Moreover, there was besides the sun god a special judge god (Madānu). Unfortunately, no text informs us, even on an introductory level, how judges were prepared for the responsibilities of their profession following their basic education as scribes. In all probability they had to participate in the legal process for a long time, and then were instructed by an experienced judge with the aid of legal cases which had already been decided. Since laws, as we have already seen, were either completely

14. There are only partial editions of the more than 1,200 previously published legal documents and letters. Cf. the series *Studies on the Civilization and Culture of Nuzi and the Hurrians* (Winona Lake, 1981–).

15. Cf. P. Koschaker, "Göttliches und weltliches Recht nach den Urkunden aus Susa," *Orientalia* 4 (1934): 38ff. A comprehensive evaluation is not yet available.

lacking or regulated only a small part of the legal material, the judges often had to reach decisions on the basis of their own free discretion, just as they had to do later following the creation of the great codices. They risked the loss of their office, however, if they did not proceed in a reasonable or prudent fashion (see above, section 1b). Nevertheless, corrupt judges could be found in every age: only the gods were incorruptible.[16] To what extent the king, governor, and mayor could influence the findings of the court is unknown; that they undertook to do just that, however, can scarcely be doubted, and in every instance they served as the final court of appeal in important cases. It is also certain that the trials were almost always public: "the gate," a place or niche in a building at the city gate, is often named as the locus of the court. We hear of judges in the Old Assyrian texts with remarkable rarity. In the Cappadocian trade colonies there were in all probability no professional judges at all, but only individuals who could decide from case to case. Since very few studies have been done on the office of judge,[17] our knowledge of many aspects is insufficient.

If we turn to the cases which the judges had to conduct, the first thing that strikes us is the almost complete lack of criminal cases in which the maximum penalties prescribed in the laws would have been administered. Only a single Neo-Sumerian murder case with a resulting death penalty has been passed down in a few transcribed copies; it was probably treated as a school exercise.[18] From the later period, only criminal judgments with monetary fines are known, and the ancient world nowhere knew of prison sentences. Other than that, a few records of proceedings exist which list criminal acts.[19] Since thieves and

16. *AHw* 1382a lists citations of the Akk. *ṭātu/ṭa'tu*, "bribery."

17. Cf. A. Falkenstein, *Die neusumerischen Gerichtsurkunden,* Part I (Munich, 1956); Part II (Munich, 1957) treats the documents superscribed with *di-til-la,* "verdict, judgment, concluded legal matter"; cf. also J. G. Lautner, *Die richterliche Entscheidung und die Streitbeendigung im altbabylonischer Prozessrecht* (Leipzig, 1922); A. Walther, *Das altbabylonische Gerichtswesen* (Leipzig, 1917). In the first millennium documents and letters are familiar with the *sartennu,* or "chief justice," in addition to the *dayyānu;* the term *sartennu* is of Hurrian origin.

18. In addition, cf. T. Jacobsen, *Towards the Image of Tammuz* (Cambridge, Mass., 1970), 193ff.: "An Ancient Mesopotamian Trial for Homicide."

19. Cf. M. San Nicolò, "Der Monstreprozess des Gimillu, eines *širku* von Eanna," *Archiv orientâlní* 5 (1933): 61ff. Under pressure from witnesses, the temple administrator Gimillu, in the temple of Ishtar Eanna in Uruk, had to admit to theft and the embezzlement of great numbers of livestock during the reign of King Nabonidus.

murderers certainly were often sentenced to death or, where it was customary, to mutilation, we can only conclude from the lack of criminal judgments that these, at least, were only pronounced orally, that is, that the principle of written documentation was only valid for civil procedures. We can only guess at the reason for this: the judges may have feared that the written death penalty might somehow, perhaps by magic, be used to their own harm. Another possibility might also be considered: in such cases one wrote on perishable wax and completely destroyed the tablet as soon as possible thereafter.

In all cases the plaintiffs had to be heard first, and afterward the accused or defendants; both parties had to bring forth witnesses who would confirm their testimony, but this, of course, was often enough impossible. Wherever necessary, the witnesses had to testify under oath; in other words, they had to take a curse upon themselves in the case that they gave false testimony. This generally took place before a symbol of the deity,[20] which sometimes had to be brought from the temple. Under these circumstances, each lie simultaneously became an insult to the deity. Certainly, the statements made under oath were often written down. Testimony under oath was unnecessary when documents could be presented which confirmed the essential elements of someone's testimony. In such cases, the judgment of the court could be announced immediately. The king frequently demanded oaths as well.

The ordeal was employed as a further means of proof when someone was accused of murder or adultery without adequate substantiating evidence. It was occasionally used also in cases of suspected theft; in Babylonia, Assyria, and Nuzi, this was always a river ordeal. Apparently at that time no one considered the possibility that someone could actually swim in the river. Therefore, people could be persuaded that the river god always threw the innocent up on land, yet he would at the same time let drown either the one who committed the crime or a person who brought a false charge. A propagandist of Nabonidus depicts quite vividly the performance of an ordeal which had already been prescribed under the law of Ur-Nammu of Ur.[21]

20. Cf. U. Seidl, B. Hrouda, and J. Krecher, "Göttersymbole und -attribute," *RLA* III (1969): 483ff.

21. Cf. J. Bottéro, "L'Ordalie en Mésopotamie ancienne," *Annali della Scuola . . . di Pisa* 10 (1981): 1005ff.; W. G. Lambert, "Nebukadnezzar, King of Justice," *Iraq* 27 (1965): 1ff. The text deals with Nabonidus!

Depending on the case, functionaries of various ranks, as well as the elders of the city, could take part in the proceedings. Studies of the particular functions of such persons are still needed,[22] and we know nothing of any kind of attorney. The indispensable person who directed the process was generally the scribe, who as a rule was named following the witnesses, and who was also responsible for preparing the documents. He was required to have mastered the conventional formulations and the juridical terminology. Texts exist from the first millennium which set the Sumerian technical terms and phrases alongside the Akkadian.[23]

Neither the documents nor the laws make any statements whatever concerning the persons charged with carrying out the physical penalties. These individuals may simply have been summoned from case to case. The collection of monetary fines and payments to the party who had prevailed, payments which often far exceeded the value of a case itself, were in all likelihood supervised by city officials. Women often entered into the procedures, and not just to protect their own interests in marital disputes. The designation "judge" was attributed to individual goddesses, though there were in fact no earthly female judges (with the possible exception of the biblical Deborah).[24]

22. Besides state commissioners, such as the *šakkanakku*, there were junior counselors with merely advisory functions. The judges may even have voted in critical cases. Professional judges would not have been on hand everywhere.

23. The most important of these texts was edited by B. Landsberger (*Die Serie ana itti-šu*. MSL I [Rome, 1937]) and also contains the Sumerian family laws. In the same series, vol. V (1957): 9ff. provides additional supplementary material (Landsberger, *The Series ḪAR-ra = ḫubullu: Tablets I-IV*). These texts served the further purpose of providing training in verb forms.

24. Ereshkigal, the queen of the underworld (see below, XII.3b), along with other gods and goddesses was simultaneously a judge over the dead, though of course with much more limited possibilities than Osiris in Egypt.

CHAPTER XI

Sumerian and Babylonian Science

1. The Sumerian Science of Lists as a Science of Order

Soon after the invention of their writing system (see above, IV.1), the Sumerians began to compile smaller lists of cuneiform signs. With a system of word signs, sign lists are simultaneously word lists, having even a certain somewhat topical material arrangement. With the gradual transition to cuneiform, the signs, which were increasingly employed as syllabic signs, were becoming less pictorial. Thus, lists arranged according to the signs could remain simultaneously word lists with a topical arrangement of the signs only in the case of a minority of signs. For this reason, distinct lists of objects were created as early as the third millennium. These contained primarily compound words: in addition to objects designated by determinatives (see above, IV.1), including those objects made from wood, reed, leather, metals, stone, wool, and so forth, the lists enumerated plants with particular subgroups, such as trees and grains, as well as domesticated and wild animals, and certain classifications of people with designations for body parts, geographic names, stars, and divine names. The tendency toward a firmly established sequence within the individual groups, however, had still not been fully realized by the Old Babylonian period. Among the local scholastic traditions, which from the beginning had diverged widely from one another, that of Nippur came increasingly to prevail after the time of the Third Dynasty of Ur.[1] The word lists migrated to some extent with the writing

1. On the science of lists and on this entire chapter, cf. W. von Soden, "Leistung

145

system to both Elam and Syria, where independent native traditions developed, as the archives of Ebla (about 2400) impressively show, though they preserve the adopted lists in a form which has undergone manifold changes.

When such lists were first compiled, practical criteria may have stood in the foreground, and these always retained a great significance for the scribal schools. At the same time, however, these considerations were increasingly surpassed by goals of a more theoretical sort. The Sumerians believed in a means of ordering the world which brought with it confirmation of the working of the gods (see below, XII.2). The lists had the task of making this order manifest in connection with the main groups of objects and living creatures, including the gods. This could be accomplished, however, only by people who knew how to handle the lists. The Sumerians were unable to present their ideas in a connected fashion, either in the realms of nature, abstract matters, and theology, or in those of mathematics (see below, XI.9) or jurisprudence. Thus, Sumerian science lacked the conceptual framework of formulated principles (what in the West has been called "natural laws"), and simply ordered nominal expressions one after the other in a one-dimensional fashion, without any kind of elucidation. Verbs in finite form and abstract terms are found only in those sign lists which are not topically ordered, but not in the lists which have been ordered according to systematic criteria. Mythic literature served to illustrate the conception of order (see below, XIII.3). During the Neo-Sumerian period, the compilers and tradents of several lists were apparently concerned to com-

---

und Grenze sumerischer und babylonischer Wissenschaft," *Die Welt als Geschichte* 2 (1936): 411-505, 509-557 (originally *Islamica* 2 [1926]: 355ff.); supplemented in B. Landsberger, *The Conceptual Autonomy of the Babylonian World*. Monographs on the Ancient Near East I/4 (Malibu, 1974). In addition, cf. von Soden, *Zweisprachigkeit in der geistigen Kultur Babyloniens* (Vienna, 1960); *Sprache, Denken, und Begriffsbildung im alten Orient* (Mainz, 1973).

A comprehensive overview of the mono- and bilingual lists is provided by A. Cavigneaux, "Lexicalische Listen," *RLA* VI (1983): 609-641, with extensive bibliography and textual examples for the important types of lexical lists. For further evidence, and as a supplement to the very brief information given here, this treatment can be drawn upon at nearly every point. There is nothing comparable either to the Sumero-Babylonian science of lists as a whole or to the bilingual lexical lists in any of the other ancient cultural spheres, although the phenomenon of bilingual culture can be found elsewhere, achieving great significance, for example, in medieval Europe as well as in the Islamic world or even East Asia.

Clay liver model, inscribed with omens and magical formulas for divinization. First Dynasty of Babylon (about 1830-1530). *(Trustees of the British Museum)*

prehend the nominal expressions in many areas as nearly completely as possible; in other cases, as with the stars, they were satisfied with a small selection of that which was accessible to observation; the reasons for these variations are still unclear.

History, for its part, was presented in the form of king lists, which were composed on the basis of the fiction that there had always been only a single king in the land. For the earlier as well as the later period, the king lists set simultaneously reigning dynasties in successive order without any explanation. Nor were mythical and historical kings differentiated; three- to four-place numbers for regnal periods are occasionally encountered, even for historical monarchs. In mathematics, an equally one-dimensional arithmetic table replaced the one-dimensional lists (see below, section 9).

2. Bilingual Lexical Lists in Ebla and Babylonia: Tri- and Quadrilingual Lists in Asia Minor and Syria

The Semites in Syria and Babylonia came to know the Sumerian sign and word lists, but they only partially understood the sense and function of the lists. These people recognized quite early, however, that one could create two-dimensional lists by the addition of a second column, or line, in their own language, as was done at Ebla; these two-dimensional lists could then aid the study of the other language. The Sumerian words and expressions were rendered with Akkadian or, as the case may be, Eblaite words, genitive constructs, or brief relative clauses, which in turn were only of provisional assistance due to the vast differences in the languages. The bilingual lists thus became the first lexical aid in human history, and for a long time nothing similar followed outside the cuneiform cultures, since the Greeks had little interest in other languages; not until the Renaissance did Western lexicography begin to develop. Until a short time ago we only knew of bilingual lists from the second millennium, so we assumed that the beginnings of lexicography lay in the early part of the Old Babylonian period. The discovery of the archive of tablets from Ebla (see above, IV.1) forced us to revise our position: in twenty-fifth century Ebla, Sumerian-Eblaite lists of considerable scope already existed. Here, as in later Babylonia, verbs were presented by juxtaposing the Semitic infinitive to the Sumerian verbal root.[2] Unfortunately, many Sumerian words in these lists were left untranslated, including particularly frequent words as well as those used

---

2. In these lists, the infinitive is represented as a nominal verbal form by being made into the Lemma-form, since this form originally specified only substantives. Cf. *Il Bilinguismo a Ebla,* ed. L. Cagni (Naples, 1984), 51ff. Cf. also Cavigneaux, 615. What has still not been taken into account from that corpus is *Materiali epigrafici di Ebla* IV: G. Pettinato, *Testi lessicali bilingui della Biblioteca L. 2769* (Naples, 1982). This work contains the Sumero-Eblaite lists and is to be supplemented by a further volume with revisions. The important essay by M. Krebernik ("Zu Syllabar und Orthographie der lexikalischen Texte von Ebla," *ZA* 72 [1982]: 178ff.) offers many further improvements. W. von Soden, "Zweisprachige Listen in Ebla und der altbabylonischen Zeit" (forthcoming) includes considerations on the intellectual-historical placement of the lists.

less often. According to the present reconstruction, the bilingual lists were first created in northern Syria around 2400; afterward, they were created anew in Babylonia shortly after 2000 without knowledge of Eblaite. It is not unthinkable, however, that the bilingual lists of Ebla were patterned after northern Babylonian models which have yet to be discovered.

For a long time, the Sumerian lists of objects were handed on in monolingual form, and not until late in the second millennium were they first prepared with the Akkadian column. Conversely, lists of different types, arranged according to signs, and even lists of grammatical forms, which were conceived from the outset in bicolumnar form, were transmitted as early as the Old Babylonian period. Certain of these lists attest a multifaceted concern with the Sumerian language and with their own. Still, grammatical rules were never formulated in terms of precepts, and one learned instead from the multitude of examples, which of course were not always of equal merit.[3]

In the age following the Old Babylonian period, certain types of lists were canonized by the creation of series of tablets, most of which were named after the initial line and which consisted of up to forty numbered tablets. To these were added completely new compilations of lists. The compilers of these new lists collected synonyms and homonyms, for example, or Akkadian root words with their multifarious usages and their real or supposed derivations, without shrinking from assembling wild etymologies. To put it mildly, these lists are still in need of thorough study. Very brief explanations, introduced by the determinative pronoun *ša*, comprised a completely novel element in the later lists. The equivalencies of the earlier lists, rightly understood, often present indeterminate relationships. This happened because the compiler was unable to formulate his knowledge clearly, owing to the fact that the Sumerian and Akkadian words often were not actually equivalent. In the later lists we find many hundreds of partial equivalencies of the type, *zi-zi = qa-ta-pu ša ḫašḫūri,* "to pluck, [said] of apples." Naturally, even such equivalencies as these must be read critically.[4]

3. Cf. B. Landsberger, *Old Babylonian and Neobabylonian Grammatical Texts.* MSL IV (1956), and, as supplements to this work, e.g., O. R. Gurney, *Middle Babylonian Legal Documents and Other Texts.* Ur Excavation Texts VII (1974), no. 97ff. An evaluation of the bilingual grammatical lists is still needed.

4. Cf. von Soden, *Sprache, Denken, und Begriffsbildung im alten Orient,* 11ff.

During the first millennium, numerous commentaries led beyond the lists. These commentaries maintained the form of the bicolumnar lists only in part. They also contained many citations from the bilingual lists and the lists of synonyms (see below) and included the verbal infinitive along with many verbal forms. Factual commentaries of different sorts, which also contain clarifications of many words, existed alongside the predominantly philological word commentaries. We will have to refer frequently to these commentaries below.[5]

Along with the commentaries, the bicolumnar Akkadian synonym lists first came into being during the first millennium and were transmitted primarily in Assyria. The synonyms enumerated in these lists are overwhelmingly "partial synonyms," a fact which is rarely mentioned. These same lists often survey little-used words of literature and poetry and therefore become a particularly important aid for understanding works of these genres.[6]

That Akkadian could for a time become the language of diplomacy and commerce from about 1400 to 1200, even as far as Egypt and the Hittite Empire, was made possible by the fact that the schools there took over, selected, and even expanded considerable portions of the Sumerian object lists and the bilingual Sumerian-Akkadian lists. Since the native languages then had to be surveyed, these were introduced into third or even fourth columns. From the Hittite capital of Hattusas we possess many Sumerian-Akkadian-Hittite word lists alongside merely Akkadian-Hittite lists; there are even quadrilingual Sumerian-Akkadian-Ugaritic-Hurrian word lists from Ugarit. These are quite helpful, of course, despite their extremely fragmentary state of preservation.[7] It would have been quite simple to introduce into such lists the Aramaic which prevailed primarily in the West during the Neo-Assyrian period. We know of no such lists, however, but only smaller groups of West

5. No comprehensive assessment of such diverse word and subject commentaries is yet available. For examples, cf. R. Labat, *Commentaires assyro-babyloniens sur les Présages* (Bordeaux, 1933); H. Hunger and E. von Weiher, *Spätbabylonische Texte aus Uruk*, Parts I-II (Berlin, 1976-1983), with commentaries on medicinal and omen texts, among other things.

6. An edition of these monolingual lists, which we know primarily from Assyria, is not yet available.

7. Cf. certain literary citations by Cavigneaux, 639; for Hattusas, cf. provisionally H. Otten and W. von Soden, *Das akkadisch-hethitische Vokabular KBo. I 44 + KBo. XIII 1* (Wiesbaden, 1968), with a survey of the various groups of texts in the introduction.

Semitic words in the Akkadian synonym lists. In isolated cases, very late copies of lists contain Greek transcriptions. Still, classical antiquity neither adopted the bilingual lists nor offered something better in their place.

3. Further Functions of Babylonian Word and Name Lists: Inventory Rolls and Compilations of Various Sorts

The purpose of the topically ordered, monolingual Neo-Sumerian lists was not to present ideas of the cosmic order, but rather to depict inventory rolls according to the main categories in the world of objects and living creatures. The Old Babylonian period expanded the corpus of compiled lists. Nevertheless, the development of these into bicolumnar and bilingual lists did not occur until toward the end of the second millennium. During this process of transition and expansion, however, there were many kinds of additions, omissions, and transpositions. In many cases particular principles were presupposed in the arrangement within individual tablets as well as within entire series of tablets, which were named after their beginning line *urra = ḫubulla,* "interest obligations." In addition, external associations often played a role, as did perhaps even chance. Trees were treated exhaustively in Tablet III, but the rest of the plants were not found until Tablet XVII. So also, most domestic and wild animals came in Tablets XIII-XIV, but birds and fish not until Tablet XVIII. There are also many kinds of explanatory additions, though much more frequently these are completely lacking or are encountered only in commentaries running parallel to the lists.[8] One would scarcely have been able to read the work at many places without preliminary instructions. Altogether the work comprises a comprehensive survey of the animate and inanimate world, geography, and stars, as well as artificially produced objects, victuals, and many other things. Similarly, the work was perceived early on as inadequate form for some important categories; thus, further compilations were created, though generally not in the form of word lists. These will be treated below. Furthermore, occasional distinctions between the real and the mythical

---

8. Cf. B. Landsberger, E. Reiner, M. Civil, and A. Draffkorn Kilmer, *The Series ḪAR-ra = ḫubullu.* MSL V-XI (1957-1974).

world were overlooked, especially when dealing with animals. In later copies, supplements were only sporadically inserted.

At the same time, because of their bicolumnar nature the lists could have functions completely different from those of the Sumerian-Akkadian word lists. Thus the great "god list," perhaps formed in the twelfth century by the insertion of much later additions into various monocolumnar Sumerian god lists, begins with *an = Anu* and generally lists in the left-hand column divine names which stand in quite different relationships to the god in the right-hand column, which often remains the same for many lines. There are variations on divine names, gods who bear essential similarities (such as the gods of the Elamites, Kassites, and other peoples), but above all, many names of originally independent gods who had evaporated into the syncretistic theology within the framework of a polytheism which reinterpreted much, and which made many divine names subsidiary names to other gods or simply relegated them to the status of hypostases of other gods. More will be said of this theology (see below, XII.3b), which the Babylonians were unable to develop systematically.[9]

Further differences are found in the functions of bicolumnar works of astronomical instruction (see below, XII.2). This list form is used in certain bicolumnar lists of pharmaceutical plants and stones which are no longer bilingual, in order to present side-by-side alternatively applicable floral, faunal, or mineral drugs, in most cases without explanation (see below, section 7). Bicolumnar king lists play only a subordinate role beside the monocolumnar king lists which the Babylonians and Assyrians had taken over from the Sumerians with some modifications. These bicolumnar king lists juxtapose the actual or sometimes conjectural concurrent rulers of Babylonia and Assyria without indicating the length of time they reigned concurrently.

In summary, we could say that the bicolumnar lists offered the Babylonians quite diverse possibilities of expression, but that these lists were seldom able to bring to tolerably adequate expression what should have been understood from them. The same is especially true even for the Sumerian and Akkadian grammatical forms preserved in many instructive lists.

9. W. G. Lambert is preparing a comprehensive edition which includes previously unpublished pieces.

4. Lists of Analogous Verbal Expressions

To the Sumerian lists of words and nominal expressions, the Babylonians added not only the previously identified lists of similar types, which generally were bilingual, but often quite comprehensive compilations of lists which arranged hundreds and even thousands of similar verbal phrases in serial order without tying them together logically or syntactically in the way we have been accustomed to do in academic study since the time of the Greeks. Moreover, no conclusions at all are drawn from the heaps of individual expressions, and no conclusions are formulated as general principles of knowledge. That conclusions and knowledge, as well as premises, were not formulated should not mislead us into thinking that the Babylonians were not interested in such forms of knowledge. Their mathematics, especially, shows clearly that they had at their disposal a type of knowledge which comprised many details, yet which was not formulated in terms of basic principles. Because of our schooling, we will perhaps never understand how they were able to realize such knowledge without either predicates or deductions. We must, however, recognize that this was possible under the determinative presuppositions of Babylonian culture. Even knowledge without formulations could be quite fruitful, though only to a limited extent. We must now attempt to explicate for ourselves some areas of science which the Babylonians especially nurtured, but which we would scarcely be prepared to regard as sciences. It could thus be considered sensible to set the word "science" in the following treatment in quotation marks; I would not want to do this, however, since this too frequently signifies a degree of denigration which would be inappropriate here.

5. The Babylonian Science of Omens

The term "science of omens" will estrange some from the outset because the belief in good or evil omens sent by the gods, which was present everywhere in antiquity, is a superstition to us. Manifold references to omens of the most diverse sorts are found throughout ancient literature, and people were convinced that these had proven true. Lesser or greater collections of omens with their interpretations were frequently compiled, and sporadically appear even as early as the Sumerians. Yet the Babylonians and Assyrians were the first to order thousands and later tens of thousands of omens with their respective interpretations according to similar categories, thereby creating a science of omens which the Hittites took over in many particulars and which stimulated the assembling of some collections. These collections must be treated here briefly according to formal criteria.

Each omen consists of a conditional clause with a final clause containing the interpretation: for example, "When the blind are numerous in a city, there will be trouble in the city"; or "When a serpent falls upon a sick person, it draws that person's sickness out; he will regain his health." In all probability only a small minority of omens were ever observed. The rest were added in the endeavor to comprehend particular categories of omens as fully as possible, since some of these could possibly take place once. What is important to us, however, are those rare cases when historical events are referred to in connection with an omen. By the arrangement of interpretations of the omens, some principles can be established, as, for example, left = good, right = bad, and vice versa. Quite often, however, no rational principle can be discerned, though one must note that there is still a dearth of studies on this subject.

In the Old Babylonian period, the collections of omens were for the most part still rather small. Omens which took place without human agency, such as encounters with animals or anomalies of birth, were given less attention, and astrology was almost completely absent. People were mostly concerned with inducing omens, primarily through inspection of the liver of sacrificial sheep, but also in figures which were formed when small quantities of oil were poured into a basin of water, or even in the curves of a rising plume of smoke. In the case of liver divination, a question which could be answered either positively or negatively was probably always posed prior to the slaughter of the sheep. The majority of these questions concerned public life, for example, the prospects of a military campaign or the acceptance of a public office. A person inquired about the appearance of twelve different parts of the liver. Usually the result was then a partial "yes" and a partial "no." In such cases, the yes and no characteristics were counted, and the greater number determined the answer. If the result was six to six, the liver divination was unsuccessful and had to be repeated, if no additional features permitted an answer to be inferred. One could also derive more sharply differentiated answers from the lists of actual or fictitious liver diagnoses which had become quite comprehensive as early as the Old Babylonian period, and which were ordered primarily according to the parts of the liver. Individuals were concerned with omina addressing the fate and relations of the family, house and property, and the chances of recovery for the sick.[10]

In the later period, none of the Old Babylonian omen collections was adopted *in toto*, but they were nevertheless widely exploited for new text compilations, even in Asia Minor. New comprehensive texts are first attested from the period after 1200, but the great series of tablets known primarily from Assyria were most likely not assembled until the first millennium. The liver divination texts comprise a great part of the aggregate omen literature down into the Hellenistic Age. Further, many omens are based on a combination of features, and clarifications are often inserted or collated for special commentary tablets. Only sporadic mention is made of oil divination.

Besides liver divination, the observation of the far more numerous non-induced omens emerged in the first millennium. These omens, supplemented through thousands of others construed according to particular schemata, were compiled into the greatest tablet series of Babylonian literature, whose most comprehensive form comprised far more than ten thousand terrestrial and astrological omens. To these must be added several thousand birth omens, calendar omens — held to be especially important for the choice of the best possible day or month — and diagnostic omens, in addition to somewhat smaller classifications, such as physiological omens and dream omens. Clear organizational principles are recognizable in all of these series, even if these are not strictly adhered to in every case. Nevertheless, only specialists with years of schooling, who are called "seers" or "gazers" (as are those who divine by sacrifice; Akk. *bârû*), were able to work with these masses of texts. It took many generations to compile this massive amount of material, and the great series in its entirety, with its hundreds of serially numbered tablets, was probably first brought together in the eighth and seventh centuries in Babylonia or Assyria.[11] These collections associate

---

10. Editions of larger groups of the immense corpus of liver omens do not exist, but R. Borger, *HKL* III (1975), 96, provides much evidence. For the reports of liver-offering divination, cf. A. Goetze, "Reports on Acts of Extispicy from Old Babylonian and Kassite Times," *JCS* 11 (1957): 89ff.; J. Nougayrol, "Rapports paléo-babyloniens d'haruspicine," *JCS* 21 (1967): 219ff.

11. Large portions of the terrestrial omens of the series *šumma ālu ina mēlê šakin* — "when a city lies on a height" — were edited by F. Nötscher in *Orientalia*, Old Series

the immense number of omens with a much smaller number of mostly quite general interpretations from the spheres of public and private life. If it were merely a question of mantic prophecy in the narrower sense of the term in these collections, supplemented by the commentaries, the collections would hold a preeminent position in a history of superstition, but they would command quite limited interest beyond this. However, the omen collections are of far greater importance.

The desire to understand as fully as possible the ominous constellations manipulated by the gods, even to the extent that one could even organize trade arrangements by them, led to ever more precise observations. Thus for the sheep livers, of which no two were alike in every respect, even the smallest oddities were observed, registered, and recorded on clay tablets.[12] Other organs were observed as well, insofar as a diagnosis could be drawn. The same was true of new-born infants and their anomalies, as well as miscarriages.[13] The body structure and behavior of various animals in highly diverse situations was observed very precisely as well, and special attention was paid to snakes.[14] The result was a level of zoological knowledge which was quite unusual in ancient times. Many plants came under observation too, though they did not receive the same attention as animals. Several kinds of omens were deduced from water, particularly the floodwaters of the rivers, as well as from meteorological phenomena of all types. In accord with the Babylonian worldview, weather omens were incorporated into the astrological omen series.

Humanity was studied with special intensity, and in this regard the science of omens worked closely with medicine (see below, section 8). The basic questions regarding human behavior had to do with morality and ethics. We learn much about the moral values then in force (supplementing other sources; see below, XII.4), as well as of the consequences of outbursts of temper, from the interpretation of good and

---

31, 39-42, 51-54 (1928-1930); since that time many texts have been added. For omens of birth which treat, following human beings, a number of ruminant animals and, particularly extensively, sheep, cf. E. V. Leichty, *The Omen Series šumma izbu* ["when there is a miscarriage"]. Texts from Cuneiform Sources IV (Locust Valley, 1970), including a large commentary on omens.

12. Cf. R. D. Biggs and J.-W. Meyer, "Lebermodelle," *RLA* VI (1983): 518ff.

13. Cf. Leichty, 31ff.

14. Cf. also B. Landsberger and I. Krumbiegel, *Die Faune des alten Mesopotamien* (Leipzig, 1934), 45ff.

evil omens, which were important for the fate of the individual.[15] Finally, dreams were also recorded in very great numbers. Since people are able to remember only a small part of these, a great many dreams admittedly may have been invented for the omen collections. From dreams, sicknesses were also diagnosed.[16] One can derive many observations relating to psychology and the study of human behavior from all of these omens and their interpretations. Still, one can speak of no more than the beginnings of these and other modern sciences nurtured on the fringes of divination in ancient Babylonia.

The situation is completely different in the case of astrology. In contrast to the later periods, the early Babylonians did not deduce from the stars the fate of the individual — that happened on occasion first in the Seleucid period[17] — but rather, the fate of noble families, the state, and larger groups, and not least of all the prospects for the harvest. In these areas, astrology primarily supplemented liver divination. But astrology could not attain a greater significance until astronomy, which was pursued from time to time for astrological purposes, had access to a sufficient number of observations. That would scarcely have been possible prior to 1200. Astronomy will be treated in its own right (see below, section 9). Here, reference will be made solely to the many thousands of astrological omens which we know from the first millennium.[18] In hardly any other instance has superstition been as fruitful for the emergence and development of a science as in the case of astronomy, which was scarcely nurtured, in contrast to opinions often represented regarding the Sumerians.[19]

15. Cf. F. R. Kraus, "Ein Sittenkanon in Omenform," *ZA* 43 (1936): 77ff.; many further text fragments have been published subsequently.

16. Cf. A. L. Oppenheim, *The Interpretation of Dreams in the Ancient Near East: With a Treatise on an Assyrian Dream-Book* (Philadelphia, 1956); supplements in *Iraq* 31 (1969): 153ff.

17. Cf. A. Sachs, "Babylonian Horoscopes," *JCS* 6 (1952): 49ff.

18. Cf. C. Virolleaud, *L'Astrologie chaldéenne* (Paris, 1908-1911) (incomplete); E. Reiner and D. Pingree began an updated new edition in *Bibliotheca Mesopotamica* II (Malibu, 1975ff.).

19. The divergent view of the Pan-Babylonians (e.g., of Hugo Winckler and Alfred Jeremias), that astronomy is to be traced back to the Sumerians in the fourth millennium, can no longer be reconciled with the known sources, although this view is still sporadically represented.

6. Theology, Historiography, and Geography

Theology will be treated only briefly here, and under formal criteria; its contents will be dealt with in the chapter on religion. Theology was primarily the teachings about the gods, but the Sumerians could only express these in monocolumnar, one-dimensional lists of deities without suggesting any clarification (see below, XII.2). The mostly bi-columnar Babylonian god lists (see above, section 3) reveal essentially more, since they have been illuminated in numerous ways, so that much more can be deduced from them about the relationships of the gods to one another. Nevertheless, they still leave the reader ignorant of much crucial information. The first millennium added cultic commentaries to these lists, drawing quite colorful pronouncements from the lists of gods, the myths, and the rituals, but scarcely exhibiting a systematic viewpoint. Wildly rampant speculations, frequently based on etymo-logical wordplays, often find expression in these pronouncements. These scarcely ever had a binding character, and they are only witnesses to Babylonian science in a very limited sense. Central theological ideas, which must be deduced from prayers and mythic poetry, were never formulated or linked together systematically.

There was fertile ground for a scientific approach to history in Babylonia and Assyria insofar as there was often a pronounced interest in the distant past. This interest was expressed among the Sumerians, although only in the monocolumnar, one-dimensional king lists (see above, sections 1, 2) and in mythic poems relating to earlier kings such as Gilgamesh. Political criteria were determinative for the exclusion of a number of dynasties from the lists. The alleged regnal years were not always correct, even for the period after the middle of the third millen-nium, and the listing in successive order of dynasties which were actually contemporary certainly led to false understandings for periods in the more distant past. Both the Babylonians and Assyrians continued these lists (see above, V.1).

The year lists down to 1530 served primarily practical purposes, but were interpreted for the king lists in the same way as the eponymal year lists (the *limmu* lists; see above, V.2) in Assyria, which were con-structed for similar reasons. Interest in particular kings was expressed primarily in epic sagas, among which those on the kings of Akkad, Sargon, and Naram-Sin (see above, V.4) were especially beloved and were repeatedly revised. However, from the Sumerian period on, times of trouble also served as themes of such poetry, for example, such events as the incursions of Elamite armies. The wrath of the gods was often referred to in these poetic compositions (see below, XIII.3).

The king lists were enriched early in the second millennium by additional information, for example, concerning a change of dynasty. It is not entirely correct to regard as chronicles later texts which, from a particular perspective, briefly recount significant events for selected kings. After about 1100, we find texts in Assyria as well as Babylonia which give brief reports primarily on wars during the preceding 250 years or so. An Assyrian chronicle from the eighth century treats the conflict between Assyria and Babylonia after around 1500 with a strong anti-Babylonian slant, and similar works exist in Babylonia. The so-called Babylonian Chronicle begins with the year 747. This work registers the most important events for each king in annalistic form, but subsequently gives shorter or more detailed treatment to each year. Some political bias can frequently be detected behind the otherwise very factual reports. Moreover, no recollection of the list form can be recognized in any of these works, though the texts themselves offer merely the raw materials for an actual historiography.[20] From the seventh century on, even the "astronomical diaries" (see below) contain short historical reports.

Geographical lists of lands, cities, bodies of water, and occasionally mountain ranges were handed down in Babylonia, and for a brief period in Ebla, from the middle of the third millennium. These were altered in later centuries through omissions and additions, but from the Old Babylonian period on they offered an increasingly historical geography, which is still more oriented to earlier than to contemporary names. Conversely, the itineraries and lists of Assyrian provinces from the later period are not part of the geographical literature. Some narrative texts, and especially Assyrian campaign reports, show that the landscape of foreign lands was observed as well.[21]

---

20. Cf. A. K. Grayson, *Assyrian and Babylonian Chronicles* (Locust Valley, 1975), which cites the earlier literature.

21. The witnesses for the geographical interest in foreign lands have still not been assembled. Especially impressive is the report of Sargon II on his eighth campaign (cf. W. Mayer in *MDOG* 116 [1984]), e.g., in lines 324ff.

7. The Beginnings of Natural Sciences

The names of trees and other plants, animals of all kinds, and minerals were included by the Sumerians in their expanded monolingual word lists, and were recorded by the Babylonians in essentially more comprehensive, mostly bilingual, and sometimes very briefly expanded lists (see above, section 3). The principles which determined the arrangement are only partially recognizable for us, primarily because we are unable to interpret very many of the names. In comparison to the other categories, however, we know most about the land animals, under which the insects and worms are ordered; we know less of the birds, and even less of the fish.[22] The body parts of animals are treated along with those of people. The distinctions made between a great many types in all areas attest to intensive observation, although naturally all types were not treated in the same manner. The initial words of word phrases allow us to discern a pre-scientific order among the Sumerians, who in any case had at their disposal only a limited number of words to be used as names; for example, *ur* designates dogs, wolves, and so forth, as well as the great predatory cats.[23]

In the first millennium, the word lists were supplemented by the above-noted lists of floral, faunal, and mineral drugs, which present a far greater number of plants than the other lists. Where these lists are ordered according to the illnesses that the drugs served to combat, numerous drugs are to be found. Names derived from foreign lands testify to the importation of many medicinal herbs at an early date. Medicinal commentaries contain further important disclosures. The works *šammu šikin-šu* and *abnu šikin-šu* — "the plants with respect to their appearance," "the stones with respect to their appearance" — which emerged in the first millennium, bring new insights and serve to facilitate the recognition of plants and minerals. In the case of the plants, the list names several parts from the flower to the root and compares these without any differentiation to the corresponding parts of other plants, following the pattern, "Plant a: its flower is plant b, its stem is

22. Cf. A. Salonen, *Die Fischerei im alten Mesopotamien* (Helsinki, 1970); *idem, Vögel und Vogelfang im alten Mesopotamien* (Helsinki, 1973), with many illustrations.
23. Cf. Landsberger and Krumbiegel, nn. 7ff., on dogs and cats; further articles on animals living in the wild are to be found in *RLA* by W. Heimpel and others, e.g., "Hirsch" (IV [1975]: 418ff.), "Leopard (und Gepard)" (VI [1983]: 599ff.).

plant c," and so forth. Naturally, the inquirer thereby gains little exact knowledge. The schema for the minerals is simpler still. Nevertheless, these descriptions presuppose multifarious observations, though the scope of both works cannot be discerned from the portions preserved.[24] On pharmacology, see below, section 8.

The great lists of terrestrial omens (see above) treat flora and fauna at length. Here the primary concern with animals is their behavior, while with plants it is their location, especially unusual locations. Unfortunately, as is elsewhere the case, floral and faunal omens based on actual observation are found alongside a great many others which were invented according to some analogy or other. The latter are easy to recognize if they make obviously absurd pronouncements, as, for example, the claim that someone had observed a lamb with ten feet; but in many other cases the invented omens can be recognized only with difficulty, or not at all. We still need someone to undertake a comprehensive evaluation of the omens. Certain literary texts give quite valuable pointers for identifying birds, and also render the birdcalls in vocalized form.[25] Collective descriptions of the body structure and behavior of certain types of animals are completely lacking: these lay beyond the possibilities of Babylonian science.

The Babylonians never possessed even the beginnings of an understanding of physics, though they did have at their disposal some knowledge of physical principles, such as the laws of leverage, which had to be used in transporting the heaviest blocks. One can speak of Babylonian-Assyrian chemistry in only the most limited sense that many kinds of experiences with the properties and behavior of elements, and their relationships, had been assembled. This accomplishment in the middle of the second millennium made it increasingly possible to reproduce chemical relationships going well beyond those of metallurgy, which had been known at a far earlier date. Thus was attained the means of working with many kinds of glazes and cosmetic media. We have learned much from chemical analysis; but we also possess, primarily from Assyria, collections of formulas for the production of glazes and

24. Neither series of texts has yet been compiled; on the second see B. Landsberger, "Über Farben im Sumerisch-Akkadischen," *JCS* 21 (1969): 151ff. The texts known up to that time are cited in *AHw* 1235a, *šiknu* B 8.

25. Cf. W. G. Lambert, "The Birdcall Text," *Anatolian Studies* 20 (1970): 111ff. On botany, cf. R. C. Thompson, *A Dictionary of Assyrian Botany.*

cosmetic pastes. Yet these collections of formulas should not be reckoned among the scientific writings in the strict sense of the term.[26]

8. The Scientific Study of Humanity: Medicine and Pharmacology

As for the scientific study of humanity, the focal point is either groups and communities or the individual person. The study of individuals attained a considerable significance in Mesopotamia, but scarcely the beginnings can be found for the collective focus. Thus, in the area of law, we are quite familar with collections of laws (see above, X.1) but find no discussion of legal questions of a more fundamental sort. One finds programs for better conduct of the affairs of state in some royal inscriptions, but nothing which one could designate as the beginnings of a political science. It scarcely needs mentioning that even the very presuppositions are lacking for more wide-ranging approaches to knowledge, such as philosophy with its various subdisciplines. Still, the so-called wisdom texts contain interesting pronouncements regarding these fields, as well as pedagogy and ethics (see below, XIII.4).

In the same way, there was no intensive concern for the healthy individual outside the religious literature. All manner of individual observations on psychology are found in the omen collections, especially among the physiognomic omens, which often deal with human behavior.[27] Particular interest in the anatomy and physiology of the human body is shown predominantly within the framework of that form of medicine concerned with the means of healing illnesses; especially intensive concern was devoted to this area. It must at the same time be noted that, in contrast to Egypt, surgery is only rarely treated in the great mass of medical texts.[28] As in Europe during the Middle Ages,

26. Cf. A. L. Oppenheim, R. H. Brill, and A. von Saldern, *Glass and Glassmaking in Ancient Mesopotamia* (Corning, N.Y., 1970), 23ff.; and E. Ebeling, *Parfümrezepte und kultische Texte aus Assur* (Rome, 1950).

27. Cf. Kraus, *ZA* 43 (1936): 77ff.; also *Die Physiognomischen Omina der Babylonier* (Leipzig, 1935); supplementing this with bibliography is W. von Soden, "Die 2. Tafel der Unterserie Šumma Ea liballiṭ-ka von alandimmû ["Gestalt"]," *ZA* 71 (1981): 109ff.

28. Cf. R. Labat, "À propos de la chirurgie babylonienne," *Journal Asiatique* (1954): 207ff. The treatment of surgery in § § 218ff. of the Code of Hammurabi is particularly bad.

surgery was considered more of a tradesman's activity. The doctor (Sum. *a-zu*, "fluids expert"; Akk. *asû*) worked primarily with orally taken or externally applied medicaments of the most diverse sort, and with magical means. Indeed, medicine and magic were so intertwined that it is completely impossible to draw a sharp line between the two. Here Babylonian-Assyrian medicine can be shown to be archaic on the one hand, while on the other the combination of medicine and magic anticipates modern psychosomatic methods. The magical practices stimulated the patient's will to be well, without which no successful healing can be expected. Incantations and prayers supplemented treatment with drugs, and one can scarcely distinguish between the magical and actual medical effects of these applications. Our understanding of the methods of that period is made much more difficult by our inability to interpret many words for plants and minerals. The situation is even worse with the designations of diseases, which primarily denote the external appearance of a disease, and so in our own medical terminology are ambiguous (cf. the treatment of leprosy in Leviticus 13–14, where "leprosy" can apply to a house or garment, as well as the human body); in many cases we do not even have a clue as to the meaning of the word. Still, an intensive study of the numerous pertinent texts would certainly bring forth new knowledge and information.[29]

Only occasional, modest collections of prescriptions and diagnostic texts, which lack exact descriptions of symptoms, are preserved from the Old Babylonian period. These lack any systematic organization and have the appearance of the records of individual doctors. The texts from the last third of the second millennium are more numerous and often far more comprehensive, as well as better arranged, and attest to considerable advances in medicine and pharmacology. The great medical works, however, did not emerge until the first millennium, and the copies on hand mostly stem from the time after 700. Letters provide us with extremely important supplementary information to the medical texts, since they often report on individual cases in great depth and make known to us famous doctors of their age, as, for example, Urad-

29. No comprehensive treatment of Babylonian medicine is yet available. Nevertheless, a chapter is dedicated to this topic in every presentation of cultural history (cf. the works cited in ch. I, n. 2). Cf. also D. Goltz, *Studien zur altorientalischen und griechischen Heilkunde: Therapie — Arzneibereitung — Rezeptstruktur* (Wiesbaden, 1974); R. D. Biggs, "Babylonien," in *Krankheit, Heilkunst, Heilung*, ed. H. Schipperges *et al.* (Freiburg, 1978), 91ff., with bibliography.

Nanâ, who served in the royal court of Nineveh after 680. Occasionally these letters even contain the patients' questions to the doctor.[30]

There are two large groups of medical texts. Those in the first group present the diagnostic omens and generally give only a few symptoms of the illness. They also state quite briefly whether the disease can be healed and, depending on the case, how long it will take, or whether death will come after a shorter or longer period. In place of this last statement one often finds "the hand of the god (or the demon) X"; the hand of each god was not equally malevolent. Such a reference may intend to indicate either that the help of the designated god should be sought, or that a ritual should be carried out against the particular demon. One such example reads,

> If he [the patient] is sick all day long,
> then his head is "devouring" him —
> he lays his hand repeatedly on his stomach and cries out,
> he stretches his hand out again —
> he will die.

The omen series begins with incidents which should enable the incanter to approach the case of the patient, then cites many diagnoses from the head to the feet, as well as the internal organs, then many maladies with various symptoms, and finally a great number of infantile diseases. As with other portents, there are certainly many invented combinations of symptoms here. But there is nowhere any mention of what the doctor can do or usually does.[31]

The collections of prescriptions, which were not assembled in as great a tablet collection as the diagnostic omens (comprising forty tablets), also begin each section with a brief, or in some cases very detailed, diagnosis. Several magical-medicinal prescriptions, and sometimes incantations which the doctor can try usually follow upon these. Occasionally, the series of plants, trees or woods, or minerals are very long.

---

30. For the Neo-Assyrian letters, cf. S. Parpola, *Letters from Assyrian Scholars to the Kings Esarhaddon and Assurbanipal*, I. AOAT 5/1 [1970]; II. AOAT 5/2 [1983]); *idem* and J. Reade, *The Correspondence of Sargon II* (Helsinki, 1987). For earlier letters, cf. H. Waschow, *Babylonische Briefe aus der Kassitenzeit* (Leipzig, 1936); A. Finet, "Les médecins au royaume de Mari," *Annuaire de l'Institut de Philologie et d'Histoire Orientales et Slaves* 14 (1954-1957): 123ff.

31. Cf. R. Labat, *Traité akkadien de diagnostics et pronostics médicaux*, 2 vols. (Paris, 1951); Hunger and von Weiher offer numerous supplements to this work.

A very large part of the tablets which have come down to us are tablets which individual doctors or incanters had abstracted for themselves from larger compilations. The prescribed medicaments frequently were mixed with water, milk, beer, or more seldom wine, and point to a developed pharmacology. It is of course improbable that all the given components of any prescription were always available. Not a few medicaments contained substances completely similar to those used today for the same sicknesses, and the doctors of the first millennium were able to build upon the experiences of many previous generations. That is true, for example, of the application of fish gall for the healing of blindness caused by a speck upon the cornea.[32]

Beyond the diagnostic omens and the various prescription texts with numerous commentaries appended, there was no further medical literature in Babylonia and Assyria. The situation was the same in medicine as in other areas of science: knowledge formulated in terms of general principles was not deduced from the many individual observations which each doctor knew how to apply. Nor was there any physiological theory as was found among the early Greeks. For these reasons, narrow boundaries constricted ancient Oriental medicine despite all of its respectable achievements. At the same time, however, it attained an entirely unique position in the history of medicine.

9. Mathematics and Astronomy

Babylonian mathematics presents us with particularly difficult problems, because in many respects it is completely different from that of the Greeks and ourselves. In the early period, mathematics was determined by entirely practical demands, namely the measuring of fields and the necessities of administration, which already by the time writing was invented required quite complex means of reckoning. Because only a limited amount of fertile ground was available in Mesopotamia, land parcels had to be measured with great exactitude so that the land could be used to its best advantage. Not only were there rectangular and triangular parcels, but also some in the form of irregular polygons. In order that the area of such fields could be calculated, they had to be

32. See above, nn. 28-31; cf. W. von Soden, "Fischgalle als Heilmittel für die Augen," *AfO* 21 (1966): 81-82.

broken down into triangles and rectangles, once the boundaries had been measured and recorded. The sum of the areas of these simple figures was then the same as the total area. One Old Babylonian tablet, in a sketch not true to scale, depicts a field which had been divided into four rectangles, three trapezoids, and seven right triangles.[33] Moreover, even cubic entities, such as pits, walls, and the like, had to be calculated quickly, or at least estimated, so one could know how much material had been excavated, or how many bricks would be needed, or even how many workers were needed and for how long. The yields of the harvests had to be figured too, along with great quantities of livestock and fish, as well as payments in kind, often to thousands of workers.

While reckoning in Syria, at Ebla, and in Assyria was done primarily according to a numerical system based on ten, the Sumerians and Babylonians used mostly a sexagesimal system (one based on sixty), which had as its basic numbers 1, 10, 60, 600, 3600, 36,000, 2,160,000, and so forth, and as the reciprocals to this the fractional numbers $\frac{1}{10}$, $\frac{1}{60}$, and so forth. The smaller cardinal numbers originally had not only their own numerical names, but also their own numerical symbols which could be repeated for the multiples of these numbers and used in varying combinations. After about 2200, however, the numbers also came to be written in cuneiform signs, and, like other cuneiform signs, could not be allowed to exceed the normal height of a line. Thus, the vertical difference between the perpendicular wedge of the 60 and that of the 1 disappeared. Sometime later, this development provided the mathematicians with the occasion to retain only the broad, slanted wedge of the 10, and the vertical wedge for the (respective) 60-, 3600-, etc., multiples of 1 as well as the fractions of 1 ($\frac{1}{60}$, etc.). In this manner, a purely positional system of numerical writing was invented, as was later found in the decimal systems of the Indus valley, the Arabs, and our own. Since, however, no sign was employed which corresponded to our comma, the positional value of numbers with multiple places was not normally evident. Thus, a sexagesimal number such as 58 45 40 corresponded not only to the decimal numeral 208800 + 2700 + 40 = 211540, but also to the sixtieth multiple of the same, and so forth, as well as to $\frac{1}{60}$ of it, and so forth, inasmuch as no designation followed to make the numerical value clear. The Babylonians understood the prob-

---

33. Cf. B. Meissner, *Babylonien und Assyrien*, II: 390-91, including an accurate sketch, drawn to scale.

lem in such a way as to make a virtue of necessity, and thus to reckon with great sophistication without any unequivocal place value, since as far as they were concerned a protracted reckoning of the place value was of no concern in the case of the intermediate sums. Only the final sums had to be unequivocally identified. Moreover, within the sexagesimal system division by 3 and its powers always led to finite sexagesimal fractions which were more exact than the abbreviated, interminable decimal fractions of our system. In the case of the measures of length, area, and volume, as well as of weights, quite diverse multiples were used, since a very ancient measuring system had been adopted. For instance, the spatial measurement *bur* corresponded to 5400 = 18 × 5 × 6 × 10 *qa* (approximately 0.8-1 l.).[34]

The primary difficulty for reckoning in the ancient Orient was that one could work out addition and subtraction for very large numbers, but the same was not true of multiplication and division. This forced the Sumerians early on to prepare multiplication tables as well as reciprocal tables, because division could be conceived only as multiplication with the reciprocal of the divisor.[35] In addition, there were tables of powers and roots. Tables other than those necessary for calculation had been created at least by the Old Babylonian period, and these allow us to deduce a theoretical interest in the properties of numbers. Thus the number 225, which appears as the sexagesimal 3 45, was carried out to the tenth power, since there are unusually similar numerical series with this number. The tables of powers for the number 2 led a scholar through to 2^{30}, and then formed in addition the reciprocals to what is for us a ten-place number, which sexagesimally is an even longer numerical series. Such unusual tables could have no practical interest, but we have no indication of why someone would prepare them.

The situation was similar in geometry, which had grown far beyond the various practical purposes. Nevertheless, this discipline developed without formulated theorems, and a proof of a geometric fact was never attempted. People could work with the Pythagorean Theorem and

34. Cf. K. Vogel, *Vorgriechische Mathematik,* vol. II: *Die Mathematik der Babylonier* (Hannover, 1959), 15ff.

35. The dating of legal tablets is often scarcely possible if they contain only numerical signs, since these signs changed only negligibly since about 2000. [The standardization of the numerical signs prevents dating them orthographically, as one distinguishes between the Old, Middle, and Neo-Babylonian syllabic signs on the basis of orthographic variations. — Trans.]

even knew that there are Pythagorean triplets in considerable number, according to the equation $[a^2 + b^2 = c^2]$, in which every number is a whole number. One tablet arranges fifteen select triplets with predominantly high numbers, as for example the decimal $13,500^2 + 12,709^2 = 18,541^2$. As for how could someone have come up with this, there are a number of conjectures.[36] The starting point was naturally the basic triplet, $3^2 + 4^2 = 5^2$, which was easily ascertained by trial and error, along with its multiples (e.g., $6^2 + 8^2 = 10^2$).

The Babylonians of the period before and after Hammurabi added to these tables thousands of texts of mathematical problems, both with and without the accompanying computations. Individual tablets compiled up to 247 problems of similar type without computations. A part of these was algebraically formulated, and among these were multifarious problems pertaining to divisions of inheritances which never appeared in actual praxis. Some texts show that the Babylonians could work with arithmetic progressions. The geometric problems are of a quite diverse sort; many have to do with building construction and excavation, including military purposes such as sieges. Often, however, only the terminology is geometric, as shown by the addition of linear and quadratic quantities, among other things, and such problems are therefore to be understood algebraically. We would formulate many of them as equations, both linear and quadratic. Still, the Babylonians never formed an equation, though they could solve numerous algebraic problems notwithstanding and only rarely had to be satisfied with estimates, which could not be avoided in geometry through circular calculations. Almost all problems work with concrete numbers. It is only in rare instances that we find problems without such concrete numbers, in which we would insert general numbers or variables, such as a, b, and the like.[37]

36. Cf. Vogel, 37ff.

37. Vogel (with bibliography) and B. L. van der Waerden (*Science Awakening: Egyptian, Babylonian and Greek Mathematics* [Leiden, 1973]) offer brief but comprehensive presentations of Babylonian mathematics. The most important text editions with detailed compilations are O. Neugebauer, *Mathematische Keilschrifttexte I-III* (Berlin, 1935-1937); F. Thureau-Dangin, *Textes mathématiques babyloniens* (Leiden, 1938); O. Neugebauer and A. Sachs, *Mathematical Cuneiform Texts.* American Oriental Series 29 (New Haven, 1945); E. Bruins and M. Rutten, *Textes mathématiques de Suse* (Paris, 1961). Cf. also J. Friberg, *A Survey of Publications on Sumero-Akkadian Mathematics, Metrology and Related Matters* (Göteborg, 1982).

The completely unique phenomenon of Old Babylonian mathematics, whose achievement we can only sketch briefly here, has still not been satisfactorily interpreted, largely because this field is examined too one-sidedly, from the perspective of the history of methodology. Such a consideration is, of course, both necessary and indispensable, but it leaves open the decisive question: How is it possible that one form of mathematics, which was far more productive in its inception than Greek mathematics, developed without any systematic formulation of the knowledge of which it made such manifold use? It has often been maintained that oral instruction had supplied the principles of mathematics which cannot be found in any texts. If so, the intellectual structure of oral instruction must have been fundamentally different from that which had determined the form of the texts. This theory is made even less probable by the fact that other scientific texts contain no systematic formulations of scientific knowledge. Thus one comes with difficulty to the assumption that there was in Babylonia a nonverbal form of thought which was able to work quite efficiently without systematically formulated principles of knowledge, yet was never able to surmount certain limitations.[38] This conclusion stands in direct conflict with what passes everywhere else as almost certain knowledge. What these limitations signified is shown quite impressively by the fact that after the great advance of Old Babylonian period, Babylonian mathematics stagnated for a thousand years, and in all probability sharply declined in productivity. There are only a few textual witnesses that during this period mathematics remained a subject of instruction.

The most important witness for the nurture of mathematics in Babylonia and Assyria in the first millennium is astronomy. As has already been mentioned (see above, section 5), astronomy emerged from the study of astrology. Astrology played a totally subordinate role during the period when mathematics flourished, but it won increasing significance toward the end of the second millennium and thus necessitated a far more exacting observation of the stars than earlier. This development then led to the demarcation of a larger number of constellations; the so-called astrolabe divided thirty-six of these among the three circles of the gods Anu, Ellil, and Ea. Bicolumnar lists of stars showed in the usual indeter-

---

38. Regarding questions of the basic principles of Babylonian mathematics, which are still diversely evaluated, cf. my own works on Babylonian science, which also deal with mathematics; see above, n. 1.

minate manner the arrangement of fixed stars and planets with respect to one another. The series *MUL.APIN* ("Plow-star") uses complete sentences and explanatory relative clauses, and makes substantially more concrete pronouncements.[39] The sun, moon, planets, and fixed stars were even more carefully observed in the first millennium, and the high temples were often used in this endeavor as observatories (see below, XII.5c). In Assyria, whose kings had bestowed upon astronomy a quite unique position after the ninth century, the royal residence-city Calah was the center of astronomical observations. The new capital cities Dur-Sharrukin and especially Nineveh, with their observatories, came later. We know a great many astronomers by name from letters and from the numerous astronomic-astrological reports of the period after 700.[40] Drawings of noteworthy phenomena in the heavens were already being made at an early date; according to Ptolemy, lists of eclipses were kept after 747 with absolute precision. An initial result of this practice was that lunar eclipses could be reckoned with approximate accuracy after 700; previously these had been seen as signs of the wrath of the gods. The same was also true with the much rarer solar eclipses, as in the case of the total solar eclipse of June 15, 763 (see above, V.1). Nevertheless, the astrological texts often mention "untimely" eclipses that took place before they were expected. Thales of Miletus, however, was able to predict accurately the momentous solar eclipse of May 28, 585, on the basis of Babylonian series of observations. Otherwise, there were only sporadic astronomical calculations in the Assyrian period.

The beginnings of astronomical calculations in Babylonia, which could be tied to the great and as yet unquenched tradition of mathematics, may lie in the sixth century. Babylonian astronomy was comprehensively pursued until the Achaemenaean period, when Greek and Babylonian astronomers began to work together; it was developed

39. Cf. E. F. Weidner, *Handbuch der babylonischen Astronomie* (Leipzig, 1915) [only vol. I appeared]; *idem, Gestirndarstellungen auf babylonischen Tontafeln* (Vienna, 1967); H. Hunger and D. Pingree, *MUL.APIN: An Astronomical Compendium in Cuneiform* (Horn, 1989). More comprehensive are F. X. Kugler, *Sternkunde und Sterndienst in Babel*, 2 vols. with 2 supplements, and a third supplement by J. Schaumberger (Münster, 1907-1935); B. L. van der Waerden, *Science Awakening*, vol. II: *The Birth of Astronomy* (Leiden, 1973); F. Gössmann, *Planetarium Babylonicum* (Rome, 1950).

40. Cf. Parpola; R. C. Thompson, *The Reports of the Magicians and Astrologers of Nineveh and Babylon* (London, 1900); I. Starr, *et al., Queries to the Sungod* (Helsinki, 1990); H. Hunger, *et al., Astrological Reports to Assyrian Kings* (Helsinki, 1992).

further still in the Seleucid and Parthian periods. The Babylonians contributed to this process the series of observations, which extended in part centuries into the past, while the Greeks brought their ability for systematic thinking and the formulation of scientific and mathematical results as well as problems. Famous Babylonian astronomers even came to bear Hellenized names. Thus, the man regarded as the creator of System A of Babylonian lunar calculations, Nabû-rīmanni (about 500?) was also called Naburianos; later one finds Kidinnu (Cidenas) and Belussur (Berossos; about 300; see below, XIII.3b). Of course, the astronomical calculations were presented without any basic discussion, as typical in Babylonia. Therefore, if historians of astronomy often speak of Late Babylonian lunar or planetary theories, they nowhere refer to formulated concepts which can be deduced from the highly complicated numerical series found in the texts, and which the Greeks could have formulated in terms of a theory. The mathematical methods of the later astronomers far surpass those which the Old Babylonian algebra had been able to achieve. Presented in the form of a graph, the figures for the size of lunar eclipses result in "peaked curves." The cooperation of the Babylonian astronomers, some of whom emigrated to Greek territory, with their Greek counterparts was a development whose significance for scientific progress can scarcely be overestimated.[41]

Great advances in the practical aspects of the calendar accrued as a by-product of these astronomical calculations. The fact that there was no connection between day, month, and year which could be expressed in terms of whole numbers created problems all over the world. For the most part these problems could be resolved fairly well by provisional alterations in the nature of the calendar. For example, the Babylonians added an extra month, VIb or, more frequently, XIIb, to the twelve months of the lunar year as often as necessary, with the aim of equalizing the lunar and solar years. For centuries this was done from time to time only by special decree of the royal administration; corresponding directives are extant. The astronomers knew approximately seven hundred

41. Cf. Kugler; van der Waerden, *Science Awakening*, vol. II; also O. Neugebauer, *Astronomical Cuneiform Texts: Babylonian Ephemerides of the Seleucid Period for the Motion of the Sun, the Moon, and the Planets*, 3 vols. (Princeton, 1955). The astronomers published ephemerides, also called "astronomical diaries," for every year after about 700, along with subsections for each month; these also contain references to the weather and other news items. Cf. A. J. Sachs and H. Hunger, *Astronomical Diaries and Related Texts from Babylonia*, I-II (Vienna, 1988-1989).

intercalary periods for this kind of calendrical adjustment, which were never put into practice. After about 380, there was a nineteen-year period with eight leap years which produced a tolerable approximation of reality. For the purpose of simplifying calculations, astronomers often worked with twelve months of thirty days each. The names of the months from the Neo-Babylonian period were adopted at an early date by the Judeans, and later by the Syrians as well.[42]

42. Cf. S. H. Langdon, *Babylonian Menologies and the Semitic Calendars* (London, 1935); and H. Hunger, "Kalender," *RLA* V (1977): 297ff., with bibliography.

CHAPTER XII

Religion and Magic

1. Basic Problems

While only that very small circle of individuals who could read and write were able to take part in the sciences in the ancient Orient, religion and magic concerned everyone, though not in the same way everywhere. In this context it is not possible to distinguish religion and magic sharply from one another, since, just as in our sources, both permeate everyday life in too many ways. We must therefore reckon with this fact in the following treatment. Because all of our texts derive from professional scribes, many questions regarding the beliefs of the common people must remain unanswered. Still, thousands of private letters from Babylonia and Assyria provide in many respects a welcome supplement to the more formal literature, and certain issues can be deduced from the theophoric names. The abundance of materials here again forces us to turn our attention almost exclusively to the Sumerians, Babylonians, and Assyrians. Reference to Syria can be made only occasionally, since those sources are more meager and uneven.[1]

1. All collective works in the history of religion treat the religions of the ancient Orient, as do all discussions of culture (see works cited in ch. I, n. 2); the most exhaustive of these, though now superseded in many aspects, is M. Jastrow, *Die Religion Babyloniens und Assyriens*, 3 vols. with a portfolio of illustrations (Giessen, 1905-1913). Cf. also G. Furlani, *La religione babilonese e assira*, I-II (Bologna, 1928-1929); C.-F. Jean, *Le milieu biblique*, vol. III: *Les idées religieuses et morales* (Paris, 1936); É. P. Dhorme, *Les religions de Babylonie et de l'Assyrie* (Paris, 1949); T. Jacobsen, *The Treasures of Darkness: A History of Mesopotamian Religion* (New Haven, 1976); C. J. Gadd, *Ideas of Divine Rule in the*

The main stairway of the ziggurat of Ur, built by Ur-Nammu at the end of the third millennium. *(Jack Finegan)*

In Babylonia, we must attempt to see the fundamental differences between the religion of Sumerians, which was marked by even earlier religious concepts native to Mesopotamia, and the religion of the Semites. At the same time, in view of the syncretism which set in at a very early date, we must not overrate these differences. In many respects, then, this approach can be only moderately successful. For Assyrian religion, the Hurrians also attained considerable significance. The fact that in many ways religion is reflected differently in the monumental inscriptions than in the artistic depictions poses problems of particular difficulty, especially since in Mesopotamia the artworks are only rarely accompanied by inscriptions which have direct bearing on their contents. Thus, subjectivity is given quite a bit more play in the interpretation of pictorial testimony, for example, regarding myths. The result is that scholars express highly diverse interpretations of the central ques-

Ancient Near East (London, 1948); H. Frankfort, *Kingship and the Gods*, 3rd ed. (Chicago, 1978); N. Schneider and F. M. T. de Liagre Böhl in *Christus und die Religionen der Erde*, I, ed. F. König (Vienna, 1951), 383-498; J. van Dijk, "Sumerische Religion," in *Handbuch der Religionsgeschichte* I (Göttingen, 1971), 431-496.

tions of the history of religions (see above, VI.2). Such a brief presentation as this must therefore stick predominantly to the texts.

2. The Gods of the Sumerians

The essence of the Sumerian belief in the gods is very difficult for us to grasp, not least of all because our understanding of Sumerian religious texts still leaves much to be desired. For this reason, more than preliminary pronouncements on religion are, in many areas, impossible. The first thing that strikes one in the study of the texts themselves is the unusually high number of Sumerian gods and goddesses recorded in the god-lists (see above, XI.6), and which run to hundreds of names as early as the middle of the third millennium.[2] Their numbers grew even further in the Neo-Sumerian period, and the Sumerians themselves gave the certainly very exaggerated round number of 3600. How is it conceivable that people could believe that such a large number of deities was active in the small area of Babylonia, where divinities were always understood as entities of power? Several things are essential here. The sources show that the city gods were thought to have a princely state in which there were functionaries similar to those in the palace of an earthly city prince *(ensi)* — in other words, administrators of all sorts and even divine artisans. Thus, the terrestrial world was carried over to the primarily heavenly world of the gods, and to the gods were then ascribed functions varying in importance according to their respective rank in the world above. On the other hand, the city prince attained a special status as the earthly representative of the city's god (see above, VI.1).[3] Finally, all Mesopotamian deities had a human form; animal heads, such as those in Egypt, are found in texts and pictures only among demons.

It is illuminating that, when people had to put their trust in them, the gods could be more than merely the guardians of an order whose particular significance for the Sumerians is manifested in their one-dimensional science of ordering. Of course, the city deities included in the term "the great gods" were not always available without mediation, since they, as we will see later, had other functions, at least in the

2. Cf. A. Deimel, *Schultexte aus Fara* (Leipzig, 1923), 9ff.
3. Despite this fact, the translation which was earlier preferred — "Priesterfürst" ("priest-prince") — for the title *ensi* (one read then *Patesi*) is not accurate.

Neo-Sumerian period. Even the prayers of the city princes were first of all addressed to the tutelary gods of the family, and the subordinate deities functioned in this role for most people. According to the official theology, these lower deities stood in the service of the city gods, where they were no mere abstractions, but rather stood as the primary powers of welfare and, necessarily, as advocates before the great gods. This understanding is expressed most beautifully in the many thousands of cylinder seal carvings from the Neo-Sumerian and Old Babylonian periods. These show how the prayerful petitioner is led before the great gods by the tutelary deity; an inscription with the name of the petitioner is usually attached.[4] Underlying these scenes of introduction and their accompanying textual pronouncements is the notion that the tutelary deity alone cannot fulfill all the wishes of the petitioner.

The city gods often had simultaneously overlapping functions outside the districts of Babylonia, too. As the god of the heavens, An of Uruk (Unug) was the sky god, and the highest of the deities, followed by Enlil of Nippur (Nibru), the god of the atmosphere; both installed and deposed the kings who reigned over the city princes (see above, VI.1). Enki of Eridu had his abode in the groundwater table, called Apsu (Abzu), which made all life possible. Next to these three leading gods, the mother goddess stood as the guarantor of fertility for both humans and animals. She was worshipped under various names in numerous cities: as Ninḫursag in Kish, as Bau in Lagash, and as Nidaba, the goddess of scribes and grain, in Umma. Among the gods of the celestial bodies, the moon god, Nanna of Ur, was considered the father of the sun god, Utu of Larsam, while the shimmering form of Inanna, at once mother goddess, goddess of love and fertility, and goddess of war, had temples in Unug and Zabalam. As goddess of the herd, her sacred beast was the sheep. Among the other chief gods were the war god, Ningirsu of Girsu, who was worshipped at Nippur as Enlil's son Ninurta of Nibru, Dumuzi of Badtibira (see below, section 5b), and Shara of Umma. Whether some of the chief gods of northern Babylonia are to be regarded as originally Sumerian divinities still needs to be clarified. For the pre-Sumerian period, the numerous small figures of naked women point to an Inanna-type, and the bull refers to the moon god. The horns of the bull

---

4. We are have no comprehensive treatment of this group of cylinder seals. The same motif is found even more frequently on reliefs.

nonetheless became the emblem for all the gods. For the divinization of the king, see above, VI.2.

The gods of the Sumerians attained their power primarily because they had at their disposal certain powers of the natural order. Among these were the divine powers, including those for maintaining and protecting the cosmic and earthly order, which were in part thought of in objective terms but as a rule in terms of the abstract *me*.[5] Of scarcely less significance is the *nam*, which is generally translated according to the corresponding Akkadian term *šīmtu*, "fate, destiny," even though this far more comprehensive concept can hardly be translated, as shown by the compounds *nam-lugal*, "kingdom, monarchy," and *nam-dingir*, "divinity, godliness," and other abstract terms. The gods "cut" *(tar)* the fate or destiny *(nam)* not only for the creation, but also in the cosmos.[6] A further "numinous term for the order" is *giš-ḫur*, actually "design, plan," which can also be understood as the "conception(s)" of the gods. Moreover, the basic ordinances for the cultic sphere were also established by the gods. This is shown above all by *garza*, which can also designate a cultic office, *billuda*, a "cultic practice" or "custom," and of less significance, *šu-luḫ*, a "rite of purification." Since these terms are assigned to the gods outright, they may be regarded as distinctive in a particular way for the Sumerian religion.

3. The Gods of the Babylonians and Assyrians

a. Chief Gods of the Ancient Semitic Peoples:
Gods of Northern Babylonia in the Sumerian Period

We know nothing of the religion of the Semitic-speaking peoples prior to their immigration into the domains where — with the exception of South Arabia[7] — they later came into contact with other peoples and over time more or less borrowed from their religious notions. Since our

5. Cf. G. Farber-Flugge, *Der Mythos "Inanna und Enki," unter besonderer Berücksichtigung der Liste der* me (Rome, 1973), where the other terms for the created order mentioned in the following discussion are also briefly treated.

6. Verbs for "cutting," in connection with treaty, covenant, and oaths, are also used in Hebrew and Greek.

7. Cf. above, III.2; also H. Gese, M. Höfner, and K. Rudolph, *Die Religionen Altsyriens, Altarabiens und der Mandäer* (Stuttgart, 1970).

written sources do not begin until centuries after the presumed time of the Sumerian immigration, these almost always reflect a certain syncretism, which is impossible to analyze with any precision. All sources demonstrate with certainty, however, that the three gods of the main celestial bodies — the sun, moon, and Venus — are Semitic. It is strange to note in this regard that the moon god is always masculine but the sun god is more often feminine, particularly in South Arabia and to some degree in Syria. By contrast, the South Arabian Venus is a male deity (ʿAṭṭar). In Syria, ʿAshtart stands beside the male ʿAshtar, whom she later supplanted. The star gods were gods of the celestial bodies, but they were not the celestial bodies themselves; thus one can nowhere speak of an astral religion, not even in Babylonia itself.[8] Much more difficult to answer is the question of whether the storm god, who was venerated everywhere in Western Asia under various names, belonged to the most ancient of the Semitic gods. Apparently, the South Arabians did not know either him, a particularly distinct god of the heavens, or a goddess of the underworld (among their already few goddesses), even though he appears already in the Ebla texts under his ancient Semitic name, Hadad (Hadda). There and at other locales, the grain deity Dagān, the god of pestilence Rashap (later sometimes Resheph), as well as Kamosh (later in Moab, Chemosh) were widely worshipped alongside other deities with non-Semitic names. In comparison with Mesopotamia, the pantheon in northern Syria was small in the third as well as the second millennium, despite its heterogeneous origins. Since the Old Testament later always speaks of the individual gods of the neighboring peoples, we are led to conclude that the Semitic tribes and peoples venerated only a few deities at any given time, but ascribed to them correspondingly more power.[9] The majority of these deities were masculine, although goddesses were always present as well and had a great deal of importance for belief as well as for the cult.

The sources for the religion of the Akkadians in northern Babylonia first emerge in the period after 2500, when groups of Northeast

8. The term "astral religion," as applied from the time of the "Pan-babylonians" who succeeded Eduard Stucken (1865-1936) down to the present, is used in quite different ways, and this has led to many misunderstandings. The relationship of Babylonian divinities to the stars must be studied anew.

9. Cf. J. J. M. Roberts, *The Earliest Semitic Pantheon* (Baltimore, 1972). The Ebla texts were not known at the time; the readings of the names of some of the chief gods of Ebla (e.g., *NI.DA.BAL* [!]) have still not been explained.

and North Semites had been settled there for centuries. At first, however, these texts yield few results. Then around 2400 the Semitic *ilum* ("God, the god") begins to appear as a nearly exclusive theophoric element in proper names. Only later do we encounter in addition to this the ancient Semitic astral triad: Su'en, later Sin, "Moon"; Shamash, "Sun," with his consort Ayya; and Ishtar (Eshtar), "Venus." There are in addition some deities whose names cannot be explained with certainty, as above all the warlike Irra (Erra). In the inscriptions of the kings of Akkad, these gods often appear with Dagān, Nergal the plague god of Mars, and the war god Zababa (Ninurta) of Kish, as well as the cosmic triad of the Sumerians, Anu(m), Enlil, and Enki (Ea), as well as the mother goddess Ninkarrak. Thus, Enlil remained for the Akkadians the god who installed and deposed kings, and beside him stood the warlike Ishtar. In this way, some of the chief figures of the Sumerian pantheon entered the ranks of the ancient Semitic gods. The later Babylonian pantheon, however, stands in contrast to this. A similar phenomenon is observed in Mesopotamia at Mari. Not only were such other ancient Semitic deities as Abba, Lim, and the mother goddess Annunitum (Mama) worshipped there, in addition to Dagān and the weather god Adad (Addu), but also, as in the Early Dynastic period, some cosmic deities of the Sumerians who may have been regarded as essentially identical with Semitic gods.[10]

b. Babylonian Belief in the Gods: Syncretistic Theology

The increasing intermixing of the Akkadians and the immigrating Canaanites with the Sumerians which took place after 2000 even in southern Mesopotamia (see above, III.2a-b) led to a thoroughgoing transformation in the religion. To be sure, the tendency to merge into the Sumerian tradition continued, but too much of Sumer remained foreign, not least of all many of the myths of various origins regarding the divine combat. Thus, people searched for gods who combined care for maintaining the creation with provision for the individual, while at the same time not leaving these characteristics to subordinate tutelary deities. The distant god of the heavens, Anu (An), took on the features of a *deus otiosus* (god without duties). Enlil retained his significance for

10. The third millennium in Mari is very meagerly attested, and we know even less about the other districts north of Babylonia.

the realm of the state. Only Enki remained close to humanity as Ea, the god of wisdom. Besides the ancient mother goddess with her various names, there now emerged the consorts of the high gods as the goddesses of intercession and provision. Among these, Ningal, the consort of Sin (Nanna), was worshipped even in Syria. In Babylonia, Ayya, Tashmētu, and Sarpānītu, the respective consorts of Shamash, Nabû, and Marduk, were probably the deities mostly widely petitioned.

Among those Babylonian deities who simultaneously represented celestial bodies, the sun god Shamash, as god of law and justice, came to be much more widely venerated throughout the land in the Old Babylonian period than the Sumerian Utu had been previously. Together with the weather god Adad, he was the god of sacrificial divination (see above, XI.5). His father, the moon god Sin, receded in comparison, other than in nomenclature. Marduk, the god of the previously insignificant city Babylon, who was also associated with the planet Jupiter, experienced a sudden elevation with the rise of Hammurabi's dynasty, beginning in northern Babylonia and even extending beyond the official cult. Although in contrast with Shamash he was also a god of battle, like Shamash Marduk was disposed to help the individual. The function of the god of white magic was carried over to Marduk from the Sumerian Asalluḫi of Eridu, the son of Enki; thus, Marduk became the son of Ea.[11] Nabû of Borsippa, associated with the planet Mercury, was regarded as Marduk's son; in time he came to be primarily the god of scribes and scholars. Alongside Nabû came the plague god Nergal, who could also be accessible to the petitioner.[12] Enlil's son Ninurta, alone among the war gods of the Sumerians as the god of Sirius, remained a vital force apart from theology and cultus, and later attained even greater significance. Ishtar, goddess of the planet Venus, was for the Babylonians a peculiarly ambivalent figure. She was goddess of both fertility and slaughter, a benevolent mother and at the same time the tutelary goddess

11. Cf. W. Sommerfeld, *Der Aufstieg Marduks: Die Stellung Marduks in der babylonischen Religion des zweiten Jahrtausends v. Chr.* AOAT 213 (1982); H. D. Galter, *Der Gott Ea/Enki in der akkadischen Überlieferung* (Graz, 1983); F. Nötscher, *Ellil in Sumer und Akkad* (Hannover, 1927); H. Wohlstein, *The Sky-God An-Anu* (New York, 1976).

12. F. Pomponio, *Nabû* (Rome, 1978); E. von Weiher, *Der babylonische Gott Nergal.* AOAT 11 (1971). Monographs are still lacking on Sin, Shamash, Ishtar, and Ninurta, as well as on the various forms of weather gods. Cf. D. O. Edzard in *Wörterbuch der Mythologie*, I, ed. H. W. Haussig (Stuttgart, 1961), 19-139; C. Wilcke–U. Seidl, "Inanna/Ištar," *RLA* V (1976): 74ff.

of prostitutes, and not limited to her city of Uruk, which she had taken over from the Sumerian Inanna. Conversely, the maternal personality alone was embodied in Annunītu in the north, in Nanâ in Uruk, and in the goddess of healing Gula in Isin. No one expected anything good from Allatu (Ereshkigal), the ruler of the underworld. Several more deities were worshipped only in certain regions, or by members of particular professions.[13]

Most of the many hundreds of subordinate gods of the Sumerians lost their significance in this period, even as tutelary deities, but they were not forgotten by the theologians and at times not even in the cult. We have just seen that nearly all of the gods of the Semitic north had been identified with Sumerian divinities. At first that had happened without system and on an individual basis, as already on occasion among the Sumerians. It has become clear, however, that after the time of Hammurabi the theologians tried to bring the theological tradition into harmony with a starkly altered image of the divine. This was done on a grand scale, using the essential identity of Semitic and Sumerian gods to reduce increasingly more deities to mere hypostases, and thus reducing the total number of gods. The Semites could not imagine such a large number of powerful gods in such a limited area as Mesopotamia, nor could they fully comprehend the idea of the conception of order (i.e., that nature was the result of divine conception) which was determinative for the Sumerians. The syncretistic theology now made it possible to hold onto the tradition, while incorporating into it new concepts. This theology found its comprehensive documentation in the great bicolumnar god list (discussed above, XI.3), as well as in the concluding section of the Creation Epic (see below, XIII.3b), which refers only to Marduk and praises him under fifty new and different names. Reflection on the deities, however, did not cease with this list, which retained two hundred gods and even called into question the autonomy of many of the "great" gods. Thus in hymns, gods are made into representatives of particular characteristics of the god who is addressed or even, somewhat tastelessly, into his body parts. Behind this practice stood the widespread assumption that all historical divine names referred only to one god or one goddess, and that prayers were largely interchangeable. In the first millennium, however, people quite

13. Among these deities are Tishpak of Eshnunna, Ishtaran/Satran of Der, and the god of judges, Madānu.

often renounced names altogether and spoke only of "the god" or "the goddess," who saw and was able to see everything. Still, a denial of the existence of many gods was only very sporadically connected to this type of speech.[14] Therefore, it is better not to speak of monotheistic tendencies in Babylonia; rather, one should speak of monotheiotetistic tendencies, which amount to the doctrine of only a single divine nature represented by god and goddess.[15]

The Babylonians also adopted the notion of religious tolerance from the Sumerians, even with respect to the gods of neighboring peoples, which often were subsequently identified with their own. Some gods of the Kassites (see above, III.4a), such as the divine couple Shuqamuna and Shimalia, were called on frequently. Only Ashur, the god of the hated Assyrians, was bluntly rejected.

Although in the later period there were only isolated cases of city gods that were worshipped only in their own cities, the chief gods did retain a certain priority in their cities, and this fact finds particular expression in the nomenclature. Since Babylon remained the capital with brief interruptions even after the age of Hammurabi, Marduk was recognized as the king of the gods with the title Bel, "Lord." This was done in agreement with the Creation Epic, which ascribes to him two faces, as depicted in some images. But the cult of Nabû also was particularly widespread (see above), as is shown by the personal names. Attempts by individual kings to favor particular cults scarcely ever met with any success. That of the last king, Nabonidus, who tried to give priority to the cult of the moon god Sin, met with a harsh rejection and consequently led to his overthrow (see above, V.10). The Achaemenaeans made no attempts at converting the Babylonians. The Seleucids, however, demanded the identification of the Babylonian and Greek gods, for example, Marduk with Zeus. For the relationship of the gods to humans, see below, section 4.

14. In the eighth century an Assyrian wrote, "Trust in Nabû; trust not in another god!" Cf. Pomponio, 69.

15. Cf. K. L. Tallquist, *Akkadische Götterepitheta.* Studia orientalia 7 (Helsinki, 1938, repr. 1974), for the extensive interchangeability of the divine attributes; for the theology of syncretization, cf. W. von Soden, "Leistung und Grenze sumerischer und babylonischer Wissenschaft," *Die Welt als Geschichte* 2 (1936): 57ff.

c. Belief in the Gods and Political Religion in Assyria

The Assyrians worshipped primarily the same gods as the Babylonians, but did not always connect the same ideas with them. Other than a few royal inscriptions, our sources for the Old Assyrian period are scarcely more than the letters and documents from the trade colonies in Asia Minor.[16] These show us Ashur, the god of the city Ashur, as the leading god in other areas besides nomenclature. He is the god of the kings; one swears by him, and one prays to him even in personal matters. Beside Ashur stands Ishtar of Ashur, who likewise is invoked frequently. Anu is paired with Adad in Assyria, perhaps under foreign influence. Many other deities are named as well, among them Ea, Su'en, and Shamash, but the texts give little information on these. Occasionally one finds references to indigenous cults in Asia Minor.

The temporary subjugation of Assyria to the Hurrians and to Mitanni also led to many changes in the area of religion. The most important concerns the character of Ashur, who then became primarily the god of the state. As such, he promoted the expansion of Assyria, though he also remained a god for the individual. That changed after about 900, because Ashur had then become solely the imperial god, urging his kings to ever-wider expansion until the great empire of the Sargonids had been created. The subjugated were required to venerate him, somewhat in the way all Roman provinces were later required to respect the cult of the emperor. The subjugated provinces were not required to worship Ashur, however, and as a rule remained free to serve their own gods. The Assyrians themselves prayed mostly to the Babylonian deities, whose cult had gained increasing acceptance after about 1400. For political reasons there was for a long time considerable prejudice against Marduk, until sometime after 800 the sick in particular came to invoke him. The Assyrian kings allowed the legitimacy of their policies to be sanctioned by Shamash, while Ninurta, who had a great temple in Calah, became along with Nergal the god of war and of the hunt.[17] Nusku, the god of light, was a frequent object of petition as well.

16. Cf. H. Hirsch, *Untersuchungen zur altassyrischen Religion*, 2nd ed. Beihefte zur Archiv für Orientforschung 13/14 (Graz, 1972); K. L. Tallquist, *Der assyrische Gott* (Helsinki, 1932).

17. In the first millennium, the battle reports of Assyrian kings often refer to a great number of gods, not only Ashur, Shamash, and the war gods.

Next to Ishtar, Nabû played an indispensable, central role in both the official and private cults in the first millennium. The Hurrian ideas of god obviously had a powerful influence on the Assyrian religion, even though the names of Hurrian gods are not often mentioned. Thus, Shaushka lived on in the Assyrian Ishtar, and the Hurrian high god Teshup continued in Adad. Yet from the texts we learn hardly anything of the gods of the hundreds of thousands of deportees in the Neo-Assyrian Empire, apart from the nomenclature.[18]

4. God and Mankind: Sin and Ethics, Theodicy, Life after Death

In every religion, people expect help from the deity if they are unable to help themselves. Conversely, they are persuaded that the deity imposes demands on them and threatens penalties if they do not fulfill these. On the one hand, service to the gods by means of all kinds of cultic practices is demanded, and these will be treated below. At the same time, a type of behavior is demanded which serves the maintenance of creation, and here it is particularly a question of the relationship of person to person. Between these different demands there are, of course, serious shifts of emphasis, even in the religions of the ancient Orient.

The cult is frequently a central topic for the sources of Sumerian religion, but human guilt and its consequences are found much less. The most important concept which is pertinent to this discussion is *nam-tag*, "encroachment" (into the divine order) or "trespass" (of the same). One scribe saw King Lugalzaggesi's destruction of Lagash (see above, VI.1) as just such a trespass, and was of the opinion that his goddess, Nidaba, should let him bear his sin.[19] Individuals too could make themselves guilty of a *nam-tag* in manifold ways,[20] though at least

18. The royal inscriptions mention foreign gods only sporadically, e.g., those of the South Arabians or Urartians; treaties of state also required an oath by the gods of the other partner.

19. Cf. E. Sollberger–J.-R. Kupper, *Inscriptions royales sumeriénnes et akkadiennes* (Paris, 1971), 82, VII. According to an earlier translation, this sin was laid upon the goddess herself.

20. The delimitation of the various Sumerian words which contrast "sin" and "misdeed" has still not been clarified. Nor was there in all probability any special word for the penalty of sin.

the prevailing view was that guilt could play no determinative role in human fate. In the songs of lament over public catastrophes (see below, XIII.5b) the guilt of the concerned party hardly plays a role. One reason for this may be that too petty a significance was ascribed to human action to allow this to bring any essential influence to bear on the decisions of the great gods. Furthermore, it is particularly significant that the Sumerian spells against sicknesses and other forms of suffering do not say that the gods had given the person over to evil spirits on account of his or her sins. That pleas for forgiveness are lacking in these laments is conclusive, and one proceeded against demons with merely magical means (see below, section 6).

In the mythic poetry of the Sumerians, the gods not infrequently run up against their own established ordinances; in some cases offenses are punished by the assembly of the gods. Not much is different in the Babylonian myths: struggles between the gods are not disavowed in principle, but a settlement at the conclusion is the normal result; only some of the primeval gods, who took their stand outside the order, are ever handed over to death (see below, XIII.3c). Besides the depiction of the gods in the myths, however, another view gained increasing credence among the Babylonians after the time of Hammurabi. According to this view, there was no longer any room for clashes among the gods. This idea first comes clearly into view toward the end of the second millennium as a consequence of the conviction that, in the interests of maintaining the creation, the gods placed increasingly higher ethical demands on humans, whose disregard for these demands qualified as sin. In Babylonia and Assyria, however, there was no unified term for sin, but rather a number of words for sins of different weight, among which *arnu/annu* and *šertu* simultaneously designate the penalty for the sin. Even the venial sins *(egītu)*, however, remained sins in the eyes of the gods and, as all sins, required "redemption," or forgiveness on the basis of divine mercy. That a human being, despite every precaution — and that is essential — cannot find the right way through his or her own strength, and that the deity is free both to punish and forgive is one of the most significant perceptions of the Babylonians.[21]

21. Cf. A. van Selms, *De babylonische termini voor zonde* (Wageningen, 1933); H. Vorländer, *Mein Gott: Die Vorstellungen vom persönlichen Gott im Alten Orient und im Alten Testament.* AOAT 23 (1975); R. Albertz, *Persönliche Frömmigkeit und offizielle Religion: Religionsinterner Pluralismus in Israel und Babylon* (Stuttgart, 1978).

What constituted sin was generally determined at first and even later casuistically. Thereby, sin for a long time concerned only the proper bearing toward the gods and the basic rules of human morality, the keeping of which was certainly demanded as early as the Sumerians. Toward the end of the second millennium, the casuistry was sharply refined, as we learn from the oath series *Šurpu*, "burning" (see below, section 6, and p. 198, n. 42). This series is directed against the "ban" *(māmītu)* which separates one from the deity. In Tablets II and III are listed two hundred behaviors and omissions considered as sins; these include speaking differently than one thinks, engendering discord in the family, neglecting a naked person, killing animals unnecessarily, and many other things. Whoever judges himself by these confession-like enumerations and the many omens (see above, XI.5) cannot help but recognize that he daily makes himself guilty. One can only rightly conclude from this that the recognition of the sinfulness of all people grew out of this system. "Who has not sinned, who has not transgressed?" asks one penitent. Even unconscious and unrecognized sins, as well as those of one's ancestors, could weigh the individual down. If the gods would not forgive the penitent, that person was beyond help.

The gods did not always forgive, but punished also, in order to show that they were serious about their demands. The normal belief, like that in Israel, was that a proportional relationship existed between the suffering of a person and the weight of the sin; thus, the person who strove to maintain his or her integrity had to fare better than the evildoer. At the same time, one had to recognize that this notion did not always correspond to reality, that is, that the wicked often fared better than the righteous. The religions that hold to a belief in life after death reckon in such cases with a just settlement after death, on the basis of a judgment of the dead, as for example in Egypt. The dreariness of the underworld in which the Babylonians believed, however, allowed little hope for a better fate after death for those who had to suffer on earth. This was especially true since the oft-mentioned judges of the underworld apparently could only penalize the wicked with additional pain. By way of comparison, only the author of the Sumerian myth "Gilgamesh and Enkidu in the Underworld" (which is appended as Tablet XII of the Babylonian translation of the Epic of Gilgamesh; see below, XIII.3e) presents a more agreeable picture for some groups of dead, for instance, for the fathers of numerous children or those who have fallen on the field of battle. Yet he can promise no liberation from the underworld. An even worse lot than the underworld befell the unburied: they flew about as dead spirits and caused spiritual torment among the living.

Under these circumstances, one had to come to doubt the justice of the gods in the case of one who suffered without having committed grievous sin. This became even more true after about 1100, when for many Babylonians the solution provided by a true polytheism was no longer viable, namely that the sufferer had offended other gods by his appeal and because of their vexation had brought harm on himself. In the poem "I Will Praise the Lord of Wisdom," the author goes beyond the injustice of the gods and raises the possibility that humans often cannot know what the deity actually requires of them; it might be that one is sometimes made ill precisely by that which one, in ignorance of the true will of the deity, holds to be particularly good. Such considerations, however, provide no actual help for those who suffer the most. Thus the question of theodicy remained for Babylonian religion ultimately as unresolved as it did for Job in the Bible. The only thing that helps is to submit oneself to the will of the deity, as it manifests itself in one's fate as a sufferer, and to petition for deliverance from suffering, even when these pleas are so seldom answered. A dialogue from the time around 800 (see below, XIII.4c) presents us with two friends. One of these defends the traditional view and the other calls it into question with complaints against the deity, but finally gives up and resigns himself to his fate.[22]

The poems just mentioned were copied even in Assyria and in the later period in Babylonia, and thus are more than the expressions of solitary outsiders. As far as we know, no one ever got beyond these poems in considering the problem of the individual before God.

22. In addition to the works cited in n. 21 above, W. von Soden, "Das Fragen nach der Gerechtigkeit Gottes im Alten Orient," *MDOG* 96 (1965): 41ff. W. G. Lambert, *Babylonian Wisdom Literature* (Oxford, 1960), contains these texts.

5. Cults and Offerings:
Priests, Temple Servants, Prophets

a. Overview: Sources

So extensive are the written sources for the temple cult that they still have scarcely been surveyed, yet they give insufficient information for many areas. Documents of all sorts, including letters after 2000, preserve a great deal of material concerning the variety and number of priests, prophets, and other members of the temple, and this material still has not been exhausted. Further very important sources are the dedicatory inscriptions of the kings and many genres of religious literature. Cultic rituals, on the other hand, are still very rare in the Old Babylonian period and are not extant in large numbers until the first millennium; the same is true of Assyria. To these sources must be added many works of sculpture, great and small, particularly from the third millennium, which present scenes of sacrifice, along with the results of archaeological excavations of all sorts of sanctuaries. The remains of sacrificial animals and grain offerings are likewise found quite frequently in excavations, but these have not yet been comprehensively edited. Only a few references to this type of evidence can be made here.[23]

We are familiar with a great many details of the official cultus, set primarily in the great temples, but we know little of the basic ideas which were determinative for the cultic activities. One thing significant is that the deity had its second abode in the form of a statue in the temple or, in small sanctuaries, in the form of his symbol. Only a few were permitted to enter the inner sanctum as the holy of holies. The sacrifices served probably to provide food for the gods, who according to the myths ate just like humans. At all times a distinction was made between the normal daily or otherwise regular offerings and those instituted for particular occasions such as the great feasts, emergencies, or in celebration of joyful events. For such there was a rather abundant terminology. It is notable that animal sacrifices were brought on occasion as holocausts only in Assyria in the first millennium; otherwise, animal sacrifices were offered only for slaughter. Besides incense, oil and butter were the primary substances burned in the cult. Much specula-

23. Cf. G. Furlani, *Il sacrificio nelle religione dei Semiti di Babylonia e Assiria* (Rome, 1932); F. Blome, *Die Opfermaterie in Babylonien und Israel* (Rome, 1934).

tion is found in the later cultic commentaries over the meaning of particular practices; but one may not conclude too much from these, not even for their time. Even on the various categories of priests and other temple personnel we are only inadequately informed.

b. The Cults in the Sumerian Period: The Sacred Marriage

From the fourth millennium, before the Sumerians' entry into the land, we know of nothing but smaller temples which offered only limited space for cultic activities, and these were only slightly accessible because they were situated on steep terraces. As early as the time of the invention of writing around 3000, high terraces with steeply scarped sides were erected for some temples. In addition, however, there stood in Uruk a great, single-story temple of immense proportions (up to 80 × 50 m.), decorated with mosaics. Such temples, along with other buildings, comprised much greater complexes. Here rituals may have taken place with great masses of people participating. We can infer from many illustrations that processions were held even on boats, and these were most likely the predecessors of the later New Year festival. Following this golden age, the temple installations became much more modest again, and occasionally even rather poor, a situation which certainly necessitated less extravagant cults. We can further draw many details from the documents, among them quite comprehensive lists of sacrifices. The carvings of the so-called drinking scenes repeatedly portray cultic meals, certainly with the frequent participation of the city prince, and often even with his wife. In many sacrificial rites, a priest had to come naked before the deity, perhaps to demonstrate thereby his complete purity.[24]

Although all kinds of temple paraphernalia are left now, as, for example, incense stands, images of gods have only survived in isolated cases where they were not made of some valuable material. One custom was limited to the Early Dynastic period and is only rarely observed in the south. This was the practice whereby numerous men and women, and by

24. Cf. G. Selz, *Die Bankettszene . . . von der frühdynastischen bis zur Akkad-Zeit,* 2 vols. (Wiesbaden, 1983); A. Moortgat, *Frühe Bildkunst in Sumer* (Leipzig, 1935), pl. XI. For the temples, cf. E. Heinrich–U. Seidl, *Die Tempel und Heiligtümer im alten Mesopotamien.*

no means only the nobility, produced small stone figures of themselves in a praying position to be set on small benches along the walls of the elongated inner sanctum, so that these might always stand, or in some cases kneel, vicariously before the deity. Other miniatures show that there were cultic wrestling matches by which the otherwise naked wrestlers tried to bring one another to a fall by pulling by jerks on their belts.[25]

There were numerous temple feasts as well as those which were observed monthly with particular sacrifices, such as the èš-èš-day (Akk. eššēšum). There were also yearly festivals at different times to which exceedingly great offerings were brought. Gudea of Lagash presents for us in minute detail the feast of a temple consecration. On this occasion, work was halted for several days and the privileges of the higher orders, such as the right of meting out punishments of workers were suspended (for the festal days). Thus all became equal before the divinity; they celebrated happily and let no strife break out. Music was a necessity on such occasions.[26] The opposite of such celebrations were the great temple laments occasioned by catastrophes, during which very long musical compositions were presented (see below, XIII.5b).

Something quite unique was the festival of the Sacred Marriage, which in all probability was celebrated in only some of the cities; this has already been touched upon in connection with the divinization of the king (see above, VI.2). The god Dumuzi, or Ama-ušumgal-anna, was able to escape the fate of remaining in the underworld only if his sister Belili declared herself ready to substitute for him there half the year. Contrary to repeated assertions, there was in fact a mourning ceremony with extensive singing for Dumuzi on the day when the demons took him down into the underworld in place of his wife Inanna (see below, XIII.3c). There was, however, no joyous feast on the occasion of his annual return, not even in the later Babylonian period when the Dumuzi laments continued to be celebrated, even though they no longer actually fit into the

25. Cf. J. Renger–U. Seidl, "Kultbild," RLA VI (1981): 307ff. Cf. the works cited in ch. XIV, n. 1, on the art of the ancient Orient, for various sacrificial scenes from the third millennium and the praying statues; for cultic wrestling matches, cf., e.g., E. Strommenger–M. Hirmer, Fünf Jahrtausende Mesopotamien, pl. 46, 48.

26. Cf. A. Falkenstein in Falkenstein and W. von Soden, Sumerische und akkadische Hymnen und Gebete (Zurich, 1953), 137ff.

27. Cf. A. Moortgat, Tammuz: Der Unsterblichkeitsglaube in der alterorientalischen Bildkunst (Berlin, 1949); T. Jacobsen, Towards the Image of Tammuz; S. N. Kramer, The Sacred Marriage Rite (Bloomington, Ind., 1969).

later cult.[27] This cultic celebration was concerned with the maintenance and restoration of the fertility of everyday life.

c. Ceremonial Worship in Babylonia

An evaluation of the essential features of the transitional Old Babylonian period is still not possible. The primary reasons for this are that (1) fragments of cultic rituals are as yet known only from Mari, and (2) the many reports in the Mari letters themselves have yet to be edited. Of interest is the growing importance of the symbols *(šurinnu)* of the gods, for example, the significance of the spade as the later symbol of Marduk in lesser cultic activities. The symbols, among them astral symbols, occur on more recent carvings in place of the deities.[28]

The most important festival of several days' duration was the New Year's festival *(akītu)*. In many cities and from early on this had been originally celebrated in the autumn, and later came to be observed in spring. Later copies preserve in detail rituals, primarily from Babylon and Uruk.[29] In the course of the *akītu,* the image of Marduk was brought in great procession, part of the way aboard a ship, into the ceremonial house for the New Year's festival outside the city wall. This action prevented the honor of the deity from being injured during the necessary annual purification of the temple. This purification was tied to rites of atonement in Babylon, which the king, as the representative of his land, had to take upon himself. At this time he received a powerful slap to his face which was recognized as expiatory only if it brought tears (presumably from the pain). Besides prayers and cultic songs, the Creation Epic was recited in honor of Marduk (see below, XIII.3b, c). There was also a procession of visitation which brought Nabû of Borsippa to his father in Babylon and back. The festival proceeded quite differently in Uruk (for Ashur, see p. 195, n. 34). Cultic commentaries provide strange interpretations for many particulars which in part have influenced even modern scholars, with the result that they have not properly

28. Cf. U. Seidl, "Die babylonischen Kudurru-Reliefs," *Baghdader Mitteilungen* 4 (1968): 7-220.

29. Cf. F. Thureau-Dangin, *Rituels accadiens* (Paris, 1921), and further ritual fragments in newer text editions; S. A. Pallis, *The Babylonian* akîtu *Festival* (Copenhagen, 1926).

appreciated the purificatory and expiatory character of the festival, in which large masses of people sometimes took part.

Cultic ceremonies were carried out primarily on the ground floor of temples, in the first millennium massive structures with many rooms in the great cities. In the same sacral precinct (temenos), or nearby, lay the ziqqurat — the high, terraced edifice of the city god, whose much smaller temple was elevated atop several massive steps. The greatest ziqqurat was that built for Marduk of Babylon, which was 91.5 m. in breadth, length, and height. No temples are preserved, although the description of that in Babylon mentions a great bed and cells for some other gods. Precisely which ceremonies could be carried out exclusively in the high temple is still not clear; but the highest platform of the ziqqurat was certainly not generally accessible.[30]

Rites in which the priest of lament (kalû; see below, section 5e) was central were borrowed from the Sumerian period. Of these, the rituals which are preserved are primarily from Uruk, and prescribe predominantly Sumerian songs. The many private ceremonies for the purpose of healing sickness and deliverance from other evils will be treated below (see pp. 199ff.), although these were by no means determined primarily by magic. Burial ceremonies apparently had no great significance. There are only a very few texts of such rites, and the items sealed in the graves were as a rule modest (see below, section 5d, on the substitute offering). One text makes a very unusual pronouncement concerning the generosity of the deity toward someone who had regularly offered and prayed: "You give him a small grain, then your profit is a talent." One talent contained approximately 648,000 "seeds," each one weighing $\frac{1}{22}$ g.[31]

d. Ceremonial Worship in Assyria: Substitutive Offerings and the Ceremony of the Substitute King

From the earliest period, a tradition of temple building existed in Assyria in which the division of rooms diverged from the Babylonian pattern

30. Cf. H. J. Lenzen, *Die Entwicklung der Zikurrat von ihren Anfangen bis zur Zeit der III. Dynastie von Ur* (Leipzig, 1942); F. Wetzel–F. H. Weissbach, *Das Hauptheiligtum des Marduk in Babylon, Esagila und Etemenanki nach dem Ausgrabungsbefund, nach den keilschriftlichen Quellen* (Leipzig, 1938); Heinrich–Seidl.

31. Cf. W. von Soden, "Wie grosszügig kann ein babylonischer Gott schenken?" *ZA* 71 (1981): 107-8.

in many particulars. This divergence in part reflects different ceremonies. In Ashur there was, besides the main temple of Ashur with his ziqqurat, a double temple for Sin and Shamash as well, along with two smaller ziqqurats for Anu and Adad, an arangement which completely departs from the usual practice. The written sources from the second millennium, however, do not contain much pertinent information, although they are abundant for the period of the Neo-Assyrian Empire. Unfortunately, we have only an insufficient understanding of the important terminology from this period. Many deities often received sacrifice in the larger temples, although some of these even had their own temples. Contracts often required that the party breaking the contract lay an offering of penance on the knees of the deity; some contracts go so far as to demand the burning of one's own child before the god. At the same time, the child sacrifices attested for Syria-Palestine were not customary in Mesopotamia. We do not know whether such child sacrifices actually were presented.[32]

In Assyria, outside of the temple ceremonies, substitution offerings, usually of lambs, kids, or suckling pigs, were probably presented more frequently than in Babylonia. These offerings were supposed to move the gods of the underworld to renounce their claims on the sick. Many rituals for substitutive sacrifices were composed bilingually or even in Sumerian alone. Related to the substitutive offering was a ceremony which, to our knowledge, was only rarely performed. This was the practice of installing a substitute king (Akk. *šar pūḫi*), normally for one hundred days; this substitute king was supposed to draw onto himself all of the particularly evil omens, along with all of their consequences, which were threatened in the omen texts. A chronicle reports on one particular case early in the Old Babylonian period. According to this account, Erra-imitti of Isin had a certain Enlil-bani installed as the substitute king; subsequently, however, Erra-imitti was scalded with hot broth and died, so that Enlil-bani now could become his successor. Nonetheless, the aim of this rite, even according to the testimony of a partially preserved ritual, could only be achieved if the substitute king freed the actual king from the burden of the omens through his own natural or otherwise induced death. Our most important sources for

32. Since child sacrifices were offered in Syro-Phoenicia under special circumstances, the Assyrians could have borrowed the ideas for such sacrifices from the West, since they are not otherwise attested in any texts.

this ceremony are the letters from the twelve regnal years of the great king Esarhaddon of Assyria (681-669), who held an especial belief in omens because of his sickliness. Thus, he had a substitute king installed three times, each time having himself entitled "Mr. Farmer." One of the three substitutes died in a timely fashion; the two others had to be killed, and were then honored by a state burial. It is very strange that after 700 people were still (or again) of the opinion that one could divert the wrath of the gods onto any person whatsoever, just as if the gods would not see through the substitution.

In this matter, the ceremony presented a disguised human sacrifice; there may have been some parallels to this practice in ceremonies in ancient Asia Minor. The ritual of the substitute king affords particularly impressive evidence for the inner contradictions of the later ancient Oriental religions.[33]

e. Priests and Cultic Personnel: Cultic Prophecy

The languages of the ancient Orient had an extremely rich vocabulary for priests and cultic personnel. However, in view of the scant informative value of a great majority of the textual attestations of cultic functionaries, our understanding of this terminology remains inadequate. Modern presentations often designate as priests even employees of the temple who only carried out auxiliary functions; included in this group were those who were allowed to enter the temple, to whom certain privileges were due in return for their various services (on the relationship of trade to such positions, see above, VI.4d). The most generic word for priest, used in Assyria as a royal title, was Sumerian *sanga,* or Akkadian *šangû.* The priests who comprised "colleges" in the great temples, and who also functioned as temple administrators, often included in their number overseers and chief priests; there is as yet no incontrovertible testimony for the position of a high priest. In Old Assyrian documents we find instead of *šangû* the *kumrum.* The purification rites which were so important in the Babylonian temples were carried out by special

33. The ritual of the substitute king is discussed, with extensive bibliography, by H. Kümmel, *Ersatzrituale für den hethitischen König* (Wiesbaden, 1967), 169ff. Cf. also W. von Soden, *Religiose Unsicherheit, Säkularisierungstendenzen und Aberglaube zur Zeit der Sargoniden,* Analecta Biblica 12 (1959): 356ff.

priests such as the *išippu,* the *gudapsû,* and others. For offerings which did not require the shedding of blood, the "anointed" *(pašišu)* was frequently responsible. The *en*-priests and *en*-priestesses held an especially high rank down into the Old Babylonian period, and they played a leading role primarily in the ceremony of the Sacred Marriage (see above, section 5b). The *gala*-priests (> Akk. *kalû)* were particularly responsible for playing the cultic songs (see below, section 7) during the temple laments (see above, section 5b) and other ceremonies. The singer-priests *(zammeru)* held similar functions in the temples of Assyria, while the ever necessary musicians *(nāru, nārtu)* probably were not priests at all.[34]

In the temple of Shamash in Sippar, and less often in other temples, numerous women served in functions that were only partially priestly. Because they were normally childless, these women were called *nadītum* ("the fallow-lying").[35] Aside from these, there were female cultic personnel, primarily in the temples of Ishtar, such as the one at Uruk. There, cultic prostitution and the employment of male homosexuals (Gk. *kinaidos,* Lat. *cinaedus)* played a considerable role, and admittedly one which was not always free of controversy.[36] Some of these were involved in rituals which employed obscene expressions. Prostitution was probably used in the fertility ceremonies.

The readers of liver offerings (see above, XI.5), the interpreters of dreams, as well as the so-called incanters (see below, XII.6), probably did not belong to the actual temple personnel. In the first millennium, dream interpreters could support themselves on comprehensive collections of dream omens (see above, XI.5; cf. also the biblical Daniel, whose stories presuppose just such a background).

Cultic prophecy such as the Old Testament attests for Syria-

34. Cf. B. Menzel, *Assyrische Tempel,* 2 vols. (Rome, 1981), with bibliography and several texts; G. van Driel, *The Cult of Aššur* (Assen, 1959); S. Parpola, *Letters from Assyrian Scholars.* AOAT 5/1-2 (1970-1982).

35. Cf. R. Harris, *Ancient Sippar, passim.* The *nadītum* had a special place in the rights of inheritance.

36. No comprehensive study is yet available. Inscriptions of the kings Merodach-baladan II and Nabonidus of Babylonia, as well as the Erra myth (see below, XIII.3c), contain references to a type of revolution in Uruk around 765, during the reign of the king Eriba-marduk. This revolution was not caused by social conditions alone, but rather was directed against the cultic practices of the temple of Eanna and the cult prostitutes there; it had only temporary success.

Palestine did not exist in Babylonia. There, as in Assyria and Asia Minor, the gods manifested their will to people through many kinds of portents. Nonetheless, we know two significant exceptions. In the first case, the Old Babylonian correspondence archive of Mari attests a type of cultic prophecy for Mesopotamia and parts of northern Syria. The prophet and prophetess, designated either as ecstatics *(maḫḫûm, maḫḫūtum)* or as respondents *(āpilum, āpiltum)*, often did not belong to the temple personnel of the gods Adad and Dagan, but could instead be laypersons who primarily directed messages or exhortations, mostly concerning the cult or politics, to the king. Persons who were not previously known were tested by magical means regarding their credibility, but it was left up to the king whether he wanted to draw conclusions from the prophetic words. Resonances with biblical prophecy can occasionally be recognized, though in contrast to Israel ethical demands were scarcely uttered in the form of threatening speeches. One may suppose that in the cultic prophecy which the Old Testament condemns, extremely ancient Canaanite traditions lived on.[37]

Cultic prophecy in Assyria after 700 was of a completely different type: here there were male "callers" *(raggimu)* and still more female "callers" *(raggimtu)* in the service of Mullissu of Ashur and Ishtar of Arbela; most of the sayings of the latter which were held to be significant were recorded in tablet collections. We have a partial knowledge of some of these from the time of Esarhaddon, often in colorful language. The sparse witnesses are insufficient for a proper description of the later prophets, whose predecessors are still unknown. It appears, however, that after 750 a prophetic movement that first became evident in Israel — cf. the prophet Amos of Judah! — temporarily swept great areas of Western Asia.[38]

Certain so-called prophecies which stem from the first millennium and draw abundantly from the omen texts to comprise oracles of both

37. Since many pertinent Mari letters remain unpublished, no comprehensive study of cultic prophecy in Mesopotamia has yet been published for the period of the Mari kingdom. Cf. the preliminary study by F. Ellermeier, *Prophetie in Mari und Israel* (Herzberg, 1968); W. J. Moran, "New Evidence from Mari on the History of Prophecy," *Biblica* 50 (1969): 15ff.; E. Noort, *Untersuchungen zum Götterbescheid in Mari.* AOAT 202 (1977); J.-M. Durand, *Les textes prophétiques.* Archives épistolaires de Mari I/1. Archives royales de Mari 26/1 (1988), 377-442.

38. The oracles of salvation, often preserved only in fragmentary form, and evidence of letters for the male and female "callers," have never been collected and comprehensively treated. Cf. attempts at translation by R. D. Biggs in *ANET,* 604ff.

judgment and salvation (for instance, for Babylon or Uruk) are only stylized as prophecy. Insofar as these contain concrete information, they are for the most part rightly classified as "prophecies after events," though in some cases they do inform us of particular problems.[39]

f. Purification in the Cult and in Magic

Purification rites played a central role among all the rites in the ancient Orient. Their purpose was to dispose first of all of the manifold external pollutions, and in addition to these the inner impurities as well. These rites were just as necessary in the temple cultus as in private ceremonies and in the palace, but were especially critical in magic. The primary means of purification was water, using flowing waters wherever possible, and then other liquids and oil. Moreover, many kinds of plants and mineral substances were thought to bring purity. Often these had to be soaked in liquids and were applied externally or, in the case of the sick, internally. The rituals quite frequently use words meaning to purify (Akk. *ullulu; tēliltu,* "purification"), wash (*mesû; mīs qātē,* "to wash the hands"), and bathe (*ramāku; rimku,* "a complete bath"). Many rituals of purification are collected in the tablet series *bīt rimki* ("bathing house)" and, for those cases that demand a ritual exclusion, *bīt mēseri,* "house of exclusion."[40] Privacy very often is required, and in most cases very precise instructions are given, in order to ensure the complete purification of the "impure" who have been exposed to the demons.

The daily purification rites and the annual purification at the New Year festival (see above, section 5c) took place in the temples. The *išib > išippu*-priest is often designated as responsible for these purifications. The consecration of temples, the dedication of cultic paraphernalia for sacral use, and the erection of statues of the deities required special rites of purification. The latter required the "mouthwashing" (*ka-luḫ-ù-da, mīs pî*) frequently demanded elsewhere and, in later rituals, the addi-

39. Cf. R. Borger, "Gott Marduk und Gott-König Šulgi als Propheten: Zwei prophetische Texte," *Bibliotheca orientalis* 28 (1971): 3ff. P. Höffken, "Heilzeitherrschererwartung im babylonischen Raum," *Die Welt des Orients* 9 (1977): 57ff.

40. For both series there are only partial editions, which in the meantime have been partially superseded by new fragments which have come to light. Cf. J. Laessøe, *Studies on the Assyrian Ritual and Series* bīt rimki (Copenhagen, 1955). R. Borger is planning a complete edition, beginning with *bīt mēseri.*

tional rite of the "opening of the mouth" *(pīt pî)*, without which the idol is only dead matter and, for example, "cannot smell." The "opening of the mouth" was also necessary after repairs to the image.[41] Many aspects of the purification ceremonies, which played a major role in Assyria as well, are still in need of special investigation. The purification of persons who have sinned is a dominant theme of many prayers.

6. Magic, Demons, Evil Powers, Sorcery

There are two major forms of magic: black magic, which brings harm to people, and white magic, which seeks to turn away the harm caused by demons, malevolent powers, and humans. Black magic was practiced in many forms in the ancient Orient. Nevertheless, instructions for its practice were never written down (although the opposite is sometimes asserted), because a written record of the demons and persons involved could be used against the very one who had concocted the evil spell. Therefore, the massive amount of magical literature preserved in cuneiform texts addresses only white magic. Nevertheless, black magical activities are often described with great precision in the introduction to the white magical incantations. Thus we know rather precisely what forms of harmful sorcery the Sumerians and Babylonians believed themselves threatened by on a daily basis.[42]

The languages of the ancient Orient know no collective term for "demon"; they employ either the word for "god" or designations of distinct groups of demons. The Sumerians, Babylonians, and Assyrians used some words for demons individually, or in some cases for good genies who held stations comparable to an angel.[43] Thus, besides the evil

41. Cf. E. Ebeling, *Tod und Leben nach den Vorstellungen der Babylonier*, I (Berlin, 1931), 100ff., with bibliography.

42. Cf., e.g., B. W. Farber, *Beschwörungsrituale an Ištar und Dumuzi* (Wiesbaden, 1977); also, the ritual tablets on the incantation series *Šurpu* — "Burning" — against spells (see above, p. 186, and E. Reiner, *Šurpu: A Collection of Sumerian and Akkadian Incantations* [Graz, 1958, repr. 1970]) and *Maqlû* (see below, n. 45), as well as many rituals cited in the texts in H. Hunger and E. von Weiher, *Spätbabylonische Texte aus Uruk*. Magic is extensively treated in books on cultural history (see above, ch. I, n. 2) and religions (see above, n. 1). Magical texts have also been found in Ugarit.

43. Cf. R. C. Thompson, *The Devils and Evil Spirits of Babylonia*, 2 vols. (New York, 1976).

udug demons, the Sumerians also knew a good *udug* (Akk. *utukku*), while in Akkadian *šēdu* could be both a protective spirit and a demon, and a *rābiṣu* could be a spy for both good and evil. Otherwise, the demons of the Sumerians, among whom *dimme* and the storm demon *líl* could be masculine and feminine, display little of their own profile; the majority of them, including the dead spirit (*gidim* > *eṭemmu;* see above, section 4), could be lumped together as the "evil seven." There were even special incantations against the "storm maiden" (*kisikil-lilla;* Akk. [*w*]*ardat lilî*) and against *dimme*. As Lamashtu, the child-murdering demoness of the cradle fever, *dimme* became among the Babylonians and Assyrians the most colorful figure of the demons. Many amulets show her as a mixed-form creature with a lioness's head and hanging breasts. *Dimme* was combatted primarily with preventive rites and sympathetic magic.[44] It is already reported in an Old Assyrian incantation that she was the daughter of Anu, the god of the heavens. Because of her evil behavior, Anu threw her out of heaven and down to the earth. Of all demons it is said that neither doors nor geographical barriers can prevent their harmful activities, which spare not even the animals. Some, such as "those who decide fate" — the *nam-tar/namtaru* — are simultaneously demons of the underworld who attack even the dead. The Sumerians did not see the attacks of the demons as the penalty for sin. Among the Babylonians, however, one finds the idea that the gods have indeed given people over to the demons on account of their sins (see above, section 4). Thus, the Babylonians required prayers with pleas for the forgiveness of sins, as well as the magical rites which had largely been adopted from the Sumerians, for defense against demons and the nullification of the evil that they worked. Finally, the "spell" (see above, section 4) often becomes the personification of demons, along with many sicknesses.

In combatting the demons, the Sumerians refused to trust those magical rites carried out by humans. For the depiction of the evil activities of the demons, many incantations present a dialogue between the god Enki and his son Asalluḫi, who corresponds to Ea and Marduk in Akkadian texts. This dialogue follows an essentially stock format, in which the son requests help from the father against the demons, but receives the answer that the divine son can do the same as the father,

---

44. Cf. W. Farber, "Lamaštu," *RLA* VI (1983): 439ff.; also S. Lackenbacher, "Note sur l'*ardat lilî*," *RA* 65 (1971): 119ff., with supplements by von Weiher, in Hunger–von Weiher, no. 7.

Ea (Enki). Individual instructions then follow the dialogue; these are hardly specialized and end with such established incantation formulas as "by heaven let it be sworn, by earth let it be sworn."[45]

In addition to the invisible demons in the air were those people who, by means of black magical practices, sought to bring harm to their neighbors. The Sumerians called them $uš_{11}$-zu, "connoisseurs of slander" = Akk. kaššāpu, "warlocks," and kaššaptu, "witches"; before about 1000 only the latter are attested. The incantations and the prayers similarly employed were composed for the most part in Babylonian and are found mostly in the series Maqlû, "burning." Of course, it may not be extrapolated from the title of this series that witches and warlocks would have been burned; but besides the magical destruction of witch images, only burning belonged to the rites for warding off their spells. Only a fragment of a single letter indicates that certain women were accused of witchcraft, and we hear nothing of witch trials.[46]

A priest, designated lú-mumun or lú-maš-maš by the Sumerians, (w)āšipu(m) or mašmaššu by the Babylonians, was responsible for reciting the Sumerian and Akkadian incantations and for carrying out the attendant rites. Since this same priest often recited prayers (see below), the translation "incantation priest" for this word is occasionally disputed today and replaced by "ritual technician."[47] Many rites, in fact, were not magically defined and consisted only of a sacrifice; in the case of the poor, a handful of meal sufficed. At any rate, one must keep in mind that not all rites fell to the designated priest, especially not the actual temple rites (for the prayers of the genre "lifting up the hands," used to designate incantations, see below, XIII.5c). No appropriate word exists which would properly characterize the activities of these men in the service of the individual. Many incanters were also physicians (see above, XI.8) and also prescribed medications. We learn important details about them, along with the names of known āšipu-priests, from the letters.[48]

45. Cf. A. Falkenstein, Die Haupttypen der sumerischen Beschwörung literarisch untersucht (Leipzig, 1931); the bibliography now needs to be supplemented extensively. Editions of the most important bilingual incantation series are in preparation.

46. Cf. G. Meier, ed., Die assyrische Beschwörungssammlung Maqlû. AfO Beiheft 2 (Berlin, 1937); in addition, much supplementary material exists today; W. G. Lambert, "An Incantation of the Maqlû Type," AfO 18 (1958): 288ff.

47. Cf. W. Mayer, Untersuchungen zur Formensprache der babylonischen "Gebetsbeschwörungen" (Rome, 1976), 59ff.

48. Cf. Parpola, passim.

Detailed studies are still lacking for the magical substances these men employed, such as plants, minerals, parts of animals, and liquids, as well as their preparation, since too much about the terminology is still unclear; important individual observations can be found in the secondary literature.[49]

Many rituals had to do with the protection of those who suffer, and not with their healing, and among these the rites to assist birth are especially important. A mythical story, according to which the moon god Sin had stood by one of his sacral cows while she was giving birth, is frequently inserted into the rituals; therefore a woman might request his aid during a nocturnal birth.[50]

7. Death and Burial

No one can outrun Death, for Death has a great lead on people: even the heroes of the primeval age had to experience this (see below, XIII.5d). When Death meets the individual, Fate makes the decision. All pray to the gods for a long life and that they may not thus have to die too early on account of their sins. To be sure, Death does not entirely extinguish the individual human: one continued to lead a shadow existence in the underworld.[51] As a mortal could only live on through his or her children, this was constantly requested in prayer. A few, particularly kings, could also live on through the notoriety of their deeds. The word for the dead, Akk. *mītu,* could also be used for the sick who had been consecrated to death. One of the two words for body, *pagru,* designated the human corpse and the animal carcass.

49. Cf. Farber, *Beschwörungsrituale an Ištar und Dumuzi;* and D. Goltz, *Studien zur altorientalischen und griechischen Heilkunde* (Wiesbaden, 1974); also R. C. Thompson, *A Dictionary of Assyrian Botany; A Dictionary of Assyrian Chemistry and Geology.*

50. A critical, comprehensive edition of these rituals and of the myth of the cow, which is preserved in several Sumerian and Akkadian recensions, is not yet available; cf. J. van Dijk, "Incantations accompagnant la naissance de l'homme," *Or* 44 (1975): 52ff. [Sumerian], with occasional bibliographic citations; W. G. Lambert, "A Middle Assyrian Medical Text," *Iraq* 31 (1969): 28ff. [Akkadian].

51. See above, section 4, with reference to the somewhat better fate of those who have fallen on the field of battle; see further the collection of lectures, *Death in Mesopotamia,* ed. B. Alster. Mesopotamia 8 (Copenhagen, 1980), which also discusses mortuary offerings. The killing of gods is spoken of in certain myths (see below, XIII.3b).

Since the unburied person had to float through the air as a dead spirit (see above, section 4), everything had to be done to lay the dead to rest (very often with his seal). The children and other relatives bore the primary obligation for this, and for bringing mortuary offerings *(ki-sè-ga/kispu)* for a period of time. Adopted children were bound by contract to this same service, and to mourning the dead.[52] As has been mentioned already (see above, section 5c), the earthen graves were almost always simple, and the generally few votive offerings were supposed to help the dead into the underworld. Individual details of burial customs varied according to land and period, and one frequently finds double chamber graves. Stone sarcophagi are only rarely attested in Babylonia (see above, VI.2, for the "royal cemetery" of Ur); in Assyria these were somewhat more common, though primarily for the kings. Sarcophagi with sculpted reliefs in all probability appeared for the first time in Anatolia and Syria after the Hittite period.[53] Precious votive gifts laid in the graves, sometimes of gold, are attested for the third millennium in Babylonia (Ur and Kish), as well as in Asia Minor; in some cases these have remained intact, though most have been lost to grave robbers. The genre of the dirge is best known to us through the lament of Gilgamesh for his friend Enkidu, and professional singers of laments, both male and female, were often hired. On grave inscriptions, see below, p. 207, n. 3.

52. Cf. J. Bottéro, "Les morts et l'au-delà dans les rituels en accadien contre l'action des 'revenants,'" *ZA* 73 (1983): 153ff. There are no certain witnesses from Mesopotamia or Babylonia-Assyria for the practice of cremation, which was customary among the Hittites. Cf. E. Strommenger, B. Hrouda, and W. Orthmann, "Grab," "Grabbeigabe," "Grabgefäss," *RLA* III (1971): 581ff.

53. Monumental structures over graves comparable to the pyramids of Egypt are not attested even for kings. At the beginning of the second millennium, from Shulgi of Ur until before the time of Hammurabi, numerous kings were venerated as gods (see above, VI.2); sometimes these kings were even interred in the sanctuaries. The focus here is not on cults of the dead, but much is still disputed; cf. P. R. S. Moorey, "Where Did They Bury the Kings of the IIIrd Dynasty of Ur?" *Iraq* 46 (1984): 1ff.

CHAPTER XIII

Literature

1. Overview: Tablet Series; Prose and Poetry

Literature is a narrower term than written material, and in the field of cuneiform therefore does not include the several hundred thousand letters and documents of all types. Within the area of literature in Babylonia and Assyria, the "scientific" writings, in the widest sense of the term, present the most comprehensive sector; this type of literature was discussed in depth in chapters XI and XII. Individual verses from poetic compositions are found primarily in commentaries, where they are quite often quoted and briefly explained (see above, XI.3). Prayers and incantations are often recorded in their entirety. More frequently, however, the beginning line is cited and must represent the missing title of a work.

Extensive poems, especially many myths and epics which could not be recorded on a single multi-column tablet, were spread over as many as twelve tablets and thus, at least formally, comprised series similar to the larger scientific works. The division into tablets was usually determined in advance. Since the end of a tablet always came at a break in the contents, only in exceptional cases did the partial tablets encompass the same amount of material. Shorter compositions, such as hymns and prayers, were not collected in series with a fixed number of tablets, but were only compiled on larger tablets from case to case. For the voluminous royal inscriptions, see below, section 2.

Literary works other than the royal inscriptions were composed predominantly in a stereotypical language in which the ends of lines

203

and verses usually coincided. Even today, we are in no position to distinguish with certainty between poetic and prose compositions, or to recognize in any reliable way prose sections in verse compositions. The attempt to analyze poetic rhythm in Sumerian poetic compositions is only in its inception, and we cannot tell whether this will ever meet with any success. We can do somewhat better with the Akkadian, even if the dominant assumption until now — that in Babylonian as in Hebrew poetry, it was always only a question of the number of accented syllables, since there was no basic principle governing the number of unaccented syllables between them — has not always proven to be true. Therefore, in order to recognize an actual rhythm we must first of all come to know the pronunciation and accentuation of individual words in the vernacular much more precisely than is now possible for us regarding the ancient Orient. Even with very careful study of the manner in which words and groups of words were written, we are often unable to get beyond working hypotheses which enable us to understand much, though not all, of the material. In all languages, even if in quite different degrees, words are shortened so that they can fit into the poetic rhythm. This is done either by omitting vowels or by adding emphasis through a clearer accentuation of open syllables with short vowels. Neither technique is always evident in written texts. On methodological grounds we do well if we reckon as little as possible with altered word forms and shifts in accents in the verses. At the same time, we cannot always determine how often we may do that, so that considerable room is left to our discretion. Thus many are of the opinion that attempts to recognize the poetic rhythm have too little chance of success to be significant. It is my view, however, that those chances are not so negligible and that the study of poetic form can contribute much to our understanding of the nuances of many expressions. Even in other fields of knowledge there is no way around assumptions which are not borne out later, and the correction of initial errors still yields much essential knowledge.

In a great portion of the Babylonian poems of the second millennium one can establish no quantitative meter by counting syllables over alternating verse lengths. According to our terminology, the iambic ($\smile$-), trochaic (-$\smile$), and amphibrachic ($\smile$-$\smile$) metrical feet alternate with one another in quite variant ways. The triptych predominates in narrative, while verses composed only in diptych lend particular emphasis to pronouncements. Two verses generally form a double-verse on the basis of what is usually an antithetical parallelism or, more rarely, a tauto-

Bearded man, possibly the Sumerian mythic hero Gilgamesh (3rd millennium), wrestling with two bulls. Limestone libation vase from Uruk. *(Trustees of the British Museum)*

logical parallelism. Without exception, the rhythmic and syntactical units are concealed by a trochaic conclusion. The strophes comprise four to twelve verses and only rarely more, or by counterstrophes only two. The verse structure of much later poetic compositions, such as the great Gilgamesh Epic and a great number of prayers, sharply departs from the older form, often in the preference for longer verses. In contrast to earlier works, there now appear to be as many as three unaccented syllables — or even none at all — between two accents. In addition, we must reckon with the possibility that, just as in many of our own songs, the strength of the accents varied, especially in the quite popular musical delivery of poetry, and that the accentuation was often quite different from its merely spoken recital.[1]

2. Royal Inscriptions

The inscriptions of kings and, less frequently, other functionaries can only be regarded as literature if they offer more than the very brief enumeration of building projects or campaign reports. The great mass of these are shorter or longer building inscriptions which sometimes also record dedications. Such inscriptions are introduced either through the designation of the god or gods for whom the building was built, and include hymnic attributes. They can also open with the self-introduction of the ruler, with brief or more extensive titles and the subsequent mention of the deities. Occasionally, an invocation of the god stands at the beginning. In the conclusion, blessings are quite often invoked for those who restore the edifice, and curses are called down upon those who neglect it. In more lengthy building inscriptions, the description of the building process itself as a literary form can go beyond the common format of the building report. Generally people were satisfied with an elevated prose using a somewhat freer word order, and in every case rhythmically metrical language can be found here and there. The inscriptions of the Chaldean kings offer particularly detailed building descriptions, in several cases with historical retrospectives. These inscriptions often replace the usual blessing and curse formulas with prayers to the god to whom the structure is commended.

The second major category of royal inscriptions, the reports of

---

1. Cf. W. von Soden, "Untersuchungen zur babylonischen Metrik, Teil I," *ZA* 71 (1981): 161ff., with references to earlier works by H. Zimmern and others; also "Teil II," *ZA* 74 (1985): 213ff. For bibliography, cf. the works cited in ch. I, n. 2; and ch. XII, n. 1, which treat the history of culture and religion; cf. also, e.g., J. Krecher, E. Reiner, "Sumerische . . . bzw. Die Akkadische Literatur," in *Neues Handbuch der Literaturwissenschaft: Altorientalische Literaturen,* ed. W. Röllig (Wiesbaden, 1978), 101-210 (with bibliography); R. Labat, *et al., Les religions du Proche-Orient, textes et traditions sacrées* (Paris, 1970). *ANET,* 3rd ed., is the most comprehensive work to date. Literary texts are only rarely dated. On the basis of the writing (as long as not dealing with later transcriptions), language, and various other internal indicators, approximate datings are nonetheless frequently possible, though these are seldom exact.

wars and conquests, is found in Babylonia in only a minority of inscriptions. In the Sumerian period, for example, these come almost exclusively in the late Early Dynastic period, and particularly fully in the vulture stela of Eannatum of Lagash. Eighty to one hundred years later, Uruinimgina uses this medium to delineate his manifold social reforms instead. Conversely, the campaign reports in the Sumerian and, more frequently, in the Akkadian inscriptions of the great kings of Akkad from Sargon I to Naram-Sin are again extensive. In the Old Babylonian period only a few kings, among them those of Mari, give brief campaign reports. Hammurabi says in the poetic introduction to his law stela only what he later accomplished for the cities he had conquered; the curse formulas at the conclusion are unusually comprehensive. After 1500, we find campaign reports from only a few Babylonian kings, who describe particular actions. Normally, one was satisfied with very brief references to victories over enemies, but without supplying any names: the actions of the gods, and of the king on behalf of the gods, were supposed to be given the primary emphasis.[2] A unique text is the grave inscription which Nabonidus dedicated in 548 to his mother, Hadda-ḫoppe, who died at the age of 103. Here the mother herself speaks at length.[3]

From a literary standpoint, the Sumerian sacral and building inscriptions on the statues of the ruler Gudea of Lagash (see above, V.4) present an exceptional case. In these Gudea speaks of himself as "he," as was customary in Lagash even earlier, and he has adopted many expressions from religious texts. The great building hymn, recorded on two or three multi-column clay cylinders, is unique. It includes many theological reflections as well as a detailed account of the dedication festival following completion of construction of the temple. Little here has been borrowed from the usual building reports.[4]

2. Cf. D. O. Edzard and J. Renger, "Königsinschriften," *RLA* VI (1980): 59ff.; A. Schott, *Die Vergleiche in den akkadischen Königsinschriften* (Leipzig, 1926); P. R. Berger, *Die neubabylonischen Königsinschriften* (626-539 a. Chr.), I. AOAT 4/1 (1973), 1-125: "Die literarische Gestalt der 'neubabylonischen' Königsinschriften."

3. Cf. C. J. Gadd, "The Harran Inscriptions of Nabonidus," *Anatolian Studies* 8 (1958): 35-92. His mother lauds her own piety before the moon god Sin; afterward Nabonidus depicts the funerary rites. The small number of grave inscriptions which are otherwise extant is treated by J. Bottéro, "Les inscriptions cunéiformes funéraires," in *La mort, les morts dans les sociétés anciennes,* ed. G. Gnoli and J.-P. Vernant (Cambridge, 1982), 373ff.

4. For the building hymn, cf. A. Falkenstein and W. von Soden, *Sumerische und akkadische Hymnen und Gebete* (Zurich, 1953); no more recent translation of the statuary

In Assyria, moreover, there are building inscriptions in which political themes are completely overlooked or resonate only on the periphery. The primary inscriptions of the conquering kings increasingly enlarged and elaborated the depiction of battles and conquests after about 1300, so that the building report often appears as no more than an appendix to the campaign reports. By the time of the Neo-Assyrian Empire, the building report was often omitted completely, and several kings even tell of their hunting expeditions. The long inscriptions were most often written on great stone tablets or clay prisms, which could hold up to six, eight, or ten columns and as many as 1,300 lines. If we overlook some kings between 950 and 725 who mainly preferred a very dry style for their reports, the style of these inscriptions was highly polished and in some battle reports could even be gripping. Despite the many conventional formulations, various kings, particularly the Sargonids, revealed elements of a personal style (e.g., sometimes impressive portrayals of nature or technical details by Sennacherib). Frequently the campaigns were not ordered chronologically, but rather according to other criteria, such as geographical considerations or others less easily discernible. In special cases, extremely detailed initial reports of particular campaigns were composed for and dedicated to the god Ashur. These, too, were literarily demanding presentations.[5] Occasionally the governors of larger provinces had inscriptions composed in the style of the royal inscriptions.

The royal inscriptions in other lands of the ancient Orient are to be distinguished from those of Assyria and Babylonia not only by their language, but in many respects by their structure and style as well. That is as true of the Hittite inscriptions as it is of those from Urartu, for the Elamite as well as for the often trilingual inscriptions of the Achaemenaean kings, and for the Phoenician and Aramaic inscriptions.[6]

---

inscriptions is available. For other Sumerian inscriptions, cf. E. Sollberger–J.-R. Kupper, *Inscriptions royales sumeriénnes et akkadiennes,* with bibliography.

5. Cf. R. Borger and W. Schramm, *Einleitung in die assyrischen Königsinschriften,* pts. 1-2 (Leiden, 1961-1973); Schott; A. K. Grayson, *Assyrian Royal Inscriptions* (Wiesbaden, 1972–; two volumes to date, still lacking the Sargonids).

6. No literary treatment of these groups of inscriptions is available yet.

3. Myths and Epics

a. Some General Questions: Historical Epics

Myths of the gods, which narrate stories of the gods and from which people could extract answers to important questions with respect to their own times, are often much older than the written versions of the myths. However, it is only rarely possible to draw more than speculative conclusions about the preliterary myths from the poetic accounts. Occasionally, remarkably original forms of the myths are briefly narrated in the context of other texts; but the bulk of poetic myths are reflective myths, which transformed the ancient mythic traditions according to certain basic themes and even enriched the earlier myths with new episodes. Most of the creation myths belong to this category. These are concerned not only with the creation of the world, life, and important implements, but also with the ordering of the world following often arduous struggles against the powers of a primeval chaos. Besides these myths there are also somewhat comprehensive poetic myths, which are tied to earlier traditions only in small part or not at all. These can be called "constructed myths," since the entire treatment has been constructed only loosely on the basis of earlier mythic poetry, and has been fleshed out using contemporary mythological schemata. In some cases impressive mythic poems could emerge through this process. It is not accidental, then, that the name of the author often appears in such poetic compositions, whereas the earlier poetic myths considered the author to be unimportant to the essential message and thus were unconcerned to name an author. In fact, anonymity is typical for the greatest portion of literature throughout ancient Mesopotamia.

In addition to those myths in which only gods and demons take part, there are those in which semi-divine heroes, or even humans, play important roles. In such myths, historical reminiscences continue to exist, at least to some degree. Not until after about 1400 did historical events — those of the distant past as well as those only a few years past — become the objects of epics with expressly political intent in Assyria and Babylonia. Small fragments are generally all that remain of these.[7] We possess larger portions from a poem which concerns the events in the last years of the Kassite dynasties and which from a Babylonian

---

7. Cf. A. K. Grayson, *Babylonian Historical-Literary Texts* (Toronto, 1975).

perspective depicts and laments the horror ascribed to the Elamites.[8] By contrast, an Assyrian poet of the thirteenth century sings in eight to nine hundred long verses of the great success of Tukulti-Ninurta I in his struggles against Babylonia. He wrings out victory with the help of the gods, who have been enraged by the crimes of the Babylonians. As in the great majority of the royal inscriptions from Assyria, the language is a dialect of Babylonian colored by Assyrian.[9]

b. Myths of Creation and the Ordering of the World: The Deluge

As far as we know, the Sumerians never treated the theme of the creation of the world in a great mythic poem. We do know their ideas from the introductions to dialogues concerning disputes in rank (see below, section 4b). According to these, the separation of heaven and earth took place at the very beginning. The further course of events involved differentiations. Thus people, who had originally lived as animals, became a special type of creature. Because there were the sick, the crippled, and the helpless elderly, one myth traces these back to a dispute over a contention between Enki and the mother goddess Ninmah.[10]

There are various ideas of creation and theogony among Babylonian myths. The Old Babylonian myth of Atrahasis, which is associated with the name of Nur-Ayya as the author or scribe, offers the most carefully thought-out presentation. By the later period this myth had been transformed several times and even came to presuppose another myth of theogony.[11] The myth of Atrahasis begins with the

8. Cf. A. Jeremias, "Die sogenannten Kedorlaomer-Texte," *Mitteilungen der Vorderasiatischen-Ägyptischen Gesellschaft* 21 (1917): 69ff. (somewhat antiquated).

9. An edition of these has been announced by P. Machinist. For earlier partial editions, cf. W. G. Lambert, "Three Unpublished Fragments of the Tukulti-Ninurta Epic," *AfO* 18 (1957): 38ff.

10. Cf. C. A. Benito, *"Enki and Ninmah," and "Enki and the World Order"* (diss., Philadelphia, 1969).

11. Cf. W. G. Lambert, *Atra-hasis, the Babylonian Story of the Flood, with the Sumerian Flood Story by M. Civil* (Oxford, 1969); W. von Soden, "Die erste Tafel des altbabylonischen Atramhasis-Mythus, Haupttext und Parallelversionen," *ZA* 68 (1978): 50ff.; *idem,* "Konflikte und Ihre Bewältigung in babylonischen Schöpfungs- und Fluterzählungen: Mit Teil-Übersetzung des Atram-hasis-Mythos," *MDOG* 111 (1979): 1ff.

words, "When the gods were [simultaneously] humans," in other words, when the types "god" and "human" had not yet been differentiated. At that time, the weaker group of gods, the Igigi, had to perform by themselves all of the works of irrigation and drainage which were necessary for life in Mesopotamia. They finally became tired of the work, went on strike, and threatened the ruling Anunnaki. Immediately before a struggle could break out, a solution was reached: it was agreed that humans should be created to do this work. Enki and the mother goddess then worked together to create the first human from a mixture of clay and the blood of a god, "who possessed the sense to plan." Rites of birth were then established. Twelve hundred years later, however, the humans had become too numerous and restless, and they had even acquired for themselves forbidden wisdom. Therefore, the gods decided to decimate them by pestilence and plagues. Enki (Ea) then advised the humans to withhold prayers and sacrifices from most of the gods, while turning only to one god in particular, so that he would hold the plagues in check. The god did this, but after twelve hundred years more the same thing recurred, and again a third time, with the same result.

At the summons of Enlil, the gods then came to the decision to exterminate humanity again, this time through the Deluge. The Sumerians already knew the myth of the Deluge, though the sole literary form of this of which we have even limited knowledge first emerged only in the Old Babylonian period, and was probably influenced by a Babylonian poem. The story in the Atraḫasis myth agrees in the order of events, at some places even in wording, with the story of the Flood inserted into the Gilgamesh Epic some five hundred years later. According to both compositions, the god Enki (Ea) betrays the plan of the gods to a reed hut, in which Atraḫasis (called Utnapishti in the Gilgamesh Epic) is sitting. As soon as this is done, the idea comes to this man to build a cube-shaped ark for his family and all species of animals, but he is not allowed to share the reason for his actions with his fellow humans. Then the masses of water break in upon the land from above and beneath; all life drowns, and only the ark is borne up on the waters, and finally lands on Mt. Nisir after the waters have receded. The gods are confounded by what they have caused, but they come to the sacrifice that Atraḫasis offers. Enlil, who has caused the debacle, is at first wroth that some of the humans have been saved, but then desists and transfers Atraḫasis (Utnapishti) and his wife to an island far to the west, where they enjoy life without death. The children of these two become the progenitors of the new humanity, which will never again be given over to an extermination such as the Deluge. Hereafter, only the guilty shall be punished. The differentiation between gods and humans, with its fearful consequences, will now be superseded by a new, well-thought-out solution that is fair for all.[12]

The creation epic Enuma Elish ("When above") first appeared in the fourteenth century, and was designed to establish Marduk as king of the gods. A very brief theogony stands at the beginning of this account. Tiamat, the goddess of the seawaters, is the first to rise from the primeval chaos with her husband Apsu, the god of the groundwater. Thereupon follow further generations of gods, just as in other ancient myths of theogony. Anu, the god of the heavens, appears as the great-grandson of Tiamat and Apsu, and as the ancestor of other gods. After Anu comes Nudimmud (Ea) with his consort Damkina. Awakened by the younger gods, the old Apsu wants to kill them, but is himself killed by Nudimmud (Ea), who uses magic and erects his own palace upon the groundwaters. There the divine marvel-child Marduk is born, and by his riotousness he arouses the old Tiamat as well against the young gods. Tiamat then commissions her "paramour" Kingu to raise an army of all kinds of monsters against the gods. The young gods then turn to some older gods with a plea for help, but when these refuse, they turn to the young Marduk, who agrees, on the condition that they make him king of the gods. This happens and Marduk, using special weapons, kills the dragonlike Tiamat and takes Kingu prisoner. Then Marduk creates the heavens and the earth from the two halves of Tiamat's body and, following this, stars, plants, and other living things. Last of all, Marduk even creates humans from the blood of the rebel god Kingu and, as everyone knows, forces them to work for all time. After founding Babylon and its temple Esagila, the gods hold a victory celebration for themselves and exclaim in laudatory fashion the fifty names of Marduk; the epic gives an explanation for each of these which partially rests on an etymological wordplay. The great struggle between the gods is mitigated here: only three gods are killed, but after their deaths they are integrated into the new order of the world in various ways. This epic in seven

12. Since the child-murdering demon Pashittu (Lamashtu) is given her place in the order, some hold that the struggle against the possibility of the overpopulation of Babylonia is an essential motif of the poem; however, the idea of overpopulation is found nowhere else in this period.

tablets[13] became the cult legend recited every year at the New Year festival in Babylon (see above, XII.5c). The Assyrians under Sennacherib substituted Ashur for Marduk in the epic. Berossus later propagated a reshaped version of the epic in his Greek *Babyloniaka* (about 300).[14] Direct influences of the Babylonian creation epic on the biblical account of creation cannot be discerned.

c. Clashes and Struggles between Gods

A few references must suffice for myths in this category, which deal with struggles against powers which are at enmity with the created order. Among these, the Sumerians and Babylonians counted the tales of the mythic eagle Anzu. This figure once stole from the gods the tablets of destiny, which are indispensable for their rule, and was then met in combat by the battle gods Zababa or Ninurta, where Anzu was killed.[15] Not adopted by the Babylonians were certain myths in which the great gods appear in somewhat too negative a role. To these belong the myth of "Enlil and Ninlil." According to this story, the young Enlil seeks out Ninlil as she bathes, lies with her, and begets the moon god Su'en. Because Enlil has now become "unclean," though not for moral reasons, the great gods banish him from Nippur. He nonetheless lies with Ninlil three more times in various disguises and thus begets more gods. The accompanying liturgy simultaneously pronounces Enlil as lord.[16]

According to the myth "Inanna and Enki," Inanna robs the

---

13. There is no edition of the epic based on all extant textual witnesses; the translation of E. A. Speiser and A. K. Grayson in *ANET,* however, takes almost all of them into account (pp. 60-72, 501-3). It is also possible that Tablet VII did not belong to the original stock of the epic.

14. Cf. P. Schnabel, *Berossos und die babylonisch-hellenistische Literatur* (Leipzig, 1923); S. M. Burstein, *The Babyloniaca of Berossos* (Malibu, 1978), including a translation.

15. Cf. B. Hruška, *Der Mythenadler Anzu in Literatur und Vorstellung des alten Mesopotamien* (Budapest, 1975); W. W. Hallo and W. L. Moran, "The First Tablet of the SB-Recension of the Anzu-Myth," *JCS* 31 (1979): 65ff. The name of the demon was earlier read as Zû.

16. Cf. H. Behrens, *Enlil und Ninlil, ein sumerischer Mythos aus Nippur* (Rome, 1978); S. N. Kramer, *Sumerian Mythology* (New York, 1961), 43-47. The relation of Enlil to Ninlil is treated by another, no doubt later, myth in a completely different fashion and not so offensively.

drunken Enki of the strength of his *me* (see above, XII.2) and then flees to Uruk (Unug). Enki sends demons after her to bring back the *me*, but without success. Finally, he himself comes to Uruk and gets back the *me*, thanks to the mediating action of Enlil.[17] Inanna also seeks to seize another's property in the myth "Inanna's Descent into the Underworld," which was translated into Akkadian in abbreviated form. As she passes through each of the seven successive gates of the underworld, the goddess must one by one lay aside all of her divine vestments and garments until she comes to stand, naked and defenseless, before her sister Ereshkigal, the ruler of the underworld, who imprisons Inanna in her realm. Since all fertility ceases on earth as a consequence, Inanna's lady-in-waiting Ninshubur, after numerous vain attempts, finally succeeds in getting Inanna to leave the underworld on the condition that someone else takes her place there. This substitute turns out to be Dumuzi (see above, XII.5b).[18]

A later Babylonian myth is found in two versions which diverge from one another. This myth is meant to explain why the god of the planet Mars, Nergal or Erra, at one and the same time is god of the heavens and of the underworld. According to the earlier version, Ereshkigal, the ruler of the underworld, demanded that the heavenly assembly of the gods send Nergal down to her realm, on account of his improper treatment of her messenger. Have entered the underworld, Nergal then overpowers Ereshkigal and thus, as her husband, becomes king of the underworld; at the same time he retains his place in heaven.[19]

One myth concerning an epic struggle of a particular sort is *Lugal u[d] melam-bi nergal* ("The King, the Radiance, whose Gaze is Princely"). This myth begins by hymnically presenting Ninurta, the god of Sirius, and his dangerous enemy, the great demon Asag, who has engendered a huge number of different stones. Asag subjugates ever more lands to himself, so that Ninurta becomes furious and, against the

---

17. Cf. D. Wolkstein and S. N. Kramer, *Inanna, Queen of Heaven and Earth* (New York, 1983), 11-27; G. Farber-Flügge, *Der Mythos "Inanna und Enki"* (Rome, 1973).

18. For the Sumerian version, cf. S. N. Kramer, *JCS* 5 (1951): 1ff., and *ANET*, 52-57. The Akkadian version is extant in two recensions, and was probably composed by Sin-leqe-unnini, the author of the Gilgamesh Epic; cf. R. Borger, *Babylonisch-Assyrische Lesestücke*, 2nd ed. (Rome, 1979), 95ff., with bibliography. For the translation, see E. A. Speiser, *ANET*, 106-9; Wolkstein–Kramer, 51-89.

19. Cf. E. von Weiher, *Der babylonische Gott Nergal*. AOAT 11 (1971): 48ff.; H. Hunger–E. von Weiher, *Spätbabylonische Texte aus Uruk*, no. 1.

warning of his divine weapon Shar-ur, attacks. Against Asag's colossal power, however, he can do nothing and is defeated. Despite renewed warnings from Shar-ur, Ninurta attacks again and likewise fails, but is saved by Shar-ur. Shar-ur warns Ninurta a third time, but this time Ninurta defeats the demon, rests, and then celebrates his victory. Now transpires the great judgment on the stones, the offspring of Asag: those who fought on the side of Asag are condemned to lowly service, for example as grinding stones. The others (either thirty or thirty-two out of forty-nine) receive the right to be made into statues and other valuable objects. The god then returns to Nippur. Blessings for the king (originally Gudea of Lagash?), along with doxologies, stand at the end of the 729 verses.[20] Another myth sings primarily of Ninurta's return to Nippur following a great victory.[21]

d. Heroic Sumerian Myths:
Enmerkar, Lugalbanda, Gilgamesh

The heroic myths of Sumer are woven primarily around the early dynastic kings of Uruk, Enmerkar, Lugalbanda, and Gilgamesh (earlier Bilgamesh), who were later divinized. The poetic myths about Enmerkar and his son Lugalbanda focus on conflicts between the kings of Uruk and of central Iran and the city Aratta. In the Enmerkar myth, Inanna comes to the aid of her king against Aratta when she brings the enemy land into dire straits by causing a drought. The Anzu bird, here portrayed as a good demon, plays a considerable role in both of the Lugalbanda poems. Parts of these epics were provided even later with interlinear translations into Akkadian.[22]

Gilgamesh stands at the focal point of five Sumerian poems. One of these, "Gilgamesh and Agga of Kish," is apparently based on historical events: Agga had besieged Uruk and had gained recognition for his

20. Cf. J. van Dijk, *Lugal ud me-lám-bi nir-gál: Le récit épique et didactique des Travaux de Ninurta, du Déluge et de la Nouvelle Création*, I-II (Leiden, 1983); part III is forthcoming.

21. Cf. J. S. Cooper, *The Return of Ninurta to Nippur: an-gim dím-ma*. AnOr 52 (1978).

22. Cf. S. N. Kramer, *Enmerkar and the Lord of Aratta* (Philadelphia, 1952); C. Wilcke, *Das Lugalbandaepos* (Wiesbaden, 1969); the second Lugalbanda poem has still not been completely edited.

sovereignty without a battle.[23] The other poems are concerned with the search for eternal life and fame through deeds; in these one finds, besides Gilgamesh, his retainer Enkidu. "Gilgamesh and the Land of the Living" portrays the campaign of the heroes with fifty men against Ḫuwawa (elsewhere Ḫumbaba), the demonic guard of the cedar forest. In spite of Ḫuwawa's pleas for mercy, he is killed with the help of the sun god Utu. "Gilgamesh and the Bull of Heaven" is poorly preserved, but no doubt had an end similar to the same episode in the Babylonian epic. "Gilgamesh, Enkidu, and the Underworld" narrates how Gilgamesh lost certain important objects, and then had Enkidu retrieve them from the underworld. However, since Enkidu despised the taboos of the underworld despite repeated warnings, he was not allowed to return. This poem was added to the Babylonian epic in translation. The Babylonian epic, however, did not adopt the badly preserved myth, "The Death of Gilgamesh," according to which the hero was accepted after his death as one of the gods of the underworld.[24]

e. Babylonian Myths of Those Who Searched for Eternal Life: Gilgamesh, Etana, Adapa

The sagas about Gilgamesh still had not been compiled into a single Akkadian poem during the Old Babylonian period; yet the extant epics from that time, although they are only preserved incompletely, do show a completely new impress in comparison with the earlier form. After 1400, there were in Syria-Palestine and Asia Minor Babylonian, Hittite, and Hurrian versions of the Gilgamesh poem. On the basis of the meager remains of these versions we can conclude that they represent very free imitations of the original Babylonian forms.[25] Then around

23. Cf. W. H. P. Römer, *Das sumerische Kurzepos "Bilgameš und Akka."* AOAT 209/1 (1980).

24. Cf. A. Falkenstein, "Gilgameš A," *RLA* III (1969): 357ff. A. Shaffer is preparing a comprehensive edition of the Sumerian Gilgamesh poem; part is included in Shaffer, *Sumerian Sources of Tablet XII of the Epic of Gilgamesh* (diss., Philadelphia, 1963). Cf. partial translations by S. N. Kramer, *ANET*, 50-52; for the pertinent literature until 1974, see *HKL* III: 60-61.

25. Cf. F. M. T. de Liagre Böhl and H. Otten, "Gilgameš B.C.," *RLA* III (1968): 364ff. A Hurrian-Hittite bilingual text was recently found at Hattusas. Cf. H. A. Hoffner, Jr., *Hittite Myths* (Atlanta, 1990).

1100, a person listed as Sin-leqe-unnini of Uruk composed the twelve-tablet epic of about three thousand verses as the most fully developed form of the material. Nevertheless, the scribes of the first millennium did·not hand on this text without alteration in every detail.[26]

The epic begins by praising the 9.5 km. city wall of Uruk, for whose construction Gilgamesh had imposed upon the inhabitants a heavy burden of forced labor. In order to hold this hero in check, the gods created as his counterpart the wild man Enkidu, who grew up among the wild animals but was led to Uruk by a cult prostitute, where he immediately confronted Gilgamesh. The struggle between these two ended with Gilgamesh and Enkidu declaring their mutual friendship and together planning and undertaking the battle against Ḫuwawa (Ḫumbaba) in the cedar forest (see above). After a long, difficult trek, and with the help of Shamash, they were victorious. Upon their return, Ishtar offered Gilgamesh her love, which he bluntly rejected with reference to her behavior toward earlier lovers. Ishtar then pleaded with her father Anu that she might have the Bull of Heaven in order to avenge herself. The Bull plunged many men in Uruk into deep pits with his snorting, but was then killed by the two friends. During the victory celebration Enkidu insulted the goddess so grievously that the gods ordered his death. The premonition of death, final illness, and the actual death of Enkidu are narrated along with the insertion of many dreams, which are presented in detail along with their interpretations, just as in the expedition against Ḫumbaba. Likewise, there is the dreadful pain of Gilgamesh, who is unable to save his friend.

Now Gilgamesh himself experiences the anxiety of death and sets out to the far west, to learn from Utnapishti, the hero of the Deluge (see above, section 3b), how he might escape death. The journey, which ran underground in some stretches, led him to the kindly pair of scorpion people, the ale-wife Siduri and the ferryman Urshanabi. They are

---

26. A translation of the barely preserved parts of the later epic and the most important Old Babylonian poems, with bibliographical information, introduction, and summary of the contents of the Sumerian poem, is given by A. Schott and W. von Soden, "Das Gilgamesch-Epos," *Reclams UB* 7235 (Stuttgart, 1982). Current editions of the twelve-tablet epic need supplementation and incorrectly arrange many of the fragments of the poorly preserved Tablets III-V and VII (most recently, R. C. Thompson, *The Epic of Gilgamesh* [Oxford, 1930]). Cf. also E. A. Speiser and A. K. Grayson in *ANET,* 72-99, 503-7; H. Schmökel, *Das Gilgamesch-Epos* (Stuttgart, 1966); K. Oberhuber, *Das Gilgamesch-Epos* (Darmstadt, 1977), a collection of essays in the series *Wege der Forschung;* J. Tigay, *The Evolution of the Gilgamesh Epic* (Philadelphia, 1982).

good to Gilgamesh, and Urshanabi brings him across the waters of death despite the ban. These meetings are portrayed in detail, with much repetition. Utnapishti relates to Gilgamesh the story of the Deluge, after which the gods gave him the gift of life without death. When Gilgamesh fails a test of sleep, Utnapishti advises him to retrieve the herbs of life from the bottom of the sea. Gilgamesh does that and starts back, but along the way he carelessly allows a serpent to steal the herbs of life, whereupon the serpent immediately sheds his skin. At this point, all becomes futile; Gilgamesh resignedly returns to Uruk, and on his arrival proudly shows the city walls to Urshanabi, who must ferry him back to mortal humanity in accordance with the ban. The epic adds as the twelfth and final tablet the translation of the Sumerian poem of "Enkidu and the Underworld," which gives a completely different portrayal of the death of Enkidu from that in Tablet VII.[27]

The Gilgamesh Epic has become one of the great works of world literature by virtue of its unique style of composition, by which the greater human concerns (e.g., the friendship between males) are given repeated expression. Members of lowly professions, moreover, such as prostitutes and ale-wives, appear as representatives of a special degree of humanity. Over long stretches of the epic, the time-bound elements recede almost entirely from view.

A myth about Etana also deals with the search for life, though it is only preserved in incomplete form in some Old Babylonian and later versions. Etana, the first king after the Flood whom the gods set on the throne of Kish, was without a son. At this point, a fablelike story of an eagle and a serpent is inserted. These two become friends and swear themselves to mutual help. Both have young and always care for the offspring of the other. But one day, the eagle takes advantage of the serpent's absence to devour that creature's young, despite the warning by its own offspring about the vengeance of Shamash. The serpent complains to Shamash about its misfortune and is advised to hide itself in a great carcass in the mountains in order to punish the eagle when it comes to devour. What transpires is this: the serpent rips the eagle's wing off and hurls the bird into a pit, where it begins to starve. The eagle then cries out daily to Shamash, pleading for forgiveness and

27. The reason for this, besides the attainment of a total number of twelve, was no doubt that with Tablet XII the inescapability of the fate of death is brought to the fore once more and a connection with human guilt is established.

deliverance. Shamash then commands Etana to go and pull the eagle out and nurse it back to health. Etana does this and then asks Shamash to show him the "plant of birth" (so that Etana may have a son). In spite of Etana's prayers, the eagle cannot fulfill his plea but is prepared to carry the king up to heaven on his back, so that he can receive eternal life there. They fly up to the second heaven, but Etana then becomes dizzy, and both crash. This myth proves impressively the ethos of prayer as a determinative power for humans and animals.[28]

The myth of Adapa of Eridu shows humorous features. Adapa breaks a wing of the southern storm, who had spoiled his fishing; he is therefore cited for punishment before the god Anu. Ea then advises Adapa not to accept any offer of Anu. Anu, however, who not always lacks in understanding for people, experiences compassion for the poor sinner, and instead of the food of death, offers him the food of life. Adapa, however, rejects this and so forfeits for himself life without death.[29]

f. Constructed Myths

Constructed myths (see above, section 3a) are known primarily from the eighth and seventh centuries. Among these, the myth of the god of pestilence, Erra, assumes a special rank. Composed by Kabt-ilani-Marduk between the end of 765 and the beginning of 763, as is evident from some historical references, these five tablets were claimed by the author to have been revealed by verbal inspiration in a single night. They were copied in Assyria, although the slant is clearly pro-Babylonian.[30] According to the plot, which was freely invented by the poet, Erra, along with the warring demons created for him by Anu and designated "the seven," is aroused after a long period of rest by his vizier, Ishum. The demons call him to take renewed action against humanity, which has again become restless, and to decimate them and their livestock. Since Marduk is the king of the gods for Babylonia, Erra must first of all move Marduk to relinquish to him his dominion for a time.

28. Cf. J. V. Kinnier-Wilson, *The Legend of Etana* (Warminster, 1985); E. A. Speiser and A. K. Grayson, *ANET*, 114-18, 517.

29. Cf. S. A. Picchioni, *Il poemetto di Adapa* (Budapest, 1981); E. A. Speiser, *ANET*, 101-3. The beginning and end of the poem, which was first attested in the Amarna period, are missing.

30. Cf. L. Cagni, *The Poem of Erra* (Malibu, 1977).

As it appears — the text is broken at this point — Marduk withdraws to be with Ea in his groundwater palace; Erra can now instruct other gods (such as Shamash, Sin, and Adad) to withhold their gifts from people as well. Among the humans, "every man is against his brother," even in the family, and many are lost to drought and the heavy fighting. In Tablet IV, Ishtum shows Erra in detail all that has transpired, and thereby moves him to restraint; in the future, such catastrophes should befall only the enemies of Babylon, such as Assyria and Elam. Marduk's return is never mentioned; the last that is reported of him is his lament over the fate of his city, Babylon. The poem is obviously rich in contemporary features that we can only partly understand, although it contains many literary reminiscences as well. Much in the long discourses of the gods remains obscure to us. The pompous style, which so sharply deviates from the earlier epics, shows that this myth was not composed for presentation at a temple festival.

The political slant of some myths from Assyria is even more obviously massive. On account of his unpopular war of extermination against Babylon, Sennacherib commissioned some theologians with the task of producing a myth which would have as its focal point a divine legal proceeding against Marduk, who would be found guilty. This myth would then be the subject of a cultic presentation. All that survives of this work is fragments of a commentary, and these appear to have interpreted the individual actions for use in the rituals of the New Year festival. The text, composed in Assyrian, has incorrectly been taken as evidence of an actual passion myth.[31] Assyrian commentaries interpret still other, often absurd mythic constructions from that country.

Under Sennacherib's successor, the nationalist party in Assyria concerned itself with the struggle against pro-Babylonian groups at the royal court, and with drawing crown prince Ashurbanipal over to their side. To this end, they employed a constructed myth of the vision of the underworld by a crown prince under the pseudonym of Kummā. The first part, unfortunately, is only poorly preserved. Later Kummā sees in a dream the gods and demons of the underworld from theological tradition, and is led before the god Nergal. The model behavior of

31. Cf. W. von Soden, "Gibt es ein Zeugnis dafür, dass die Babylonier an die Wiederauferstehung Marduks geglaubt haben?" *ZA* 51 (1955): 130ff.; supplement, *ZA* 52 (1957): 224ff. Conversely, but in my view incorrect, L. Cagni, "Misteri a Babilonia? Esempi della tematica del 'dio in vicenda' nell'antica Mesopotamia," in *La Soteriologia dei culti orientali nell'impero romano,* ed. U. Bianchi and M. J. Vermaseren (Leiden, 1982), 565ff.

Sennacherib is displayed to him, and Kummā is given a harsh warning and sent back to earth.[32] This myth also shows that belief in the gods was often degraded into a purely political measure.

4. Wisdom Literature and Humorous Poetry

a. The Literary Term "Wisdom"

In direct dependence upon the Hebrew word *ḥokmâ,* "wisdom," theologians have coined the term "Wisdom Literature" as a collective designation for works with predominantly moralistic and didactic purposes, ranging from collections of proverbs and religious stories to the animal fables and dialogues of Babylonia. In many of these texts, humor also comes to the fore as more than simply a brief, relaxing element. Texts of this sort were not compiled into larger works.[33]

b. Composition and Collections of Sayings

For the most part, sayings and jokes are passed on orally everywhere. Many are tied to a particular period and thus are quickly forgotten; others, however, express something that is universally human, and these are often passed from people to people. In Babylonia, the Sumerians were the first to compile larger collections of sayings, which are preserved mostly in transcriptions of the Old Babylonian period. Many of these sayings are difficult to understand, and their interpretation is therefore disputed. Included among the sayings are animal fables. The themes are manifold and various: they comprise the personal, as well as the social and the religio-cultic realms. More than a few sayings and jokes are richly elaborated and are in all likelihood only the products of scribal schools.[34]

The Babylonians adopted only a portion of the Sumerian collec-

32. Cf. W. von Soden, "Die Unterweltsvision eines assyrischen Kronprinzen," *ZA* 43 (1936): 1-31; E. A. Speiser, *ANET,* 109-110.

33. Cf. W. G. Lambert, *Babylonian Wisdom Literature.* Today, several of the texts can be restored better.

34. Cf. E. I. Gordon, *Sumerian Proverbs: Glimpses of Everyday Life in Ancient Mesopotamia* (Philadelphia, 1959); for additional collections of Sumerian sayings, see R. Borger, *HKL* I: 163; II: 88-89.

tions and passed them on in Akkadian translation. Larger collections of purely Akkadian proverbs are unknown. It is said of an informant: "A scorpion stung a human, what profit did he get from it? An informant brought someone to his death; what advantage did he get?" In a smaller collection of humorous short stories from Assyria, one finds similarities with Arabic short stories. These are often quite well formulated. They frequently contain only a few lines and include many brief fables, as well as human anecdotes which warn against perverse behavior. Sayings are occasionally quoted in letters, and in a few cases there are references to riddles, though we have no collection of riddles.[35]

c. Dialogic Controversies and Animal Fables

The dialogic controversy between two partners was one of the most polished genres of Sumerian literature. In it, the respective parties stress the merits of their own arguments while denigrating those of the other. Since the partners cannot agree, a god is called upon, or in some cases a king, who should conclusively establish who has the advantage. It does not seem to happen that both partners are recognized simultaneously to be right to the same degree. The dialogue partners can be gods or humans, as for example the shepherd represented by Dumuzi and a farmer, or the (scribe)-father and his son, and even the annual seasons summer and winter, the sheep and the barley, the sickle and the plow, and many others. In every case the controversy must concern the order of the world and also be relevant to humanity: that is, it must present more than a trivial issue. Most of the mythic introductions which precede these dialogues point to the same thing: they draw one's attention back to the creation of the world. Occasionally the behavior of one of the partners resolves the controversy, as for example in the dispute between the heron and the turtle, when the turtle devours the heron's nest of eggs; unfortunately, the conclusion to this dialogue has not been preserved. In a departure from the pattern of the fables, the animals in the dialogues of controversy do not represent people.[36]

35. Cf. Lambert, *Babylonian Wisdom Literature*, 150ff., with texts of quite distinct types.

36. Cf., e.g., G. B. Gragg, "The Fable of the Heron and the Turtle," *AfO* 24 (1973): 51ff.; J. J. A. van Dijk, *La sagesse sumero-accadienne* (Leiden, 1953); cf. also *HKL* III: 84.

As already mentioned, the concisely formulated animal fables constitute a portion of the aphoristic literature in which the behavior of animals occupies a very wide space. The few comprehensive compositions in the Akkadian language occur only in the tradition of the dialogues of controversy, as, for example, the dispute between the ox and the horse. Occasionally there are several disputants, such as a fox, wolf, hound, and lion. Plants such as the Euphrates poplar, the dogwood, the tamarisk, and the date palm also serve as important dialogue partners for humans, along with emmer and wheat. In later texts, the dialogues of controversy are more animated and less bound by pattern.[37]

Another form of dialogue is represented by the dialogue between two friends concerning divine justice, which was briefly discussed above (see above, XII.4). This richly elaborated form allows no deity to mediate this ample display of speeches and counter-speeches, showing liberal application of theological erudition.[38] In a thematically related dispute from the Old Babylonian period, the case was different: there the deity himself spoke at the end, promised the sufferer his help, and exhorted him: "Anoint him whose skin is parched; feed the hungry; give drink to the thirsty!"[39]

Finally, the dialogue form is satirized in a later conversation between a lord and his slave, in which the lord always says what he wants to do and the slave responds by praising him. The lord then states the opposite, and again receives praise, this time with supporting argumentation. When the lord finally says that he wants to kill the slave, the slave responds quick-wittedly: "My lord will survive me by no more than three days!"[40]

d. Humorous Stories

The few stories of this type which we know from the Sumerians belong for the most part to the composition *É-dub-ba* (House of Tablets), which has not yet been published in its entirety. This composition concerns

37. Cf. Lambert, *Babylonian Wisdom Literature.*

38. Cf. *ibid.,* 63ff.; R. D. Biggs, *ANET,* 601-4.

39. Cf. J. Nougayrol, "Une version ancienne du 'Juste Souffrant,'" *Revue biblique* 59 (1952): 239ff.; W. von Soden, "Das Fragen nach der Gerechtigkeit Gottes im Alten Orient," *MDOG* 96 (1965): 41ff.

40. Cf. Lambert, *Babylonian Wisdom Literature,* 143ff.

the school of that time. One fragment depicts the daily life of a pupil, both at school and at home, in the form of a conversation, then briefly describes a dismal day in his life during the course of which he is beaten seven times for various reasons. Consequently, the father invites the teacher home for supper and gives him a gift in the bargain; afterwards, the black sheep of the family becomes a model pupil.[41] Some texts which deal with the methods of summoning and examining have come down to us in bilingual form. These instruct not aridly, but often humorously in the form of discourse and counterdiscourse by teacher and pupil. Another passage presents us with a father's conversation with his son, in which the father repeatedly holds up the son's refractory behavior and his slovenliness, at the same time holding up his own claim to have always been especially careful.[42]

A Babylonian story which is completely unique for its time, about 1100, deals with the case of the impoverished Gimil-Ninurta, who out of desperation gives his only possession, a goat, to the mayor of Nippur in the hope of receiving a commensurate gift in return. The mayor, however, contemptuously dismisses the man after giving him a mug of beer. As Gimil-Ninurta is leaving, he tells the gatekeeper that he will avenge himself three times, and requests as the first item an elegant chariot from the king. With this, he drives forth as the commissioner of the king, demands a private audience with the mayor, and then beats him thoroughly "from the crown of his head to the soles of his feet." Afterward he takes from the mayor the amount in gold for the rental of the chariot. Gimil-Ninurta next disguises himself as a doctor seeking to treat the ill-handled mayor, then beats the offender as before. The mayor and his retainers then take up the pursuit of his tormentor, but he is trapped by Gimil-Ninurta under a bridge and beaten a third time. The text concludes with the words: "The mayor could only crawl back into the city [again]." Many would certainly have had similar fancies regarding the powerful in that age, and just as today they would have smirked over this story.[43]

---

41. Cf. S. N. Kramer, *Schooldays: A Sumerian Composition Relating to the Education of a Scribe* (Philadelphia, 1949).

42. Cf. Å. W. Sjöberg, "Der Examenstext A," *ZA* 64 (1975): 137ff.; "Der Vater und sein missratener Sohn," *JCS* 25 (1973): 105-169.

43. Cf. O. R. Gurney, "The Tale of the Poor Man of Nippur," *Anatolian Studies* 6 (1956): 145ff.; "The Tale of the Poor Man of Nippur and Its Folktale Parallels," *Anatolian Studies* 22 (1972): 149ff.

5. Hymns, Prayers, Laments, and Incantations

a. Difficulties in Differentiating Genres

Sharp boundaries can rarely be drawn between the various genres of prayer literature, since so many of the prayers can be classified under a particular genre only with great difficulty. Moreover, careful investigations exist for only a part of the known collections of texts as well as their genres. There are also transitional forms between prayers and incantations. Therefore, the following delineations of the most important genres can have only a provisional character.

b. Sumerian Hymns of Gods and Kings, Laments, Prayers, and Letters to the Gods

As far as our present knowledge goes, the oldest Sumerian hymns are the temple hymns which are attested as early as the middle of the third millennium, focusing on the great temples; a tablet collection which was copied quite often after 2000 contains 545 lines and comprises forty-two of these hymns.[44] Many, often very long hymns to the gods are known after the Ur III period. These describe the descent, the great power, and the place of the deity in the pantheon, as well as his or her significance for humanity; they often end with intercessions for the king. Narrative pieces are often inserted. The hymns to kings, who are in most cases divinized (see above, VI.2), are almost entirely written as self-laudatory compositions in the first person singular; the same is true of many hymns written primarily to goddesses. The dominant themes in these are the origin and legitimation of the king, his favor with the gods and his care for their temples, and his care for the poor, the orphans, and the widows, as well as for justice. Along with these one finds the king's physical strength, his exploits in war, and his accomplishments for the economy of the land. This singular genre of hymns ceased after 1650 with the Babylonian kings Hammurabi and Samsu-iluna, who no longer had themselves divinized. The Babylonians translated no royal

---

44. Cf. R. D. Biggs, *Inscriptions from Tell Abû-Salâbîkh* (Chicago, 1974), 45ff.; Å. W. Sjöberg, E. Bergmann, and G. R. Gragg, *The Collection of the Sumerian Temple Hymns, and the Keš Temple* (Locust Valley, N.Y., 1969).

hymns and passed none on. In addition, some myths contained hymnic prologues.[45]

The Sumerians had no specific literary genre of prayer. Very short prayers are found at the end of several ancient Sumerian commemorative inscriptions. Longer prayers have been inserted into the great building hymn of Gudea of Lagash (see above, section 2), as well as a number of myths, a long didactic poem, and as intercessory prayers at the ends of hymns; these follow no established structural schema. The letters to the gods comprise a strange substitute for prayers; in these the petitioner brings his desire before the god in the form of a letter of request. The drafting of such letters was practiced in the schools.[46]

The late Sumerian literature developed new genres after 1500, such as the summary prayers on cylinder seals of the Kassite period and some prayers, generally passed on in bilingual form, which were used in certain rites. The "laments to comfort the heart" are modeled on the Babylonian prayers in particular; these laments are different from all earlier prayers and contain confessions of sin and petitions for redemption from one's sins.[47]

The last genre to be mentioned is that of the Sumerian songs of lament. The quite comprehensive and tiresomely monotonous laments over political catastrophes, such as the destructions of Akkad and Ur, are included. To these must be added primarily ritual laments in the "woman's dialect" Emesal from a later period — including the *er-šemma*-songs, performed in concert with the *balang*-harp, and laments for the god in the distant underworld, above all, Dumuzi (see above, XII.5b). These were recited down into the Seleucid period. The same elements, with the variation of a member, are very frequently repeated in the litanies of lament in a refrainlike fashion, though they are preserved on tablets only in abbreviated form. Finally, there are some

45. Cf. J. Klein, *Three Šulgi Hymns* (Ramat-Gan, 1981); W. H. P. Römer, *Sumerische Königshymnen der Isin-Zeit* (Leiden, 1965); C. Wilcke, "Hymne A," *RLA* IV (1975): 539ff., with bibliography; see also R. Borger, *HKL* III: 67ff.

46. Cf. R. Borger, "Gottesbrief," *RLA* III (1971): 575-76, which also deals with Babylonian letters to the gods; W. W. Hallo, *Individual Prayer in Sumerian: The Continuity of a Tradition.* American Oriental Series 53 (1968): 71ff.

47. Cf. S. Langdon, *Babylonian Penitential Psalms* (Paris, 1927); for a comprehensive edition of the "laments to console the heart" (Sum. *ér-šà-ḫun-gá*), see S. M. Maul, 'Herzberuhigungsklagen': *Die sumerisch-akkadischen Eršaḫunga-Gebete* (Wiesbaden, 1988). See below, n. 50.

personal laments, such as "A Man and His God," in which the motifs of Job resonate.[48]

c. Babylonian Hymns and Prayers

Hymns to the gods are preserved for us as early as the Old Babylonian period. Strangely, these are overwhelmingly addressed to goddesses; they repeatedly end in intercession for the king and reveal quite a diversity of forms, along with an unevenness of scope. Myths are imbedded in some of these hymns. The song of Agushaya is a hymn to Ishtar which depicts Ishtar's unruliness. Ea creates Ṣaltum, the goddess of discord, to oppose her, and then Ṣaltum goes against Ishtar in battle. Not until the creation of Agushaya can there be peace again.[49] Only fragments remain of other hymns of this type, as is true also of a myth of Ishtar in the first person singular. A very long hymn concerning Ishtar of Nippur probably goes back to the Old Babylonian period. The language of the later hymns, which often comprise two hundred verses and more, is more artistic than that of the Old Babylonian hymns. Some of these are also hymns of repentance. The literary merit and content of the pronouncements found in the great hymn to the sun god Shamash stand out markedly; at the same time, a hymn to Gula in the first person singular which is just as long, is quite meager in content. Finally, some royal prayers from Assyria are to be reckoned among the hymns, and there is a note of self-criticism in these.[50]

Stylistically related to the hymns in many respects are the limited

48. Cf. J. Krecher, *Sumerische Kultlyrik* (Wiesbaden, 1966); S. N. Kramer, " 'Man and his God': A Sumerian Variation on the 'Job' Motif," *Supplements to Vetus Testamentum* 3 (1955): 170ff.; *idem,* "Klagelied," *RLA* VI (1980): 1ff.

49. Cf. most recently, B. Groneberg, "Philologische Bearbeitung des Aguśaya-Hymnus," *RA* 75 (1981): 107ff.

50. Cf. W. von Soden, "Hymne B," *RLA* IV (1975): 544ff., with a listing of all known hymns up to that time. The great hymn to Shamash has frequently been translated; cf., e.g., Lambert, *Babylonian Wisdom Literature,* 121ff., with editing. A representative selection of Sumerian and Akkadian hymns and prayers has been translated by Falkenstein and von Soden, with introduction; a new two-volume edition is in preparation. An even more extensive selection of Akkadian hymns and prayers is found in M.-J. Seux, *Hymnes et prières aux dieux de Babylonie et d'Assyrie* (Paris, 1976). Cf. also W. G. Lambert, "The Hymn to the Queen of Nippur," in *Zikir šumim: Assyriological Studies Presented to F. R. Kraus,* ed. G. Van Driel, *et al.* (Leiden, 1982), 173ff.

number of psalms of lament and repentance. Among these is one from Tukulti-Ninurta I of Assyria during the last years of his reign, when the revolts against him were by no means able to break his sense of self-righteousness. The only great hymn of repentance to Ishtar from the Old Babylonian period is unfortunately very badly preserved. The hemerologies often demand the recitation of prayers of repentance of the *šigû*-genre for certain days in which calamity threatens. As in a great prayer to Nabû, the priest sometimes speaks for the penitent and asks for forgiveness.[51]

A further group of prayers which is richly represented are the prayers of oracular sacrifice of the genre *ikribu;* these usually include a formulaic conclusion. Finely formulated references to the previous life of the sacrificial animal in its pasture, as well as descriptions of the deep stillness of the night, are found in prayers of this genre from as early as the Old Babylonian period. Petitions for redemption from sin seldom occur in these hymns. Moreover, many personal names are very short prayers of petition or thanksgiving in sentence form; the contents of these vary greatly. We have referred to royal prayers in many inscriptions above (see above, section 2).[52]

The so-called individual prayers of lament comprise by far the largest group of prayers. These prayers are often called prayers of incantation because their superscriptions occasionally contain magical formulas and are frequently imbedded in rituals. These begin with shorter or longer sections praising the deity; then follows the lament with the self-introduction, the plea for release from suffering, reconciliation with the guardian deity, and forgiveness for sins. A generally formulaic promise of thanks forms the conclusion. Some of these prayers are among the most beautiful pieces of prayer literature because of the earnestness of their confession of sin. A prayer begins with the petitioner's complaint that he has not yet been heard; not the slightest echo of magic can be found here. The situation is different with so-called "special prayers" of this genre, which deal with completely distinct forms of suffering and sickness. These often present mixtures of prayer and incantation and are imbedded in extensive

---

51. Cf. W. von Soden, "Der grosse Hymnus an Nabû," *ZA* 61 (1971): 44ff.; "Zwei Königsgebete an Ištar aus Assyrien," *AfO* 25 (1977): 37ff.

52. Cf. W. von Soden, "Gebet II," *RLA* III (1959-1964): 160ff. For translations, see the works cited above, n. 50.

magical rituals which have to be carried out by the incantation priest (see above, XII.6). This priest directs himself primarily to Shamash, Marduk, and Ea, individually or all together. The so-called "cultic medium" prayers apply to the substances which are used in the rituals.[53] There are many echoes of the individual prayers of lament in the biblical psalms, but the constraints of the genre left the Babylonian poet much less freedom to formulate these.

The psalm of lament "I Will Praise the Lord of Wisdom" (see above, XII.4) holds a special place in the religious literature of the ancient Orient. In this composition of 480 verses, a very long lament is put in the mouth of a high official of the period around 1100, who laments his many illnesses and his loss of social status, which have brought him to the brink of death. In a scene that is presented only slightly more briefly than his suffering, Marduk finally announces the man's deliverance through a messenger in a dream. The praise of Marduk by all who experienced these events provides the final note. Just as in the book of Job, the quantity of suffering heaped on the individual surpasses all that he considers imaginable. The meaning is this: regardless of what form one's suffering may take, everyone should find himself in the poem and find hope in a similarly miraculous solution.[54]

d. Sumerian and Babylonian Incantations

The incantation literature is quite extensive among the Sumerians as well as the Babylonians. Sumerian incantations have survived in monolingual form mostly in Old Babylonian transcriptions and were later handed on accompanied by Akkadian translations. In many cases, of course, even the Sumerian text is post-Sumerian. The texts of Sumerian demonic exorcisms have been discussed above. In some of them, which were later compiled in the great series Evil *udug/utukku's* and Bad *asag/*

53. Cf. primarily W. Mayer, *Untersuchungen zur Formensprache der babylonischen "Gebetsbeschwörungen"* (Rome, 1976), with complete discussion of the problems and many textual editions, as well as the works cited above, n. 50; W. G. Kunstmann, *Die babylonische Gebetsbeschwörung* (Leipzig, 1932).

54. The latest edition is by Lambert, *Babylonian Wisdom Literature,* 31ff., 343ff. (Tablet IV must be partially rearranged). D. J. Wiseman, "A New Text of the Babylonian Poem of the Righteous Sufferer," *Anatolian Studies* 30 (1980): 101ff., which deals with Tablet I, is a good supplement.

asakku's, the activities of the demons are portrayed in lively fashion, and we often find long successions of similar pronouncements. Depending on one's purpose, various types of incantations with particular emphases can be distinguished.[55]

The post-Sumerian incantations, which were no doubt translated from the Akkadian with some frequency, were not compiled into their own larger tablet series. They have not yet been studied from a literary standpoint. Among these are the incantations directed against spells (see above, XII.4). By contrast, we still have no evidence for Sumerian incantations against witches.

The number of Akkadian incantations of different sorts is very large, and these were generally compiled, in part with the associated rituals, only in smaller series, as for example those against the Lamashtu, against spells, and against witches (see above, XII.6). Many of these are found scattered among the collections of medical prescriptions, as well as among rituals against suffering of all kinds. They have not yet been the subject of a literary investigation. Until now, only a few have been found from the Old Assyrian and Old Babylonian periods.

Finally, there are the so-called Abracadabra texts. These are found on small tablets of the Old Babylonian period, and later occur as parts of other incantations. Mostly they consist of what are for us — and no doubt were for most Babylonians as well — senseless combinations of syllables. It has been observed, however, that at least some of them were derived from other languages (e.g., from Old Elamite) and subsequently became incomprehensible through the deterioration of texts.[56]

6. Scientific Literature

The works which can claim to be "scientific," in both the widest sense of the word and their structure, have been treated above in chapter XI and in those parts of chapter XII which have to do with the teachings about the gods and the syncretistic doctrine of identification. Estab-

---

55. Cf. A. Falkenstein, *Die Haupttypen der sumerischen Beschwörung* (Leipzig, 1931). New editions of both of the series named here are in preparation.

56. Cf. J. van Dijk, "Fremdsprachliche Beschwörungen in den südmesopotamischen literarischen Überlieferungen," *Berliner Beiträge zum Vorderen Orient* 1 (1982): 97ff.

lished supplements for school are found in the series, House of Tablets (*É-dub-ba;* see above, section 4d). One finds in this series, for instance, tables of special dialects and technical languages and types of information which are important to us. The writers of scientific works were rarely concerned with a polished literary form, since they were largely bound by a rigid schema.[57]

57. A Phoenician historical work on the Phoenicians and their religion ascribed to Sanchuniathon has been preserved only in Greek excerpts and paraphrases, primarily by Philo of Byblos.

CHAPTER XIV

Building, Art, and Music

The building and art of the ancient Orient have been treated frequently in a variety of recent works, with abundant illustrations.[1] In the present work it has often been necessary to refer to works of art and architecture as indispensable supplementary sources, along with monumental inscriptions and all kinds of archaeological excavations. Still, some remarks on the significance of art and music within the whole framework of ancient Oriental culture are necessary, even though it is impossible to address detailed questions in these few pages and without extensive illustrations.

1. Cultic Buildings and Palaces: Form and Decoration

Since there are almost no monumental burial structures in the ancient Orient, only cultic buildings and palaces as a rule can be considered

---

1. Among German works, several deserve mention: A. Moortgat, *Die Kunst des Alten Mesopotamien* (Cologne, 1967) (a new and revised edition has been announced by U. Moortgat-Correns); A. Parrot, *Sumer* (Munich, 1960); *Assur* (Munich, 1960); *Sumer/Assur: Ergänzung* (Munich, 1969); E. Strommenger–M. Hirmer, *Fünf Jahrtausende Mesopotamien;* W. Orthmann, *et al., Der Alte Orient.* Propyläen Kunstgeschichte 14 (Berlin, 1975) (presently the most comprehensive work on the subject, with extensive bibliography); P. Amiet, *Art of the Ancient Near East* (New York, 1980); on the architecture of temples and palaces, cf. primarily E. Heinrich–U. Seidl, *Die Tempel und Heiligtümer im alten Mesopotamien;* J. Margueron, *Recherches sur les palais mésopotamiens de l'âge de Bronze* I-II (Paris, 1982); E. Heinrich, *Die Paläste im alten Orient* (Berlin, 1984).

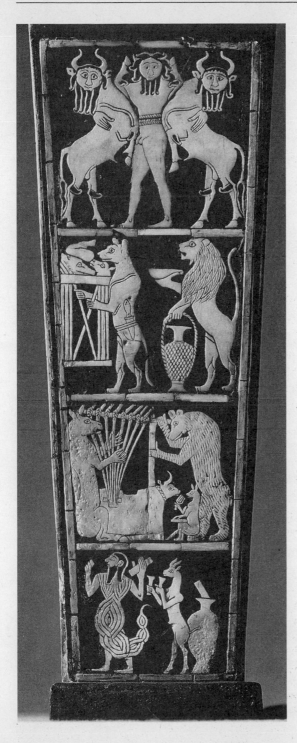

Celebratory scenes on sound-box of a lyre. Shell inlay mosaic set in bitumen. Ur, 25th century. *(University Museum, University of Pennsylvania)*

edifices; practical structures, however, such as fortifications and dwellings, must be disregarded. The temples and palaces had to make visible the superhuman position of the gods and the particular position of the ruler, even when the dimensions of those structures were rather modest. Basically, the temples assumed primacy of place before the palaces, though many periods (primarily Early Dynastic Sumer and, much later, the Assyrian and Persian empires) witnessed the use of far more than simply greater quantities of material for the palaces than for the temples, which they often somewhat overshadowed. In the third millennium the difference is especially striking between Early Sumerian Uruk, dominated by the massive temple, richly decorated with inlaid mosaics, and Early Dynastic Kish, with its great palace. Even in Old Babylonian Mari, the great palace, decorated with "al-secco" paintings, was obviously the most important building. Scarcely an equilibrium between the temple and palace can be ascertained in the Old Assyrian capital of Ashur: as far as can be determined, both were poor in decorative art. Nevertheless, the gigantic palaces in Calah and particularly Dur-Sharrukin and Nineveh, with their abundant pictorial decoration, must have drawn most of the attention after the time of Ashurnasirpal II in the ninth century. These palaces were the primary focus for their royal masters as well as for the artists. The rather modest temple at Dur-Sharrukin lay within the palace itself. In pictorial series at Calah, traditional religious and mythological motifs predominated at first, but these were later predominantly replaced by battle and hunting scenes as well as other attestations to the king's renown. It is not yet clear whether temples were among those Syrian edifices of the first millennium which had rich pictorial decorations (such as the Solomonic temple; cf. 1 Kings 6:14-35), though we are familiar with numerous images of deities there as early as the second millennium.[2]

We still know relatively little about the form of the outer facades of temples and palaces, since their walls are rarely standing to any height today. After the Early Sumerian period, when great pleasure was taken in color, not much appears to have been given to decoration of the outer walls beyond the arrangement of the monumental facades in niches and salients. An external reason for this was certainly that before the invention of glazes many types of stone and colors were hardly impervious

2. Cf. H. Bossert and R. Naumann, *Altsyrien* (Tübingen, 1951); W. Orthmann, *Untersuchungen zur späthethitischen Kunst* (Bonn, 1971); H. Genge, *Nordsyrisch-südanatolische Reliefs: Datierung und Bestimmung* I-II (Copenhagen, 1979).

to water. Even on interior walls, color could last only as long as the buildings were intact. Painting was done primarily by the al-secco technique on clay or plaster. Painted pictorial scenes are found less frequently, predominantly on the middle Euphrates in the palace at Mari (see above) and in the eighth century at Til-Barsip. Series of figures have been found in the Kassite capital of Dur-Kurigalzu in northern Babylonia. Elsewhere, great ornamental friezes were frequently painted; these probably imitated tapestries and display carefully arranged pictorial surfaces next to geometric and floral motifs, as well as animal figures and human faces.[3]

Grand compositions of pictorial reliefs were perhaps never found in temples, and even in the second millennium they were still not found on the walls of the palaces; even in the first millennium the Babylonians did not yet have at their disposal the stone necessary for such work. It was a long time before they could incorporate into stone buildings reliefs covering any extensive surface. That did not change until toward the end of the second millennium in northern Syria, when someone had the idea of dividing up large pictorial scenes between the smaller individual orthostats that were to be fashioned. At first, the stonecutters rarely cut more than a single figure from one stone, and the assembly of figures into pictorial scenes remained at that level for a long time. These limitations were not overcome until the ninth century, when the Assyrians first put together smaller orthostats to form large wall panels. They went on to refine to the utmost their work in miniature for the great royal scenes, even to the extent of reproducing with painstaking exactitude the details of wall embroideries (see above, VIII.2). For a long time battle scenes covering several panels remained rather two-dimensional, but after 750 spatial depth could be incorporated to a limited extent. Artistic limitation to a direct frontal style of depiction often necessitated strange combinations of elements of frontal and profile views. This was first overcome to an extent by some of Sennacherib's artists, who introduced foreshortenings in the interest of perspective, such as in depicting the eye in profile. The actual breakthrough to effective use of perspective was made outside Assyria. Very intensive use

3. Cf. the works cited in n. 1 above, as well as A. Moortgat, *Altvorderasiatische Malerei* (Berlin, 1959), with further evidence. Normally, there were no gradations of color; when multiple colors were used, fine lines were employed to separate the different parts of the picture from one another.

of traditional as well as entirely new artistic approaches did find expression in the Assyrian palace reliefs. Here the portrayal of moving animals, especially in hunting scenes, was somewhat more successful than that of humans, whose faces were almost always depicted without expression. Tender thematic scenes from the lives of animals and humans came to soften the generally brutal war illustrations. The depiction of sea battles along the coast of the Persian Gulf was particularly successful, and included life in the reed thickets and the fish and crustaceans in the water.[4]

Babylonian influence apparently had no important significance for the relief series distributed over many rooms of the Assyrian palace walls. After the catastrophe which befell Assyria in 612, the composite reliefs made from colorfully glazed bricks found on some of the palace walls of Nebuchadnezzar II in Babylon and on the Ishtar Gate there were no more than rather poor imitations of Assyrian wall decorations. By contrast, the depiction of scenes from the royal court at Persepolis in the relief series of the Achaemenaean monumental buildings show that the Persians had advanced beyond the Assyrian masters. The latter no doubt had a direct influence on Median art, which is otherwise unknown. Very little is found in the surviving royal art of the Achaemenaeans that recalls the thematic variety of the neo-Assyrian battle and hunting scenes, and nothing even remotely comparable to the palatial forms is as yet known from Syria.[5]

Since none of the great Assyrian palaces has been completely excavated, we are insufficiently informed about the overall architectural design and the exterior facades. It may be regarded as certain, however, that design was determined by both practical considerations and the pursuit of extreme magnitude. The palaces of the Chaldean kings far surpassed all earlier Babylonian structures in their dimensions. They deviated sharply, however, from the Assyrian palaces and, like other buildings in Babylonia, were constructed almost entirely of brick. There is still no comprehensive history of ancient Oriental palace architecture.[6]

4. Judging from the extant remains, many reliefs were originally done in color, though we do not know whether the colors were as vivid as those found in the wall paintings.

5. Cf. R. Ghirshman, *Iran: Protoiraner, Meder, Achämeniden.* Universum der Kunst 5 (Munich, 1964); E. Porada–R. H. Dyson, Jr.–C. K. Wilkinson, *The Art of Ancient Iran,* rev. ed. (New York, 1969).

6. See above, n. 1.

Babylonian temples have already been discussed in some detail (see above, XII.5a) in connection with the cult, with special attention to the difference between temples built on level ground and those on elevated terraces (Bab. *ziqqurratu*). The characteristic recessed architecture of the temple facades imitated older wooden structures; in the great temples, it accentuated the right angle as that dimension which pointed upward. In all but very small temples the inner sanctum was reached through a courtyard; the axis of the sanctuary would then be straight, so that the statue of the deity could be viewed directly from the main entrance. At the same time, we often find a bent axis where one had to turn 90 degrees to the left or right, as well as more complicated structural forms. The predominant form of the inner and outer chambers in Babylonia was a transverse, quadrilateral room; further to the north this was a narrower room running lengthwise along the axis. To the left of the inner sanctum often lay a room accessible only through it, which housed the temple treasure. Sometimes there was also a second inner chamber, for the consort of the deity or for another deity. The inner chamber was often illuminated only from the door or from above, but sometimes from small windows as well, as we can deduce from models of temples. Additional images, and not merely those of deities, were often set up in both the inner and outer chambers (see above, XII.5b, for the "praying statues" of the Early Dynastic period). The walls of the cultic chambers were often brightly plastered or covered in several colors. Unfortunately, we know scarcely anything about this, since usually only the lower parts of walls remain standing, and excavators have not always paid attention to the meager vestiges of color. The walls of the elevated terraces (see above) were generally scarped and articulated in the verticular. The main stairs, often three, were arranged in various fashions; at the most no more than one staircase ever went more than five stages. In every city, the elevated terrace with the temple upon it was the highest building and thereby pointed to the honor of the deity. As elsewhere, worship in these edifices involved more than merely words.

In Syria, where stone played a salient role in building, the form of the temple deviates in many respects from those of Babylonia and Assyria. Thus, small temples predominate, and these often display only an outer chamber and an inner chamber. The inner chamber could be either a transverse or lengthwise room, and the axis of worship could be either straight or geniculated. Quite frequently one finds an open vestibule, called by the Assyrians a *bīt ḫilāni*. Little is otherwise known about the furnishings of the cultic chambers.[7]

2. Sculpture and Modeling, Inlaid Work, and Miniature

Only by using different criteria can one classify those forms of sculpture and modeling which are only partly or not at all associated with architecture and the mosaiclike inlaid works. One way is to proceed from the materials on which the artists and artisans made very dissimilar demands. Chapter VIII dealt with the technical problems faced by artisans in working with stones of varying hardnesses, with metals, clay, and other minerals, as well as with organic materials such as bone and wood. Only rarely have artistic works from wood been preserved in Western Asia, and ivory was no doubt used only for works of miniature. Works of stone had to be produced individually, often with great difficulty; smaller sculptures made from clay and metal could frequently be formed into many similar copies by using clay models. Quantities of sculptures, ranging from monumental colossi to the smallest miniatures, sometimes have great significance for understanding artistic themes. Very often, however, we find the same artistic concepts presented in miniature as well as monumental art. Finally, one must distinguish between the larger and smaller three-dimensional sculptures and between the two-dimensional and high reliefs. Groups of figures in three-dimensional sculpture were certainly quite rare.[8]

In contradistinction to Egypt, three-dimensional sculpture in the ancient Orient preferred basically cylindrical forms.[9] Rulers are the primary subjects of this form of art, and they often appear praying; in addition, gods are frequently portrayed, generally in a rather rigid posture,

7. Cf. H. Lenzen, *Die Entwicklung der Zikkurat von ihren Anfängen bis zur Zeit der III. Dynastie von Ur* (Leipzig, 1942); A. Kuschke, "Tempel," with numerous diagrams and bibliography, in *Biblisches Reallexikon*, 2nd ed., ed. Kurt Galling (Tübingen, 1977), 333ff.

8. The lower portion of a bronze statue of a collapsed warrior, with an inscription of Naram-Sin of Akkad (see *Sumer* 32 [1976]: 58 [table]), is held by some to be a fragment of a larger group of figures.

9. Cf. A. Scharf, *Wesensunterschiede ägyptischer und vorderasiatischer Kunst. Der Alte Orient* 42 (Leipzig, 1943).

especially in miniature. The numerous praying figures of the middle of third millennium present a special case; they are far less than half life-sized (see above, XII.5b). Seated figures are rather seldom encountered; in Babylonia these display rounded forms, while in Syria as in Egypt the legs, together with the throne, can form an ashlar block. We are familiar with very slender bronze statuettes of deities primarily from Syria. A number of sculptures from third millennium Babylonia are distinguished by a particular strength of expression, as in the case of a sculpted woman's head in three-quarter view from Early Sumerian Uruk. To these must be added some statues of Gudea of Lagash and especially some sculptures of stone and bronze from the period of Akkad, though these are preserved only in fragmentary form. Otherwise, there are terra-cottas from every period, and these attest to more than mere artisanry.

Three-dimensional figures of animals were produced in large numbers as terra-cottas at least from the fourth millennium, and as metal and stone figurines at least from the Early Sumerian period. Cattle and sheep are attested with particular frequency as sacred animals (see above, XII.2). At the same time, one finds other mammals, including even lions, as well as birds and fish, though strangely enough no equids. Four-footed beasts are often depicted standing, or lying down and having only suggested legs. Gazelles or cows lying down, with the head turned back over the body, have a particularly graceful appearance. The colossal bulls with the heads of humans placed as guardians of the gates are of a completely different order: the bodies, with one side set against the wall, frequently have five legs, so that one can see two from the front and four from the side. In addition to these colossi, one finds lions with wide-open mouths at the gates in Syria.

Sculpture in the ancient Orient was developed with disproportionate richness as compared to painting, which followed largely the same pictorial motifs, but of which only very meager remains have survived. The reliefs are normally two-dimensional surface graphics which have been hewn out to various degrees; there are even examples of "high" reliefs, on which the figures are almost entirely three-dimensional. In the myriads of cylinder seals, the figures were cut into their backgrounds as mirror-images; when rolled onto soft clay, they then display the figures in normal, often minute relief. Besides the stone reliefs, one finds among the Sumerians, although rarely, bronze or terra-cotta reliefs; bronze reliefs and both large and small terra-cotta reliefs are also found from the first millennium, when clay models were produced for them. To these must be added other types of reliefs from later periods, often of brick and with multi-colored glazes. Insofar as these were mounted in buildings, they have been mentioned along with the wall paintings above. Many smaller relief panels, primarily from the third millennium, were designed for the temples; frequently these were not fastened to the walls, but instead were hung on heavy pegs and thus could be replaced. In addition to the cylinder seals, the much older form of stamp seals was used further also after 3000, primarily as clay seals. Objects of artisanry were rare in Babylonia and Assyria in the earlier period; not until the first millennium are primitive pictorial scenes found with any frequency, and from the Neo-Babylonian period on these increasingly came to replace the cylinder seals. As a pictorial medium, the cylinder seals were unique, since the pictures on them (e.g., continuous series of animals) could be transferred to successive clay surfaces. The various pictorial motifs of the reliefs and seals can be only partially interpreted with certainty (see above, XII.2), and religious and other scenes cannot always be distinguished from one another. Only some hints can be given here.[10]

In the Early Sumerian period important themes could only be depicted pictorially because there were as yet no literary texts. War and hunting played only a subordinate role in this art, with emphasis on cultic scenes and the protection of the holy flock. A large cultic vessel from Uruk combines a scene of sacrifice with an outline of the stages of life, from plants to humans and deities. In the Early Dynastic period cultic and mythological themes become still more diverse. Mythological themes are found primarily on cylinder seals and can still be only partially understood. The protection and feeding of the holy flock are brought to life along with other themes on different sorts of pictures composed of inlaid shells. On these, as on the dedicatory panels, the pictorial surface is used in grand scale. In contrast, many seal images are crowded with gods, people, and animals standing on their hind legs; perhaps this is meant to call attention to the mutual dependence of all forms of life. A unique theme is the sacral meal in the "drinking scene."[11]

10. Cf. A. Moortgat, *Frühe Bildkunst in Sumer* (Leipzig, 1935); P. Amiet, *La glyptique mésopotamienne archaique* (Paris, 1961); R. M. Boehmer, in *Der Alte Orient*, ed. Orthmann, *et al.*, 213ff., 336ff.

11. See works cited in ch. XII, n. 24. Details of the interpretation of this scene are still the subject of controversy.

The themes of two-dimensional pictures are completed by the depiction of battles, as for example those on the so-called vulture stela and the royal inscriptions from Lagash.

The period of Akkad compensated for an excess of abstract pictorial constructions through the composition of quite lively battle scenes, such as on the famous victory stela of Naram-Sin, where all figures appear erect on the mountain that has just been stormed. The seal pictures attest a rich mythology in which the sun god plays a special role (see above, XII.3). The entirely new motif of the tutelary god introducing the supplicant before the high gods seems first to have become the dominant theme of a mediocre two-dimensional pictorial and seal art during the Neo-Sumerian and Old Babylonian periods (see above, XII.2, and p. 176, n. 4). This art had generally abandoned the mythological themes to literature. After 2000, the investiture of the king by a god became a new theme in both word and picture.

Pictorial art in Old Babylonian Syria exhibits its own peculiar characteristics in form and in mythological and cultic themes; pictorial scenes on cultic vessels from Ebla provide an impressive attestation of this.[12] Examples of metallic art in the form of embossed work stand alongside two-dimensional graphics on stone from the same period and the thirteenth century. A golden crater from Ugarit with a hunting scene is a masterpiece.

The same pictorial themes as in the two-dimensional representations are often found in inlaid work from Early Dynastic Sumer. These are frequently done with shells in bitumen and include the "standard" and the pictures on the "barrels" of lyres from Ur. In these as well as in the small mosaics, much must be attributed to skilled craftsmanship.

After 1500, boundary stones were the principal bearers of two-dimensional representation in Babylonia. Still, there are only sporadic cases where these depict more than one figure. In the first millennium, one finds only a few more works of quality in Babylonia, usually among the terra-cottas.

The ninth century brought the great rise of pictorial art in Assyria, where the best can be found on the walls of the palaces (see above). From Ashur-bel-kala (about 1060) through Tiglath-Pileser II and down

---

12. Cf. G. R. Castellino, *et al.*, *Missione Archeologica Italiana in Siria . . .* (Campagna, 1965), 103ff.: P. Matthiae, *Le Sculture in Pietra* (Rome, 1966), pls. XLIIIff.

to Shalmaneser III, great obelisks as well as a throne pedestal also bore two-dimensional illustrations, predominantly with battle scenes. Primeval motifs from the themes centering on the "holy flock" were composed not only for monumental wall reliefs but also in miniature on colorfully glazed ceramic vessels. The latter bear witness to the revival from a state of near extinction of the ancient art of ceramic painting.[13] Occasionally, small works of art were successful in this area. The same is true of the generally primitive mass-produced amulets against the Lamashtu (see above, XII.6); a small bronze relief from the time of Sennacherib impressively supplements in pictorial form the depiction of the rites for warding off evil spirits in the incantations.[14] The art of the Assyrian Empire even outside the royal court can be richly informative.[15]

The later Assyrians were indebted to the Urartians for rich artistic stimulation, not least of all in connection with thrones decorated with figures. The Urartians created works of art in both architecture and representative art from 800 on, and their influence reached beyond Media and included also the courtly art of the Achaemenaeans. The Assyrians undertook monumental rock reliefs from the high mountainous regions of Anatolia as far as western Iran. One of the themes here was the king's presence before the gods, who stand upon their sacred animals. The Achaemenaean Darius I later carried on this tradition. Moreover, western Iran was for centuries a center for fine metalwork. The parts of horse bridles and other objects known as the Luristan bronzes can be dated as early as the second millennium.[16] These found their way in very large numbers into museums and collections, but have not yet been uncovered in excavations.

Finally, the ivory carvings which are known throughout Syria after about 1400 are completely unique to miniature art. The largest quantity of these carvings must be regarded merely as works of artisanship, but we do have early works of high artistic merit from Ugarit and Megiddo. These depict deities and mixed-form beings, humans and animals (in some cases in a struggle to the death), individual

13. Cf. W. Andrae, *Farbige Keramik aus Assur* (Berlin, 1923).

14. Cf. W. Farber, "Lamaštu," *RLA* VI (1983): 442; Amiet, *Die Kunst des Alten Orients,* figs. 568, 574.

15. Cf. J. Reade, *Assyrian Sculpture* (Cambridge, Mass., 1983).

16. Cf. P. Calmeyer, *Datierbare Bronzen aus Luristan und Kirmanshah* (Berlin, 1969).

figures as well as compositions of manifold likenesses. When the Assyrians invaded Syria after 900, they carried away many of these pieces as plunder and even forcibly deported ivory-carvers to Assyria, where some workshops were found after 850, especially in Calah. Thus, the Assyrian works cannot always be distinguished from the Phoenician. One outstanding work shows a lion in a thicket, killing a cub.[17] Strangely enough, the artistic carving of ivory never took root in Babylonia and, as far as is known, did not survive the collapse of the Assyrian Empire in the East.

Works of miniature, such as terra-cottas and small bronzes, may have been available to many people. How much access was had to great works of art by people who did not belong to the temple personnel or to the palace functionaries is beyond our knowledge. On some days the great pictorial series on the palace walls of Assyria presumably could be seen by many people. At the same time, only a few religious poems would be heard by the masses during the temple feasts.

3. Music and Musical Instruments

Prior to the invention of an actual system of written musical notations, music designed for the ear was the most transient of all the arts. That there was much singing in the ancient Orient, not least of all in work settings, is clear from the texts. There were male and female singers in the temples, where they sometimes served as priests, and in the royal courts. These were charged with performing cheerful songs as well as laments, and were often accompanied by musical instruments (see above, XII.5e), although nothing is yet known of notations for the pitch of male, female, and children's voices in the languages of the ancient Orient. For the musical delivery of literary works, see above, XIII.1.

We are tolerably informed on the subject of musical instruments, since we are familiar with many pictorial representations, primarily from reliefs, in addition to information derived from texts. Instruments have also been found, for example, in graves. The stringed instruments were designed to be plucked. The earliest and most important of these were the lyres, with a basically quadrilateral form, and the harps, on

17. Cf. Strommenger–Hirner, pl. XLII; cf. also R. D. Barnett, *A Catalogue of the Nimrod Ivories* (London, 1957).

which the strings ran obliquely to the sound-box. There were numerous varieties of both. We have not only representations of both of these from the royal cemetery of Uruk (about 2500), but also well-preserved exemplars with gold trim and ample pictorial decoration on the sound-box. Harps and lyres were later played widely throughout Western Asia, while the lute, which was first introduced from the mountains in the second millennium, is less well-attested. It is very doubtful that the zither (Gk. *kithara*) was known.[18]

The most important wind instrument was the reed pipe, which is also attested as a double pipe; in translations these are generally rendered "flutes." Trumpets and, especially in Israel, the ram's horn or shofar were used more as signal instruments than as musical instruments. Among percussion instruments were various types of drums, kettledrums, and cymbals, which were used both with and without sticks. Smaller bronze bells were no doubt used as well.

It is quite significant that numbers of musicians sometimes appear on the monuments; these carry harps and lyres, but also various other instruments, and several different kinds of instruments are also mentioned in the texts with some frequency. Therefore, music from a variety of instruments, and having a particularly full and differentiated sound, must have existed as a preliminary stage of orchestral music. Such music could accompany songs of diverse contents, though it could also be presented presumably without lyric accompaniment in the temple festivals and the royal court.

Concerning the type of music that prevailed in the ancient Orient, one could for a long time only conjecture based on comparisons from the history of music. Sixty years ago it was thought that a text with written musical notations had been found, but the interpretation of the cuneiform signs was incorrect. We have known since 1960, however, that texts from the second millennium in Babylonia and Assyria as well as in northern Syria (Ugarit) named the strings of a harp (which contained up to nine strings). These strings were given in different sequence, along with the possible intervals between their respective pitches. We are familiar with the Babylonian terms even in their Hurrianized forms.

18. Cf. W. Stauder, "Harfe," *RLA* IV (1973): 114ff., citing further works by the author on Babylonian music and the other musical instruments; A. D. Kilmer–D. Collon, "Laute," *RLA* VI (1983): 515ff.; "Leier," *RLA* VI: 571ff., with extensive bibliography and references to the "system of musical notation."

The texts, which are difficult to interpret but which do appear to require double stops for stringed instruments, cannot simply be translated into our system of musical notation. After much controversy, philologists and historians of music continue to advance diverse interpretations. What appears to be certain is that Babylonian music was structured heptatonically on the basis of the octave, as with our own, and not pentatonically, as with the early music in Greece. Recordings have even been produced on the basis of certain earlier interpretations of the texts; still, without the discovery of new sources for musical notation, a consensus regarding the sound of music in the ancient Orient can scarcely be reached.[19]

The gods expected people to sing to them in various ways, but we only hear of sporadic instances in which a goddess is able to sing. A god of the lyre, Kinnāru, is attested in Ugarit; the word *kinnāru* (Heb. *kinnôr*; Gk. *kinyra*) has migrated considerably, though it is first attested at Ebla. The Old Testament testifies to the significant role of music in the temple cult of Jerusalem, but many questions still need to be answered (especially concerning the composition of spontaneous lyric poetry by a minstrel [cf. Psalm 45] and the role of women in the service [cf. Psalm 68:25, where women are listed as musicians, and Exodus 15:21; Judges 11:34, which presuppose a key role for women as leaders of music and dance in victory celebrations]).

19. Cf. A. D. Kilmer, *RLA* VI (1983): 574ff., with bibliographical references. Other perspectives are represented by M. Duchesne-Guillemin, "Sur la restitution de la musique hourrite," *Revue de Musicologie* 66 (1980): 5ff.; cf. also A. D. Kilmer, *Iraq* 46 (1984): 69ff.

Tablet of late third millennium lament, "A Man and His God," called the Sumerian Job. Nippur, 18th century. *(University Museum, University of Pennsylvania)*

CHAPTER XV

Concluding Observations and Remarks

We have been able to present and discuss only a small selection of the inestimable abundance which the material remains, written sources, architecture, and art tell us about the ancient Orient — or the problems they frequently yield which remain to be solved. Many deficiencies as well as perhaps fortuitous choices in the selection of material have resulted from the limited time available for preparing such a brief presentation as this. As in similar works, subjective judgments in the intellectual sphere, in the broadest sense, were not always avoidable, and sometimes even necessary. A presentation without critical evaluation can never do justice to its task. In any case, some subdisciplines of the study of the ancient Orient do afford certain insights into the essence of that civilization. Therefore it has been all the more important to refer repeatedly to tasks which, in the current research, have been relinquished to the near or more distant future. Even that we have only been able to do in an eclectic fashion.

In terms of world history, the early civilizations can be considered from various perspectives. According to the length and duration of each, they present a greater or lesser series of steps from the very old, preliterate cultures, which we call prehistoric, to cultures which were much more highly developed. These prehistoric cultures can then be seen as preliminary steps to the later, in many respects more highly developed cultures. Such a perspective is thoroughly legitimate as long as it does not remain the only one. The earliest literate cultures tested the possibilities for the use of writing over many hundreds of years; thus the later literate cultures were able to begin with improved systems of

247

writing, which they could then develop even further. The beginnings of an economy based on the division of labor certainly lie long before the emergence of the earliest civilizations. Yet these cultures developed economic structures with no little aid from writing, and these structures led, in turn, to regular trade in goods even across vast spaces and made mass production possible, where necessary, in addition to the manufacture of valuable tools, trade items, and the construction of large buildings. Great progress could also be gained in the areas of higher technologies, although much of this was lost again, usually as a consequence of political catastrophes. As in every age, several of these technologies served primarily for waging war. Far less frequently can one speak of real progress in the realm of human coexistence and cooperation. Here catastrophes often brought severe reversals and the loss of freedom for smaller groups and individuals. The similarities of regulations in the area of family law must not always point to dependencies; rather, in spite of language barriers, administrative practices — especially of the great powers — were probably adopted from neighboring regions. The particulars here will be proven only in rare instances.

The high cultures of the ancient Orient do not merely provide developmental phases from the preliterate cultures to the Hellenistic world, nor do they serve as a mere composite of ancient cultures. Rather, they also represent unique and unduplicated realizations of human possibilities in many respects, particularly in the religious, intellectual, and artistic spheres. It is these materializations that, having often been insufficiently appreciated, make the study of cultures beyond a merely antiquarian interest so rewarding. I am thinking, for example, of the religiously grounded patriarchal absolutism of a Hammurabi and, though somewhat different in its individual aspects, of Shamshi-Adad I of Assyria, who admittedly scarcely influenced the course of the later monarchy there. In religion, the unique stamp of the Sumerian notion of order was indispensable for the emergence of any kind of science. In addition, the syncretistic theology of identification reinterpreted the excessive polytheism of Mesopotamia, and then led to the relativizing of polytheism in the cult through monotheiotetism, even though the doctrine of a divinity which expressed itself in many forms was never formulated and polytheism was never abandoned. This development took place in conjunction with the Babylonians' perception of the ethical interest of the deity and resulted in the upsurge of the problem of theodicy. Certainly, however, there is no direct route from this to the monotheism of revealed religions (such as Judaism), as was once thought. Babylonian science is also unique, and it led to astonishing accomplishments in mathematics and astronomy without the aid of formulated principles of knowledge. The path of this science ultimately led into a dead-end, from which only astronomy found its way out, thanks to the collaboration of Babylonians and Greeks in later times.

That which is timelessly unique among the leading works of poetry and art cannot be grasped so easily in brief formulations. Among these works are the Gilgamesh Epic, the representations of animals on the Assyrian palace reliefs, as well as prayers and works of sculpture of special quality. Here, as with many other enterprises, individuals displayed particular ability and attained a capacity to empathize — with humans and with animals and their respective needs — which few have ever reached.

Finally, the question arises as to the continuing influence of the ancient Oriental cultures beyond their own age. Here it must first be said that, in literature, even quite striking similarities need not be explained in terms of the influence of older works on later ones. Thus, when we find linguistic evidence of very similarly structured or even quite closely related thoughts about the relationship of humans to the deity, such as in Babylonian prayers and biblical psalms, the reason may frequently be that an extremely ancient religious heritage of the Semitic peoples emerged historically in different settings and developed in the same directions, in spite of all the differences between these peoples.

We probably should recognize Babylonian influences in the book of Job, although this work far surpasses the very impressive Babylonian poems of similar thematic concern (see above, XII.4). Babylonian influence is probably also to be found in the composition of Hebrew proverbs, since this art frequently transcends political and geographical boundaries. The influence of Babylonian myths on Israelite myths has often been overestimated. It certainly was not very great, particularly where the myths of creation are concerned. Yet we still have the idea that from early on people were not content with the role assigned to them by the deity; this theme ties the Atraḫasis myth to the biblical story of the Fall (and the Tower of Babel!).[1] Conversely, in the story of

---

1. Cf. W. von Soden, "Der Mensch bescheidet sich nicht: Überlegungen zu Schöpfungserzählungen in Babylonien und in Israel," in *Symbolae biblicae et mesopotamicae Francisco Mario Theodoro de Liagre Böhl dedicatae*, ed. M. A. Beek, *et al.* (Leiden, 1973),

the Flood, which the Bible also localizes in Mesopotamia, the corresponding motifs are so striking (e.g., in the sending out of the three birds while the waters recede) that direct connections must exist, at least between preliminary stages of these traditional stories. In purpose and in many individual features, however, the stories from Babylonia and Israel are quite different. For instance, the Bible could not adopt the idea that the human couple saved from the catastrophe had been transported away to live a life without death. Even the Greek saga of the Flood is hardly independent of the Babylonian tradition in its entirety, but it too is quite different.

Apart from astronomy and the calendar (see above, XI.9), the influence of Babylonian culture on Greece was not very strong, given the vast geographic separation. Many ideas (e.g., in mythology) did in fact make their way successfully across Asia Minor to Greece, but they had no lasting significance for fundamental concepts there. Individual questions, such as the possible borrowing of technology in the Mediterranean basin, still need to be studied.[2] For one thing, Babylonian units of weight, such as the mina and talent, certain did pass to Greece by way of Syria.

The importance of Babylonia was far greater for the Hellenistic world than it was for ancient Greece, even in the form in which it was manifested alongside the Iranian heritage at the time of the Parthian Empire. Yet here also, scholarship is only in its initial stages. Only with greater cooperation among related disciplines than at present can we anticipate results which will enrich our historical picture. What is necessary for the further study of the ancient Orient is that problems of intellectual history be addressed anew, though without neglecting economic and social research. Once this is done, the enterprise will quickly show how rewarding it is.

349ff.; cf. also M. Eliade, *Die Schöpfungsmythen: Ägypter, Sumerer, Hurriter, Hethiter, Kanaaniter und Israeliten* (Zürich, 1964); M. Schretter, *Alter Orient und Hellas: Fragen der Beeinflüssung griechischen Gedankengutes aus altorientalischen Quellen, dargestellt an den Göttern Nergal, Rescheph, Apollon* (Innsbruck, 1974).

2. Cf. R. J. Forbes, *Studies in Ancient Technology,* I-IX, some parts of which have been thoroughly revised (Leiden, 1955-1972).

Selected Bibliography

Frequently cited works and suggestions for further reading

Beyerlin, W., ed. *Near Eastern Religious Texts Relating to the Old Testament* (Philadelphia, 1978).

Borger, R., ed. *Handbuch für Keilschriftliteratur.* 3 vols. (Berlin, 1967-1975).

Bottéro, J., *Mesopotamia: Writing, Reasoning, and the Gods* (Chicago, 1992).

————, Cassin, E., and Vercoutter, J. *The Near East: The Early Civilizations* (New York, 1967).

Brinkman, J. A. *A Political History of Post-Kassite Babylonia, 1158-722 B.C.* (Rome, 1968).

————. *Prelude to Empire: Babylonian Society and Politics, 747-626 B.C.* (Philadelphia, 1984).

Buccellati, G. *The Amorites of the Ur III Period* (Naples, 1966).

van Buren, E. D. *The Fauna of Ancient Mesopotamia as Represented in Art.* AnOr 18 (1939).

Cameron, G. G. *History of Early Iran* (Chicago, 1936, repr. 1976).

Cohen, M. E. *The Cultic Calendars of the Ancient Near East* (Bethesda, 1993).

Collon, D. *First Impressions: Cylinder Seals in the Ancient Near East* (Chicago, 1988).

Cooper, J. S. *Sumerian and Akkadian Royal Inscriptions.* Vol. I: *Presargonic Inscriptions* (New Haven, 1986).

Dalley, S. *Myths from Mesopotamia: Creation, the Flood, Gilgamesh, and Others* (Oxford, 1989).

Dandamaev, M. A., and Lukonin, V. G. *The Culture and Social Institutions of Ancient Iran* (Cambridge, 1989).

Driver, G. R. *Semitic Writing from Pictograph to Alphabet.* 3rd ed. (Oxford, 1976).

————, and Miles, J. C. *The Assyrian Laws* (Oxford, 1935; repr. 1975).

————. *The Babylonian Laws.* 2 vols. (Oxford, 1952-1955).

Foster, B. R. *Administration and Use of Institutional Land in Sargonic Sumer* (Copenhagen, 1982).

Frankfort, H. *The Art and Architecture of the Ancient Orient.* Rev. ed. (Baltimore, 1970).

————. *Kingship and the Gods* (Chicago, 1948; repr. 1978).

————, et al. *The Intellectual Adventure of Ancient Man* (Chicago, 1977).

Frye, R. N. *The History of Ancient Iran* (Munich, 1984).

Gordon, E. I. *Sumerian Proverbs* (Philadelphia, 1959).

Grayson, A. K. *Assyrian and Babylonian Chronicles* (Locust Valley, N.Y., 1975).

————. *Babylonian Historical-Literary Texts* (Toronto, 1975).

————. *The Royal Inscriptions of Mesopotamia: The Assyrian Periods.* 2 vols. (Toronto, 1987-1990).

Gurney, O. R. *The Hittites.* Rev. ed. (Baltimore, 1964).

Harris, R. *Ancient Sippar* (Istanbul, 1975).

Heinrich, E., and Seidl, V. *Die Tempel und Heiligtümer im alten Mesopotamien: Typologie, Morphologie, und Geschichte* (Berlin, 1982).

Hrouda, B., et al. *Methoden der Archäologie: Eine Einführung in ihre naturwissenschaftlichen Techniken* (Munich, 1978).

Hunger, H., and von Weiher, E. *Spätbabylonische Texte aus Uruk,* pts. I-II (Berlin, 1976-1983).

Jacobsen, T. *The Harps That Once . . . : Sumerian Poetry in Translation* (New Haven, 1987).

————. *Towards the Image of Tammuz* (Cambridge, Mass., 1970).

————. *The Treasures of Darkness: A History of Mesopotamian Religion* (New Haven, 1976).

Kramer, S. N. *The Sumerians* (Chicago, 1963).

Labat, R. *Les Religions du Proche-Orient asiatique* (Paris, 1970).

Lambert, W. G. *Babylonian Wisdom Literature* (Oxford, 1960).

Larsen, M. T. *The Old Assyrian City-State and Its Colonies* (Copenhagen, 1976).

Leemans, W. T. *The Old Babylonian Merchant: His Business and His Social Position* (Leiden, 1950).

Lipiński, E., ed. *State and Temple Economy in the Ancient Near East*. 2 vols. (Louvain, 1979).

Liverani, M. *Prestige and Interest: International Relations in the Near East ca. 1600-1100 B.C.* (Padua, 1990).

Luckenbill, D. D. *Ancient Records of Assyria and Babylonia*. 2nd ed. (1927; repr. Portland, Ore., 1989).

McQueen, J. G. *The Hittites and Their Contemporaries in Asia Minor*. Rev. ed. (London, 1986).

Matthiae, P. *Ebla: An Empire Rediscovered* (Garden City, N.Y., 1981).

Meissner, B. *Babylonien und Assyrien*. 2 vols. (Heidelberg, 1920-1925).

Moorey, P. R. S., *Materials and Manufacture in Ancient Mesopotamia* (Oxford, 1985).

Moscati, S., *et al.*, ed. *L'Alba della civiltà*. 3 vols. (Turin, 1976).

Neugebauer, O. *The Exact Sciences in Antiquity*. 2nd ed. (New York, 1969).

————. *A History of Ancient Mathematical Astronomy*. 3 vols. (Berlin, 1975).

Nissen, H. J. *The Early History of the Ancient Near East 9000-2000 B.C.* (Chicago, 1988).

Olmstead, A. T. *History of the Persian Empire* (Chicago, 1948).

Oppenheim, A. L. *Ancient Mesopotamia: Portrait of a Dead Civilization*. 2nd ed. (Chicago, 1977).

————. *Letters from Mesopotamia* (Chicago, 1967).

Parpola, S. *Letters from Assyrian Scholars to the Kings Esarhaddon and Assurbanipal*. 2 vols. AOAT 5/1-2 (1970-1983).

Pettinato, G. *Ebla: A New Look at History* (Baltimore, 1991).

Porada, E., Dyson, R. H., Jr., and Wilkinson, C. K. *The Art of Ancient Iran*. Rev. ed. (New York, 1965).

Postgate, J. N. *Early Mesopotamia: Society and Economy at the Dawn of History* (London, 1992).

Powell, M. A., ed. *Labor in the Ancient Near East* (New Haven, 1987).

Pritchard, J. B., ed. *Ancient Near Eastern Texts*. 3rd ed. (Princeton, 1969).

Ringgren, H. *Religions of the Ancient Near East* (Philadelphia, 1973).

Roaf, M., and Postgate, N. *Cultural Atlas of Mesopotamia and the Ancient Near East* (New York, 1990).

Roberts, J. J. M. *The Earliest Semitic Pantheon* (Baltimore, 1972).

Roux, G. *Ancient Iraq*. 2nd ed. (Baltimore, 1980).

Saggs, H. W. F. *Civilization before Greece and Rome* (New Haven, 1989).

————. *The Encounter with the Divine in Mesopotamia and Israel* (London, 1978).

————. *Everyday Life in Babylonia and Assyria* (London, 1965; repr. 1987).

————. *The Greatness That Was Babylon.* Rev. ed. (New York, 1991).

————. *The Might That Was Assyria.* 2nd ed. (New York, 1991).

Saporetti, C. *The Status of Women in the Middle Assyrian Period* (Malibu, 1979).

von Soden, W. *Akkadisches Handwörterbuch.* 3 vols. (Wiesbaden, 1958-1981).

Sollberger, E., and Kupper, J.-R. *Inscriptions royales sumeriénnes et akkadiennes* (Paris, 1971).

Strommenger, E. *5,000 Years of the Art of Mesopotamia* (New York, 1964).

Thompson, R. C. *A Dictionary of Assyrian Botany* (London, 1949).

————. *A Dictionary of Assyrian Chemistry and Geology* (Oxford, 1936).

Thomson, M.-L. *The Sumerian Language.* 2nd ed. (Copenhagen, 1987).

Veenhof, K. R. *Aspects of Old Assyrian Trade and Its Terminology* (Leiden, 1972).

Westbrook, R. *Old Babylonian Marriage Law. Afo* Beiheft 23 (Horn, 1988).

————. *Studies in Biblical and Cuneiform Law* (Paris, 1988).

Wilhelm, G. *The Hurrians* (Warminster, 1989).

Wolkstein, D., and Kramer, S. N. *Inanna, Queen of Heaven and Earth* (New York, 1983).

Yadin, Y. *The Art of Warfare in Biblical Lands.* 2 vols. (New York, 1963).

Index

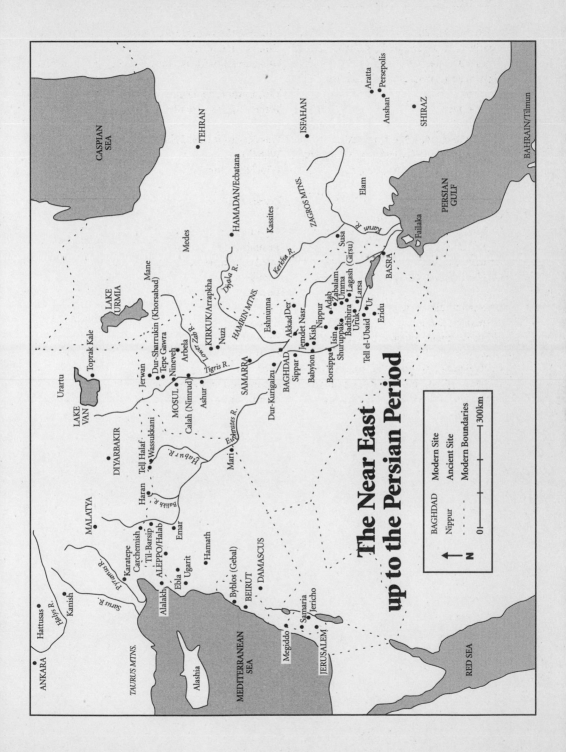

The Near East
up to the Persian Period

ANKARA

Hattusas

Halys R.

Kanish

TAURUS MTNS.

MALATYA

Karatepe
Carchemish
Til-Barsip
ALEPPO/Halab
Alalakh
Ebla
Ugarit
Emar

Pyramus R.
Sarus R.

Hamath

Byblos (Gebal)
BEIRUT
DAMASCUS

Samaria
Jericho
Megiddo
JERUSALEM

MEDITERRANEAN
SEA

Alashia

RED SEA

DIYARBAKIR

Haran
Balikh R.

Tell Halaf
Wassukkani
Habur R.

Mari
Euphrates R.

Dur-Kurigalzu

SAMARRA

Calah (Nimrud)
MOSUL
Ashur

Jerwan
Dur-Sharrukin (Khorsabad)
Tepe Gawra
Nineveh
Arbela

LAKE
VAN

Urartu

Toprak Kale

LAKE
URMIA

Mane

Tigris R.
Lower Zab R.
Upper Zab R.

KIRKUK/Arrapkha
Nuzi

HAMRIN MTNS.

Eshnunna

Akkad/Der
Jemdet Nasr
BAGHDAD
Sippar
Babylon
Borsippa
Kish
Nippur
Isin
Shuruppak
Adab
Badtibira
Umma
Zabalam
Uruk
Larsa
Lagash (Girsu)
Tell el-Ubaid
Ur
Eridu

Djala R.

Medes

Kassites

ZAGROS MTNS.

Kerkha R.
Karun R.

Susa

Elam

BASRA

CASPIAN
SEA

TEHRAN

HAMADAN/Ecbatana

ISFAHAN

Aratta
Persepolis
Anshan
SHIRAZ

PERSIAN
GULF

BAHRAIN/Tilmun

Failaka